More Praise for *The Language of Miracles*

"Amelia Kinkade is wicked smart, wicked funny, can write like crazy, and has an amazing ability to take the most complicated workings of the universe and make them seem clear and simple, even to those who may be a little science- or miracle-challenged. If you have a pet or love animals, this book is a real treat. But even if animals aren't your thing, and even if healthy skepticism is, it's still a treat. Why? Because *The Language of Miracles* isn't just about communicating with critters — it's actually a crash course in love."

— Raphael Cushnir, author of *Setting Your Heart on Fire* and
The One Thing Holding You Back

"Move over, Dr. Dolittle. Welcome, Amelia Kinkade! *The Language of Miracles* shows us how easy it is to open our minds and hearts to the spirit and soul of animal beings. This wonderful and long-awaited book is a mind-bender that shows that we can indeed talk to and with other animals if we respect who they are, what they know, and what they feel. Animals have a point of view just as we do, and Kinkade's lively text and deep caring show that timeworn and demeaning views of these individuals really don't work. We need close interconnections with animals, and in their absence we lose our sense of place and our wholeness."

— Marc Bekoff, professor of biology at the University of Colorado,
author of *Animal Passions and Beastly Virtues*,
and editor of the *Encyclopedia of Animal Behavior*

"Amelia Kinkade has written a book that will make believers out of those who don't know it is possible to communicate with animals. Her straightforward, engaging style and wealth of experiences enable anyone to enter the portal and discover what animals are thinking and feeling. As sentient species, animals inhabited our planet long before humans. Now we can all become proficient in speaking and listening to the language of the animal world. What an enlightening and delightful way to gain ageless wisdom!"

— Allen and Linda Anderson, founders of the Angel Animals Network and
authors of *Angel Dogs*, *Angel Cats*, and *Rainbows & Bridges*

"*The Language of Miracles* is a celebration of inspiring stories that help us navigate our way through the human-animal communication experience. Regardless of our circumstances, Amelia Kinkade shows us how to honor the sacred presence and beauty in all things."

— Gary Quinn, bestselling author of *May the Angels Be with You*
and *Living in the Spiritual Zone*

"Amelia Kinkade has a beautiful and clear vision of a world where all sentient beings are able to communicate directly. I have seen her work with animals and watched her teach this skill to others. She is able to do both in a kind and loving way that gets immediate responses from all around her. In *The Language of Miracles*, there are many wonderful and amazing stories of human-animal communication, as well as guided exercises to help readers learn this skill for themselves. This is a must-read for anyone interested in opening and exploring the unspoken world between humans and animals. I highly recommend it.

— John G. Myerson, PhD, coauthor of
Riding the Spirit Wind: Stories of Shamanic Healing

"Those of us who love Amelia know that she has cracked open the frontiers of communication with our animal friends, and she has generously shared this precious gift for us humans through her books, seminars, and ongoing listening and talking to the animals. She has improved and often saved the lives of countless animals. She has given us the tools to have deeper, happier, more loving relationships with our animal companions. But more than anything, what is beautiful is Amelia inside and outside. Amelia is pure compassion, goodness, and joy."

— Nadia Sutton, founder of PAWS (Pets Are Wonderful Support) LA

"Amelia Kinkade is already recognized worldwide as a lucid and compassionate animal communicator. In this informative, deeply moving, and immensely entertaining book, she proves to be an accomplished human communicator as well."

— Linda Kohanov, author of *The Tao of Equus* and *Riding between the Worlds*

The Language
of Miracles

ALSO BY AMELIA KINKADE

Straight from the Horse's Mouth:
How to Talk to Animals and Get Answers

The Language of Miracles

A Celebrated Psychic Teaches
You to Talk to Animals

Amelia Kinkade

NEW WORLD LIBRARY

NOVATO, CALIFORNIA

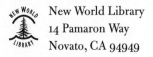 New World Library
14 Pamaron Way
Novato, CA 94949

Interior design by Tona Pearce Myers

Library of Congress Cataloging-in-Publication Data
Kinkade, Amelia.
The language of miracles : a celebrated psychic teaches you to talk to animals / Amelia Kinkade.
     p.   cm.
ISBN-10: 1-57731-510-3
ISBN-13: 978-1-57731-510-0 (pbk. : alk. paper)
1. Pets—Psychic aspects. 2. Human-animal communication. 3. Extrasensory
   perception in animals. I. Title.
SF412.5K55 2006
304.2'7—dc22   2005035060

First printing, April 2006
ISBN-10: 1-57731-510-3
ISBN-13: 978-1-57731-510-0

Printed in the United States on partially recycled, acid-free paper

g A proud member of the Green Press Initiative

Distributed by Publishers Group West

10   9   8   7

This book is dedicated to two little boys. In the early 1940s, one looked up at the stars in the West Texas sky and said, "Mama, when I grow up, I'm going to walk on the moon." About the same time, a boy his age, across the country in Brooklyn, New York, tugged on his mother's apron and said, "Mother, when I grow up, I'm going to find a cure for cancer." I love a man who is true to his word. This book is not just a tribute to Dr. Edgar Mitchell and Dr. Bernie Siegel and the icons they became — but to the little boys inside them they never let die, who can still look at the world and its animals with eyes filled with awe and wonder.

Contents

AUTHOR'S NOTE

I have written this book with the desire to help you learn to communicate with your nonhuman loved ones. This book isn't intended as a substitute for medical care or the expert diagnosis of a trusted veterinarian. Please take care to cross-reference your intuitions with professional opinions and diligently seek feedback from your veterinarians.

I have disguised the names and identifying characteristics of some of my animal friends (such as Captain Harris) to protect their privacy. However, most of my most treasured students/friends have generously granted me permission to use their real names in the stories. You will find a list of the animal communicators I've trained in the back of this book.

Foreword

What Would Amelia Do?

I BECAME A BELIEVER IN OUR ABILITY to communicate with animals after Amelia Kinkade, while sitting in California, told me via email that she was seeing through the eyes of our lost cat, Boo Boo, who had disappeared from our son's home in Connecticut. Amelia described in detail the house and yard and told me where the cat was hiding. The next morning, I went out and rescued Boo Boo from the exact place Amelia had described to me.

From that day on, I learned that when in doubt I should simply ask myself "WWAD?" or "What Would Amelia Do?" One barrier to my own intuition is my tendency to mentally move into a place of fear when one of our pets is missing or acting strangely. I know this interferes with my ability to communicate. I try to force them to do my will by every means available to me, or I go into my head and *decide* what the animal is thinking, neither of which works. Instead, asking "WWAD?" always resolves the issue.

My first experiment after becoming a believer was to try to find out why our beloved house rabbit, Smudge Elizabunny, would allow my wife, Bobbi, to walk out into the front yard and pick her up to bring her into the house each evening, while when I attempted to do it, Smudge would run around for ten or fifteen minutes until I finally caught up with her. (Smudge spent her days in our fenced-in front yard with our other creatures.) So my first WWAD was to step out into our front yard the next evening and mentally ask Smudge, "Why don't you let me pick you up the way you let Bobbi pick you up?"

The unexpected answer, which for me verified that it came from the animal and not my head, was "You don't treat the cats that way!" I asked what she meant by that, and Smudge explained that I don't make the cats come in at any specific time but give them the freedom to go in and out until my bedtime. Also, I realized she reacted to my wife differently because I was the zookeeper and guardian, while my wife often brought her treats and rarely forced her to come inside. I then explained to her that the cats could defend themselves should a predator get into the yard, and I was worried about Smudge being out late when it grew dark. With those words, Smudge hopped over and let me pick her up, and that's how she behaved every day thereafter. I will admit that some days when I tried to pick her up, she would smile coyly at me for a minute or two, reminding me of the old days, but I could tell it was just her sense of humor. And when I had appointments, I could go into the yard and tell her I had to leave the house now and would feel better if she needed her to come right in. After we'd communicated, she'd hop right over when she knew I had a schedule to keep.

When Smudge died, Amelia told me Smudge would be in heaven with someone named Rose who loved her. Little did Amelia know my mom's name was Rose, and she died shortly after Smudge. Now I know they are together again, sharing stories about me.

I also have two outdoor cats at our son's house, Eanie and Meanie, and they have proven that they can read my mind. The only time I can count on seeing them is in the morning when I serve them breakfast, so on one occasion I made an appointment with our veterinarian for an early morning visit. For that entire week, neither cat showed up for breakfast. I had to call the vet to cancel the appointment and not waste his time. The next morning, bright and early, the two cats were sitting waiting for breakfast to be served.

Our cats Miracle, Penny, Dickens, and Gabriel read my mind also. I take care of all of them every week — toenails, teeth, fur, hairball medication, and more. Whenever I think about grooming them, they all disappear. It is my way of testing our ability to communicate. If, however, five minutes later, I think about going down the hall to get something from my home office, I have to step over them to get to my desk.

Last year, I went shopping with our two dogs, Furphy, a Lhasa apso who thinks our house is his Tibetan monastery, and Buddy, a Griffon mix who loves to chase anything that moves, from squirrels to oil trucks. We three piled into my new minivan, which had all the remote-control door mechanisms on the key. After shopping, I returned to the car and was horrified to see that the side door was open because I had accidentally hit the key. Buddy, whom I was worried most about, was sitting in the car, while Furphy was nowhere to be seen. My first reaction was panic — I ran around calling out his name and searching the areas around the parking lot. Then I suddenly realized I was not doing what Amelia had taught me, so I asked myself "WWAD?"

I quieted down and went into Furphy's head to find out what he was thinking. Immediately I realized he was searching for me, and that he was probably at the front desk of the market with someone asking over the loud speaker, "Whose dog is this?"

As I approached the front of the supermarket, I saw a security guard sitting in his car. He lowered the driver's window and asked, "Are you looking for a dog?" I answered yes, and he said, "Here he is, on the front seat with air conditioning, water, and treats." The guard went on to tell me he had seen Furphy walking toward the front of the market and didn't want him to be hit by a car, so he had picked him up. My intuition had been right — Furphy had simply gone to look for me. He followed me back to the car, and we have never had that problem again.

It is interesting that Buddy stayed in the car while I was in the store that day — this is thanks to Amelia, too. After adopting Buddy from the animal shelter, I could never get him to climb into a car, and he even jumped out of the car once when I stopped for gas. At home, if I didn't have him on a leash, trying to get him into the car was a frustrating, time-consuming experience. Finally, one day I thought "WWAD?"

I then calmed myself and asked Buddy why he wouldn't get in the car. I was amazed at his answer. He said the woman who owned him before me had been very nice, but when her husband came home from work she would ask him to take Buddy for a walk. Buddy went on to tell me, "He would put me in the car and then drive to a bar and leave me in the car. When he came out, he would be abusive because of his drinking and just take me home and never let me out of the car. So, getting into a car scares me and reminds me of all the abuse I received." I was stunned as I listened to this intuitive message.

From that day on, Buddy's disobedience ended. Suddenly, we understood each other and quickly worked it out. Buddy now loves the car because he knows we are always going out to share the day together. He also loves to chase things in the woods near our home, but I no longer have to worry about him not coming home.

The only problem is, now that Furphy and Buddy know we can communicate, Furphy never stops telling me what to do. The other day, I drove off thinking they were both in the car, but after a half mile I realized no one was telling me where to go or what to do. I turned to look in the back of the car and saw only Buddy. I immediately connected with Furphy and told him I was sorry and was coming back for him. I turned around and drove home, knowing Furphy would be sitting in the driveway giving me that "Boy, are you a dumbbell!" look that God's complete creations give to us incomplete human beings.

My hope is you will all read on and let Amelia open your minds and increase your communication skills so you won't get that look from your animals anymore. With time and training, thanks to Amelia's communication tips, I even get along better with people, too.

— Dr. Bernie S. Siegel,
author of *Love, Medicine and Miracles*

Introduction

THE QUESTION I AM MOST OFTEN ASKED, particularly on TV talk shows, is: "How did you become psychic? Were you *born* like this?" To which I am always tempted to reply, "Actually, I was born with two heads, so I spent my formative years in a traveling circus until the surgery..."

Most psychics don't bother to break down and explain the complicated process of how to send and receive extrasensory information. It took me a while to learn this. I'll never forget the time I was on a talk show alongside some other psychics when we were questioned about the origins of our taboo abilities. I was blathering on and on about EEG studies on the fluctuations in brain wave activity when the hostess cut me off to question a more media-savvy psychic sitting next to me.

"It's a gift!" the old pro blurted out, and they snapped the camera off. The too-pat nonsense answer was just what the hostess was looking for, and it fit neatly into the time allotted before they cut to a commercial break.

I'm still seeking the perfect ten-word-or-less answer for this question, along with, "What exactly does psychic mean? Can you teach us all how to be psychic? How does all this work?"

The stupidest definition of psychic development I've ever heard came complete with a cartoon diagram. The theory stated that "somnambulists" (psychics) have a sheath missing in the top of their brain that's meant to prevent psychic data from "dropping in." The cartoon diagram depicted a hole on the top of the human brain, not unlike a blowhole in the skull of a whale, complete with before-and-after pictures of the lid and missing lid.

I realized this might be the perfect sound bite for American talk shows. I vowed that from that moment on when asked, "Why are you psychic?" I would simply blurt out: "My sheath is missing!" Or better yet, "There's no lid on my blowhole!"

Thankfully, the skepticism and condescension in America about animal communication are melting away daily. Even better, other parts of the world are much more open right now to these ideas. When I was interviewed on BBC radio, the first question out of the hostess's mouth was, "Well, Amelia, after you've taught *every* person on *every* continent to talk to animals, how do you think this will affect us globally?" And in Germany, Switzerland, South Africa, Australia, and the UK, we can actually talk about EEGs and brain wave studies without being "cut off."

Indeed, interspecies communication is fascinating and important and more people are taking it seriously. And it's not something that only gifted people can do. It's something you can do, too. Obviously, we need more intelligent ways to describe psychic ability in order to help you learn to make meaningful contact with your animals.

Meaningful contact with animals can help to answer a lot of important questions: Is your animal in pain? Do you wonder what your dog's life was like before he came to you? Is your cat sick? Does your horse have cancer? Do you need to know if your animal's problem is emotional or physical? Are you hoping your animal can let you know when she's ready to die? Are you wondering whether bunny rabbits and kittens and birds go to heaven? Do you want to know if you'll ever see your loved one again? How far will you go to find out?

I know the reasons you're reading this book are really important, so I thought the scientific research around these ideas would be important to you, too. These ideas may sound heady, but I promise that if you'll stay with me, we'll be able to create a new context for what most people consider magic: the ability to talk to animals and actually get answers. This is the first book on interspecies communication to hold telepathic processes analogous to quantum processes, to explore what the latest cutting-edge discoveries in quantum physics may have to do with amazing real stories of interspecies communication, and to provide instructions for how you can do it. But don't worry, I promise it'll be fun.

We have some of the world's most brilliant scientists to assist us in this fascinating adventure and to provide us with some bona fide references that may help explain why animal communication works. But before this can happen, we'll need to invent some new words. We need to formulate a new language for the twenty-first century that is both meaningful to mystics, respected by the scientific community, and understandable to everyday people who love their animals. We'll explore techniques designed to help us "pick up" the thoughts, feelings, and sensations of animals and fine-tune our intuition so that we can better understand the psychological and physical problems of our four-legged loved ones. Within this new technology, Gestalt Therapy, remote viewing, and mediumship are tools that everyone can claim, sharpen, and use daily to bless the beings around them. I will teach you how to hone your "sixth sense" until it is as clear and reliable as your other five senses.

This practice has a wider significance as well: communicating more effectively with animals makes us more conscious of their intrinsic value. It can help us to raise awareness about the rights of endangered species, the dangers of factory farming, and the evils of vivisection. It can help us to spur the human race into making a wild quantum leap in comprehension and compassion. The magic of saving this planet and communicating with her animals starts with you and you alone, and I hope this book ignites a flame in you that will warm the world around you.

As my mentor, Dr. Edgar Mitchell, the lunar module pilot of Apollo 14, says, "In my opinion, consciousness raising is the only game in town." I'm going to do everything in my power to help you understand how the latest, most breathtaking discoveries in science and spirituality will help us champion the lives of animals and inspire positive change in humans, too.

I'm giving you all I've got; you've got my heart, my soul, and my secrets inside this book. And I hope maybe you'll love yourself and the creatures around you enough to employ these tools and bless every animal in your pathway. I hope this book satisfies your intellect *and* your heart, your need for objective analysis *and* your spirit of childlike wonder. In short, I hope this book thrills the sheath off of you and blows the lid off your blowhole.

CHAPTER ONE

The New Animal Alchemy

> A clear distinction should be made between what is not found
> by science and what is found to be nonexistent by science.
> What science finds to be nonexistent, we must accept as nonexistent;
> but what science merely does not find is a completely different matter....
> It is quite clear that there are many, many mysterious things.
>
> — HIS HOLINESS THE DALAI LAMA, 1999

THE BIG IRON GATES SLAMMED OMINOUSLY behind me as the high-ranking official, the assistant adjutant, ushered me through the guarded private entrance, closed off to the public. It was my second visit to Buckingham Palace. During my first trip the autumn before, I had stood outside the front gates with the rest of the tourists, popping off snapshots, gaping at the spectacle from a distance, separated from the Queen's abode by imposing guards and big, black wrought-iron fences.

Now, barely five months later, I was inside those gates. My floral scarf whipped in the wind, so I nervously tucked it into my beige cashmere jacket to sop up the trickle of perspiration dripping down my chest. I hurried to keep up with the quick stride of the captain of these barracks, the assistant adjutant. It was a cool, crisp May day in London, a far cry from the 100-degree-plus temperatures I weathered in my native Los Angeles, but the last time I'd sweated like this, I'd been in a Beverly Hills spa, inhaling eucalyptus. I tried to remember to breathe. As I strode across the palace yards, flanked on both sides by British military officials, the cheerful sun beamed down on my flushed cheeks and lit the castle walls in pink pastel hues, like a watercolor painting. Every ounce of my courage and talent was about to be tested.

As a "corporate enabler" and international translator with a growing reputation for solving problems in management and for creating cooperative teamwork, I'd been brought in as a troubleshooter on "official royal business." The military was having problems with a few of its personnel. Some of the older employees were growing discontented, and a few of the new foreign recruits were having difficulties adjusting to their environment and workload. None of these employees spoke English.

I was met by many more men in brass-buttoned uniforms who saluted me and clicked the heels of their shiny black boots as I passed. The assistant adjutant ushered me inside the building and down a long corridor, lined with cubicles where employees worked. The adjutant said, "I'm not sure we picked the best time for you to talk to them. We just served them lunch."

"It's okay," I said nervously. "Maybe they'll speak to me while they're eating."

"This is Captain Harris," the adjutant said. "His performance has been excellent for years, but lately he's been quite argumentative. He's seems to have lost his spirit. He's not nearly old enough to consider retirement, but he seems a bit discontented with this job. Ask him what the trouble is."

As I walked into Captain Harris's cubicle, he was facing the other way, eating a bowl of oatmeal. When he saw me, he did a double take, and then went back to his lunch.

"Oh, I thought you were a carrot," he said.

I was utterly bewildered. I'd worked with a number of mentally challenged employees in the past, but no one had ever mistaken me for a carrot before.

"What?" I asked.

"Your sweater," he said. "It's my favorite color." I looked down to find I was wearing a bright orange sweater under my jacket and the hot coral color did actually form the elongated triangle-shape of a carrot.

"Well, his peripheral vision is not very good," I said, jotting notes in my notebook, "especially not on his right side."

"Did you bring me any carrots?" he asked.

"No. I'm sorry, I didn't. I understand you haven't been feeling yourself lately. Are you having problems with your diet?"

"It's very boring," he said, moving over to a plate of dry-looking salad.

"And your digestion?" I asked.

"Not very good since my coworker left. Have you seen the cat?"

"No, not yet. What color is it?"

"She's gray and white striped. She visits my cubicle at night. She's been cheering me up since my friend got transferred."

"Do you know there's a gray and white cat in this building?" I asked the assistant adjutant.

"Oh, yes. That's Emma. I didn't know he liked her."

"Tell him everyone likes Emma. She does wonders for morale," Captain Harris told me.

"Ask him if he wants to retire," the assistant adjutant urged me.

"Of course not!" Captain Harris answered indignantly. "I'm one of the Queen's favorites! I've won many awards! I could never retire. It would disappoint her. We have to practice marching in the parade this Saturday, and the entire team is counting on me to be in charge."

When I relayed the message, the assistant adjutant's eyes bulged.

"Yes!" he confirmed. "They have a practice on Saturday. Well, if he enjoys his work, and he's looking forward to the big event, ask him why he hasn't been able to concentrate lately."

"Your boss has been concerned about your performance," I prodded. "Are you not happy working here anymore?"

"I miss my friend. Bernard. They moved him into the cubicle on my left. We enjoyed working side by side and talking after work. The little cocky whippersnapper was so full of himself. He made me laugh and feel young again. I was just beginning to show him the ropes when they shipped him out. He got transferred up north to work in the beautiful countryside while I got stuck down here. I want to go up there, too. Or I want him to come back. I miss him terribly. We need to be together."

When I relayed this message, the assistant adjutant was visibly shaken.

"Please tell him to bring Bernard back," Captain Harris said.

"He's lonely," I said to the adjutant. "He misses his friend who used to stand on his left. He gives me the name Bernard. He says Bernard has been shipped up north to the beautiful countryside to work, while the Captain has to stay down here all alone." The adjutant was speechless. When he found his voice, he said excitedly:

"Yes, it's true! There was a boy standing on his left named Bernard! I never knew he meant that much to the Captain. Bernard got transferred up to Prince Charles's hunting facility in the Midlands a couple of weeks ago. It's true! The countryside is green and beautiful, and all these boys have more fun up there hunting in the woods. We ship them back and forth so they get a change of scenery. We thought the Captain was too old to want to do that anymore. Bernard! That's astonishing! How could he possibly tell you his name! Whoever would dream he could call his friend *by name!*?"

What's wrong with Captain Harris? Why wouldn't he know his best friend's name? Is he senile? Is he deaf?

No. He's a horse. Captain Harris is one of the royal procession horses of Queen Elizabeth II. I was invited to Buckingham Palace in May of 2002 to work with the Queen's household cavalry just as the horses were training for Her Majesty's Royal Jubilee. A few days later, I was further honored by an invitation to Prince Charles's hunting facility, where I got to meet Bernard in person and give him a kiss on the nose. Animal lovers, have no fear. Both boys were joyfully reunited shortly after my visit. Welcome to the new animal alchemy where all animals — two- and four-legged alike — can "talk" to each other, quietly, peacefully, and without misunderstandings.

YOU CAN DO IT, TOO

"ANIMALS CAN'T TALK!" That's what you've been taught. Well, what I propose is a revolutionary new idea. Animals do talk — all day long! And psychic ability is not a miraculous talent allotted to the lucky. It's a *learned skill*. And shutting out your intuition (and the thoughts of animals) is also a learned behavior. Someone taught you to do that. But the belief system that limits you to your five outer senses is not your own. It was the belief system of your parents, you grandparents, your teachers in high school, and the poor professors who wrote your textbooks, with what little they had to go on — yesterday's outdated science taught to them by *their* professors. We are about to embark on the most exciting time in the history of the human race. We are finally at a point of choice, where we can expand our senses to become "super" human and create an umbrella of compassion so that we can shelter our fellow earthlings with our love.

People often ask me, "Can you telepath with humans, too, or only animals?" To this, I always reply, "Do you mean *other* animals?" I'm about to blow the whistle on the big lie that animals are just furry blobs, and with this, I'm proposing two paradigm shifts. The first has to do with the way we view our fellow animals. They are far more intelligent and emotionally complex than we ever suspected. They can think and feel and yes, even reason. They have complicated relationships and experience the entire spectrum of emotions we call "human." The second quantum leap involves how we view *ourselves*. We have amazing powers that we never before dreamed possible. Our minds are capable of perception beyond the five senses — we all have extrasensory perception. It's innate in our neurophysiology, our bodies, and our brain chemistry. God hardwired it into the blueprint of your design. It just takes concentration and patience to harness it, develop it, and distill it.

Of course, you'll have people in your life who say, "I don't believe in any of that psychic stuff," but they're only hurting themselves. To deny the power of the mind is no different from refusing to plug in a refrigerator, a toaster oven, or a computer because one "doesn't believe" in electricity. Psychokinetic energy is the electricity of the new millennium. And with that I say, welcome to the twenty-first century! But how do we learn to talk to other animals? Stay with me here. I'm going to teach you how to "plug in." But first, let's look at the nuts and bolts of the new physics.

USE THE FORCE

"ALL MATTER IS HELD IN PLACE by a 'force'. . . behind this force we must assume the existence of a conscious and intelligent mind. This mind is the matrix of Creation."

Who said that? When? Did Gary Zukav say it last week on Oprah? Did Obi-Wan Kenobi say it to Luke Skywalker in *Star Wars*? Nope. This very modern Idea was blurted out eighty-nine years ago by a gentleman who was just a wee bit before his time. Genius physicist Max Planck made that reference to God after he accepted the Nobel Prize in 1917 for developing the quantum theory. This very daring statement almost blew his fellow eggheads out of their chairs. It wasn't enough that Max was accepting the Nobel Prize for developing quantum physics, the first concept to explain physics at the subatomic level. This new concept could also bridge the gap between science and spirituality — a gap filled with a battalion of trumpeting religious zealots who would condemn you to hell if you didn't bow down to worship their God, and an even more intimidating army of atheist scientists who at the mention of angels, telepathy, or mystical powers would dismiss you as a deluded nincompoop.

This brilliant man dared side with the nincompoops at the most conspicuous moment of his career. But he joined their camp with new ammunition: he had just created a "language" that was impossible for the scientific community to dismiss — a seemingly willy-nilly world of tiny bouncing lights (electrons) that could be either particles or waves and change form on a whim. In the realm of the itsy-bitsy, he found the keys to the secrets of the humongous, and thus happened upon the "force" and its "matrix," the mysterious energetic field that appears to be the blueprint of our world. Dear old Max may have been the first pioneer in the realms of consciousness who could actually prove the scientific validity of God. How I wish the wizard were still around so I could buy him a beer.

I am not a quantum physicist, and you probably aren't either, but that doesn't mean we don't have a right to talk about quantum physics. If we're going to discuss metaphysics, telepathy, and consciousness, we need a new language. The language of magic, which assumes a supernatural power beyond and separate from the natural world, no longer works; the condescending brainiacs were right: the mere mention of fairies, angels, and conversations with poodles — if spoken frankly without examination —

makes you sound like a knucklehead, or at least like someone who's been eating the wrong kind of mushrooms on her pizza.

Nor did the religions of our parents provide us with a precise way to describe our most intimate transcendental states of consciousness. The Bible is simply brimming with references to mind-blowing miracles, but intelligent descriptions of how to reenact the miracles mentioned are non-existent. It's like the Holy Book should have been accompanied by a Holy workbook. When I read it, I feel like I'm looking at pictures of elaborately decorated cakes, with no recipes. Science and God have rarely been introduced on the same pages. I think it's time we fixed that.

"SCIENCE, MEET GOD"

ONE PLACE SCIENCE can begin to investigate the transcendent is at the subatomic level. Our intuitive process, through which we experience the mystical and communicate telepathically, may be paralleled by the quantum process of subatomic communication. We may be bigger (and have more legs) than atoms, but there is exciting new scientific evidence to support the theory that we big, clumsy, multi-celled beings communicate with each other in the same manner as the cells inside our bodies, and that our cells may have a more effective way of communicating, too. Recent discoveries suggest that our cells may not actually have to ooze out chemicals to communicate with each other (which is the traditional theory), but that they may have an exquisite system of signaling each other by tapping into each other's "Signature Frequency," which is more akin to sending a wireless message on a cell phone. This would mean that the same laws that govern micro-scale objects (itty-bitty things) also apply to macro-scale objects (big lugs like us). Up until lately, scientists have agreed that bigger things like planets and solar systems and galaxies operated according to different rules than those that govern quantum physics, the mysterious world of microscopic electrons that can function as both particles and waves simultaneously. There's always been a gaping abyss between Newtonian physics (how scientists think things bigger than atoms operate) and the theory of quantum mechanics (how scientists think itty-bitty things operate). Human beings and our mysterious relationship to the universe have always been left free-falling in that abyss. And animals have never even been mentioned.

This vacuum left plenty of room to germinate the depressing ideas of dudes like Friedrich Nietzsche and that animal-hating crumb René Descartes. In short, our present philosophies about our world were built on the shoulders of scientists and philosophers who believed that Mother Nature is basically just throwing a lot of spaghetti at the wall to see what'll stick. These grim messages are still being displayed over humanity's head like a bunch of tacky advertisements dragged behind propeller planes. These messages, now deeply embedded in our collective unconscious, say things like: "Life's just a crap shoot," "Everything is random," "There's no such thing as psychic phenomenon," "Synchronicity is just a fluke," "Animals don't have feelings," "If anything good happens to you, you just got lucky," "Shit happens," and "Life's a bitch and then you die."

Descartes believed in God but thought that animals were just non-thinking, nonfeeling automatons put here for us to exploit. And Nietzsche was so sold on the idea that every event on earth is "pure chance" that he wrote a lengthy, verbose discourse about the mathematical possibilities of two dogs sharing one flea. (It made me laugh so hard I almost coughed up a hairball.) These guys bet the whole farm on the elements of chance, and they didn't put a nickel on the phenomenon of "intentionality," the power of our minds to impact and influence the world around us.

"Pure chance" is how these other killjoy philosophers would dismiss every single piece of telepathic communication you experience. Say your mother calls, and you know it's her on the line before you pick up the phone. If Descartes were standing in your kitchen, he would have said that your knowing it was your mother was "pure chance." Happily, there are new discoveries in science that leave these tired old excuses in the dust and replace them with exciting new paradigms that support the ever-expanding power of the human mind and the underestimated sensitivity of your four-legged loved ones. We're embarking on a revolution in consciousness, but as we move forward into virgin territory, we need to invent words to describe our findings.

WHAT IS THE LANGUAGE OF MIRACLES?

ACCORDING TO MY FAVORITE HERETIC, the astronaut Dr. Edgar Mitchell: "Quantum physics is the language the Occidental scientist uses to find the ghost in the machine of the everyday world. Without it he cannot explain it so fully. Quantum physics is the language one uses to express the mystery and miracle of interconnectedness in all of Nature. Science has displayed convincing evidence that electromagnetic energy is a basic building block of physical reality and the source of sunlight that brings life to our Earth." The atoms that make up your body might once have been part of an ancient star system; the basic components are eternal and indivisible. At this very moment, the atoms in your body are even exchanging electromagnetic energy with the chair you're sitting in. Energetically, you are in flux with the world around you.

About now, you may have a few questions. Do animals have electromagnetic energy? Indeed they do. Can this electromagnetic energy be perceived as thought? You bet. How can you learn to telepath with animals? Well, we might first need to reframe some of your big ideas about reality. In the next ten chapters we're going to talk about animals, not science, but let's explore this new idea first. I know it sounds intimidating, but if you'll be daring and just stick your toe in, I'll ease you into the "Zero Point Energy Field." Don't be scared. Come on in. The water's warm and inviting.

COME SWIM IN THE ZERO POINT ENERGY FIELD

PICTURE A GARGANTUAN SPIDERWEB of silver light. Every living being is connected on this web. Now let's expand on this idea. Instead of a two-dimensional web, let's picture this web in 3D, as wide as it is deep and spreading out in every direction throughout the universe, indefinitely. It's a sparkling ocean of energy that contains every thing in our universe. It includes every living being and the history of every being. What's more, not only is it made up of matter, but this sea of energy also occupies the space between the stars, and the empty space between your cells, and even the space between the nuclei and the electrons in your atoms.

Remember, matter itself is almost completely insubstantial. It's made up of 99 percent empty space. Now, instead of seeing the absence of matter as a vacuum, envision that this void, along with the rest of creation, is electric, vibrating, and alive. And not only that, this ocean is logging information into a gigantic library of "records" in microscopic interference patterns as we move along through our history. (An interference pattern results when light from two sources meets up while traveling through the same medium. If two coherent laser light beams are mixed and projected on a screen or film and one of those light beams carries the image of an object, the interference pattern is called a hologram.)

The Zero Point Energy field ("ZP field" from now on) theory facilitates the idea that all living beings are able to communicate naturally, through the laws of nature. Why? Because it surmises that we are all just parts of one big organism. If we are all simply puzzle pieces in one giant puzzle, doesn't it make sense that we should be able to connect silently with each other? Human beings can be viewed as cells in the body of God, and so is every animal, every plant, and every star in our universe. When I say "God," I mean a loving and nonjudgmental infinite force. You could also call it Universal Intelligence, Divine Creativity, or Nature's Mind. I don't care what you call it; just call it. Your ability to communicate with animals will hinge on your ability to communicate with God because that relationship is your gauge for how well you communicate with *you*.

If we erased your body and we erased the body of your cat, horse, or dog, all that would remain would be electrically charged energy fields — little clouds of spinning lights. You are made up of tiny packets of energy that are always in communion with the world around them. Your dog is made up of these little packets of information, too. Now, if we look at this with the new knowledge that we are all inside the ZP field, your animals are no longer separate from you. Take away the outer form and sharp edges and you'll find there is no more division between what is "you" and what is "not you." Your energy does not stop at your fleshy fingertips but can soar out into the world around you.

Taken one step further, you and your dog or cat are not in sequestered containers or imprisoned in carbon-based bodies, isolated from each other by empty space. If we viewed space as an ocean of energy that is as tangible outside our bodies as it is inside our bodies, that would change everything, wouldn't it? You could wade out into that ocean and swim into your animal's energy field, where you would feel their physical and emotional aches and pains, and maybe even see the pictures in their minds. This may sound outlandish, I know, but given our current understanding of science, there is no easy way to explain it. I'm giving you my version of the ZP field, so let's talk for a moment about its scientific origins.

Before the ZP field, the latest head-spinning theory was quantum physics. Quantum physics is just the physics of the incredibly small. While Newtonian physics can suitably describe the orbit of the planets or the energy transformations during a game of pool, quantum physics describes subatomic actions like how electrons surround the nucleus of the atom and especially how subparticles within the nucleus dance with each other. One would assume that all matter interacts with other matter in the same fashion, be it orbiting planets in a solar system or orbiting electrons around the nucleus of an atom, but unfortunately, that is not the case. The common laws of physics begin to deteriorate on small scales.

Quantum physics tries to explain the behavior of the building blocks of matter: electrons, protons, and neutrons, and even the subparticles that make these particles! Each proton and neutron is built from six "quarks," which are held together by "gluons." One type of gluon has been deemed a "Higgs bozon," and one type of bozon is called an "exotic meson." (To me, these terms invoke visions of ducks flapping around in vats of superglue while microscopic parasites with red rubber noses and floppy shoes ride unicycles up and down the ducks' waterproof backs.) There are also "antiquarks" and "tetraquarks" and, God help us, maybe even "pentaquarks." Scientists decided to categorize the quarks according to "flavors" and the gluons according to "colors." And they named the six quarks "up, down, top, bottom, charm, and strange."

Who made up these names? Don't ask me. It sounds like too many scientists were smoking pot in the middle of the night. (And maybe doing the Hokey-Pokey.) But in addition to their original particle-naming abilities, these genius physicists presented a new theory that indicates that the model of an atom you were taught in high school is wrong. Electrons don't orbit like planets; they form blurred clouds of probabilities around the nucleus. Quantum physics even plays a part in black holes, where regular physics is thrown out the window.

The discovery of quantum physics was a big "wow," but it left many questions unanswered. Einstein was working on a unified field theory and struggling with paradox all the way to his grave. But even he could not make sense of the willy-nilly world of quantum mechanics, where electrons are playing hide-and-seek, blinking in and out of existence, and hopping around like a bunch of microscopic clowns on fire. Big Al never accepted quantum mechanics as the fundamental physical theory because, among other objections, he didn't buy the "pure chance" aspect. In the famous letter to physicist Max Born, he wrote, "Quantum mechanics is very impressive . . . but I am convinced that God does not play dice." Bless his soul and his Don King hairdo! He went to his deathbed trying to find order in God's universe.

A small group of daring scientists all over the world has continued to experiment, picking up where the pioneers of quantum physics left off. The ZP field theory evolved from the mathematical "black sheep," a few equations that had always been booted out of the quantum physics family but were not forgotten. The scientists realized that if the ZP field were factored into our natural perception of the material world, it would mean our entire universe is one indivisible ocean of energy, one gargantuan, quivering resonating energy field, and that each tiny piece is concert with this glorious divine symphony at all times. Here's the real kicker: These scientists discovered that we are not only connected but unknowingly exchanging information with the entire orchestra of life. We're already doing it. But most people aren't aware of it.

So, then, what exactly is a thought? It's an electrical charge. What is an emotion? It's an electrical charge. What is a sensation? That's right, it's an electrical charge. And I want to teach you how to recalibrate your energy so that you may become so sensitive that you can sense the thoughts, feelings, and physical sensations of your world, especially of your animals. You'll become more aware of what you're already receiving. How do we fine-tune our intuition? By learning to perceive quantum holograms, of course.

WELCOME TO MY HOLOGRAM

BUCKLE YOUR SEATBELTS, kids; you're in for a wild ride. This information comes to us again from Dr. Edgar Mitchell, a man who tickled the moon with his toes in 1971 and will tickle your imagination with his space-age, head-spinning lingo. If you're under the age of thirty, let me recap for you exactly who Dr. Mitchell is. Remember in 1970 when the astronaut on the Apollo 13 said, "Houston, we have a problem!" He said it to Edgar Mitchell, who was listening in mission control. Mitchell was on the ground because their team had been delayed from going to the moon until the next launch. When this SOS came in from the jeopardized astronauts of the Apollo 13, Mitchell went into a simulator at NASA for three solid days and nights with relatively no sleep to help solve the problem of how to use the lunar space craft as a lifeboat. This saved the astronauts lives and enabled them to return to earth safely. Dr. Mitchell holds degrees in Industrial Management from Carnagie Mellon University and Aeronautics and Astronautics from MIT. He taught at the Air Force Test Pilot School and was a Navy carrier pilot before he was invited to embark on his first Apollo mission.

When Dr. Mitchell returned from the moon, he founded the Institute of Noetic Science, the first forum in America where scientists collaborate to explore new theories concerning consciousness, physics, mysticism, and evolution. I approached a man whom I consider to be among the most brilliant minds of the twentieth century to explain to us why telepathic communication is possible with animals. Dr. Mitchell was generous enough to give me this interview in person in 2002 while the love of his life, a schnauzer named Miss Megs, sat at my feet and begged for a piece of cheese. I'm going to translate for Dr. Mitchell as we go along.

DR. MITCHELL says: "Recent research suggests that we, and every physical object, have a resonant holographic image associated with our physical existence. It is called a Quantum Hologram (QH). One can think of this as a halo, or 'light body,' made up of tiny quantum emissions from every molecule and cell in the body."

AMELIA says: Do you have a little bright-eyed blob of fur looking up at you right at this moment, trying to tell you something? Perhaps she wants a piece of cheese? Your dog or cat is not really a blob of fur. It's a blob of QHs.

DR. MITCHELL says: "The QH was discovered and experimentally validated by Professor Walter Schempp in Germany while he was working on improvements to the magnetic resonance imaging (MRI) technology. He discovered that the well-known phenomenon of emission/reabsorption of energy by all physical objects at the quantum level carries information about the history of that physical object."

AMELIA says: Are you wondering what your dog's life was like back when she was in the shelter? The history of your animal is contained in every cell of her body. I'm not talking about memory banks in the brain alone here; the holographic history of your animal's life is stored in your animal's every molecule.

DR. MITCHELL says: "An additional and important property of QH is that it is nonlocal, meaning that it is not located in space-time but, like particles, carries the information everywhere."

AMELIA says: We're getting tricky, here. Dr. Mitchell believes that the records of your animal's experience are not literally logged in the physical body but in the ZP field itself, the vast cosmic library that records the history of every living being and stores it. Reading the holographic history of an animal is like walking into a huge Blockbuster video store, picking up the movie you want to watch, and watching it. With Dr. Mitchell's approach, you don't "read" the animal. You "read" the records and download the information directly from God.

DR. MITCHELL says: "What some quantum physicists call nonlocality, Albert Einstein called "spooky-action-at-a-distance.""

AMELIA says: I would have liked dear ol' Al. Any scientific genius who would name a phenomenon "spooky-action-at-a-distance" is one egghead I'd like to have over for breakfast! "Nonlocal" means that the animal and/or information you perceive is outside the range of your sight, smell, hearing, or sense of touch. The phenomenon of nonlocality may help account for what is commonly called "remote viewing," the ability to sense animals, humans, locations, and events that are not within range of the five senses. But if all living beings are just one big organism, and the entire world is your home, then everything is local, right?

If the ZP field theory is valid, it would allow the same laws to apply to all the objects in the universe, from the teensy-weensy ones to the gargantuan ones, and all the furry critters in between. It would mean that we live in an orderly world, created and operated by some sort of Divine Intelligence, and that our universe makes sense. It would mean that science would have to say to mysticism, "I understand you can telepath with animals. Telepathy has become a completely acceptable quantum process. I've burned your shamans at the stake and humiliated them on innumerable talk shows. Guess I've been wrong for the last six hundred years. Oops. Never mind." And that would be nice, wouldn't it?

Quantum hologram is a bit of a mouthful, and I want to introduce a short-hand version. Thus, hereafter we will use the term "Q-form" when referring to quantum holograms. O-tay?

Allrightythen, assuming you're still alert, let's put these new ideas to work. Our starting point in developing your intuition may not have anything to do with animals whatsoever. Let's take a look at how you receive information. Everybody receives nonlocal information. The real question is how much you pay attention to the signals you get. You can begin to find out by taking the quiz below.

POP QUIZ: HOW INTUITIVE ARE YOU?

1. Have you ever heard the phone ring and knew who was on the other line before you picked it up?
2. How often does this happen?
3. Do you think about the other person before or after the phone rings?
4. How do you perceive that information?

5. Do you see the person's face? Or their entire whole image?

6. Do you hear his or her voice in your head?

7. Do you hear their name spoken in your head?

8. Do you smell their cologne or perfume?

9. Do you feel their energy buzzing around you?

10. Do you have flashbacks of memory about the person before they call?

11. Have you ever been thinking about an old friend you haven't spoken to in years only to come home and find they called or emailed or sent a letter?

12. Do you ever know what's in your mailbox before you actually look?

13. Have you ever had a sinking feeling that you shouldn't date a certain person and, sure enough, you went out with them anyway and wish you hadn't?

14. Have you ever met someone and distrusted them immediately?

15. Have you ever known someone was lying, only to find out you were right?

16. Have you ever felt a strong sense of friendship for someone you've just met?

17. Have you ever had the sense that something was wrong with one of your loved ones only to find out that you were more right than you wanted to be?

18. Have you ever suspected you should have taken an alternative route on the road only to get caught in a traffic jam?

19. Have you ever had a sinking feeling you shouldn't have bought a particular stock?

20. Have you ever been in danger and knew something was about to go wrong before it did?

Think about how many "yes" answers you have. As you look back on your experience, ask yourself: How intuitive am I? And how much do I trust my intuition? Do I have a tendency to second-guess myself and override my initial gut instincts? We all do this to some extent, but your success with learning to talk to animals will depend on your level of trust.

TYPED ON THE BACK OF YOUR EYEBALLS

NOW LET'S LOOK AT HOW YOU PERCEIVE incoming information. The majority of my students will say, "I just feel it," or "I just *know*," when asked how they knew someone was calling on the phone before they picked up. At this, I accuse them of copping out. You perceive Q-forms in very specific ways, and I'm urging you to pay closer attention to this lightning-fast process. Does the person at the other end of the line appear in your mind as a picture, a smell, a memory? Do you hear the person's name in your internal voice, inside your own head, or do you actually hear *her* voice in your head?

I once posed this question to a group of students in a workshop in the British Midlands. "When you get this information, how do you receive it? In pictures? In words? Do you hear that person's voice?"

An older lady raised her hand and said, "I see it typed on the back of mee eyeballs! White on black! From right to left!" Most people aren't that perceptive. But this is not an unusual experience. Now that so many of us are spending hours a day on a computer, many people will actually see the answers "typed out" in their minds' eye. Some of my students see the words handwritten. I, too, spend many hours a day staring at a computer screen and since I began this change in my routine, my psychic machinery has adapted as well. When I pray, I can often see the answers to my questions printed out like a ticker tape flickering across my third eye.

We want to start paying attention to this inner system — your intuition is like an organic smoke-alarm system that God installed in your body to help you survive. There's no hocus-pocus to it. It's a survival mechanism, and it can be developed to help you maintain the well-being of your human loved ones and your animals.

How do you know you're not "making it up"? When you have the courage to blurt out your intuitive data and then, later, it turns out you're right, you discover you're not manufacturing it from the inside but perceiving data from the outside. The information you receive from an animal may be subtle, but our goal is to honor the fact that when you're communicating psychically, the feeling is somewhat akin to riding a bicycle for the first time.

The second after you first experienced that ecstatic thrill of balancing on a bicycle and flying down the street, you may have thought, "Did I really do that?" But you did not accuse yourself of "making it up." You knew you did it because of the way it *felt*. Telepathic communication is exactly the same. I want you to memorize the *feeling* of being right. This will encourage the neurotransmitters in your brain to create new pathways by which you can "get back" to this place and strengthen your intuition. To quote my favorite art teacher, Karl Gnass, "You don't want your talent to be like a drunken sailor, something you read about on the front page of the newspaper the next day and wonder 'Who did that?!' " Our goal is to develop a method of recreating the process and establishing continuity, and that can only be attained by paying close attention to what you were doing when you did it.

Now, even if the number of "yes" answers on the above questionnaire is only one, we established that you can "do it." But I want you to do it consistently and often, until it becomes a learned skill that is as well-integrated in you as riding a bicycle or driving a car. I want this to become so automatic to you that it'll be like cooking pasta. If you do it often enough, you won't have to stop every time to read the instructions on the box.

In the next chapter, we explore how to use your intuition as a tool so you can make this sensitivity work for you at will, whenever you need to. We'll dive right in to "reading" photographs so that you can establish an energetic connection — and maybe even a conversation — with an animal no matter where he is in the world.

CHAPTER TWO

Tuning Your Sonar

Imagination is more important than knowledge.

— ALBERT EINSTEIN

ORANGE STICK!

JUST UP THE STREET FROM MY HOUSE, I met two enormous Technicolor parrots in a pet food store: Cosmo, a blue and gold macaw, and Carlos, a green-winged macaw. Both birds were squashed into tight cages. (A bird in a cage is the equivalent of you or me trapped in a shower stall.) Cosmo looked to be painted by Picasso in God's parrot painting factory — French ultramarine blue, alizarin crimson, thalo green, and cadmium yellow straight out of the tube, and all displayed as shamelessly on his wings as laundry hanging off a balcony in the barrio. His buddy, Carlos, was dressed a bit more demurely; he simply looked to be sporting one of Elvis's Hawaiian shirts.

As I walked past their aisle, Cosmo glowed in the distance like a Vegas marquee. I always stopped in on these colorful characters to offer my condolences that they were so far from home — their native habitat is central South America — but because their lives were quite dull, I never knew what to talk about. I felt like I was trying to make conversation with two old Brazilian men in a toll booth. So every time I visited Cosmo, the flirtier one, I'd ask, "What's your favorite food?" to which he would mentally reply, "Orange stick." I would hear the words inside my head. It's called "clairaudience," and I'll explain it in depth later in this chapter. Not all of my students hear words. That's just how it works for me.

When I looked in the parrot's cage and found nothing to eat but a tub of seeds, I'd ask again, "*What* do you like to eat?" (With this, I'd send the picture of him chomping something in his bill.) He'd reply with exasperation, "Orange stick!" I'd peer into his cage, totally puzzled, never finding anything that resembled an orange stick, but Cosmo never varied his story.

This was our little ritual for a year and a half. The poor parrot must have thought I was a moron (or had a dull life) because I always asked the same question. I'm sure when he saw me coming down the aisle, he'd say to the other parrot, "Look, Carlos. Here comes that idiot animal communicator again. Watch this." He'd yell, "Hey, dingbat! Orange stick! Orange stick!" To which the parrots would laugh their tail-feathers off.

I actually contemplated buying the parrots myself, so anxious was I to free them from their cages, but I was scared all hell would break loose at home with my five cantankerous cats.

Then one afternoon when I entered the store, I noticed Carlos was missing. When I questioned Cosmo, he sent mental pictures of Carlos's cage getting dragged out of the store. The owner of the store told me Carlos had been sold, so I assured Cosmo that his friend had gone to a good home and would have a happy life. As I stood there fidgeting, not knowing what else to say, I asked Cosmo for the gazillionth time, "What's your favorite food?"

"Orange stick," he replied.

Eager to get this mystery solved once and for all, I asked, "Can you show me a picture of it?" Immediately, he produced an image of something in his bill about the size of a large slice of carrot, an eighth of an inch deep and two inches wide. For the hundredth time, I wondered what on earth this could be.

"Do they feed you bright orange seed sticks after hours, or do they give you slices of carrots to gnaw?"

"No! No! Orange stick!" he insisted. That's when the revelation occurred. Without taking his beady eyes off me, he frantically sidestepped toward me across his perch, giving me a good scare. He hopped down onto the floor of his cage and retrieved a teething ring of human baby toys. I had never noticed it before, hidden in the back of the cage. Hauling it in his beak, he climbed back onto his perch, all the while locking me in his intense gaze. As he held the key ring firmly with one scaly foot, he used his beak to rifle through the colored slices of plastic, the way one might push aside beads on an abacus. With great dexterity, he shoved aside the blue, the yellow, the red —

When Cosmo reached the orange toy, he snatched it up in his beak, leaned forward, and gazing deliberately at me, shook it in my face. The orange plastic toy was shaped like a giant car key, about an eighth of an inch deep and it *did* resemble a thick slice of carrot.

"Orange stick!" he repeated. My knees buckled. I steadied myself to keep from fainting straight away on the floor in front of his cage. Even after all my years of communicating with animals, I didn't know this kind of thing was possible.

I ran to the front desk, determined to buy him, ready to throw caution, feathers, and cat fur to the wind, when the owner told me, "Oh, he's been sold. A woman bought him yesterday and can't pick him up until tomorrow."

Cosmo knew he would never see me again. He had to make his point to the slow-witted animal communicator who had needled him for over a year about his orange stick. That miracle was his parting gift to me.

Since that day with Cosmo, I've had many other parrots reveal to me the shocking ability to demonstrate what they're talking about *while* you telepath with them. In one workshop in Frankfurt, Germany, we had a giant parrot as our guest teacher. I had the group ask him questions about his life that his human guardian could absolutely confirm. He was perfectly still and quiet as the crowd mentally quizzed him and jotted down their answers. He sat silently on his human's arm as she discussed the answers my students had received. But when the group asked him, "What is wrong with the other bird at home? She has a problem. What is it?" the bird suddenly went wild!

He flew around the room in a huge swoop of feathers, then returned to his human guardian's arm. Everyone screamed, it was so unexpected. The problem with the bird at home was that she *couldn't fly*. This upset the homebound bird very much and apparently it upset our parrot as well because he went so far as to "act out" the answer to our question.

You might dismiss that as mere coincidence. But then, another participant brought out a tortoise as our animal teacher. The parrot did not know the tortoise. Per the guardian's instruction, the group mentally asked the tortoise what she did to show her frustration when she was upset. The parrot had been silent and quiet since his boomerang flight around the room. He gave the group a few minutes to struggle with the answer before he burst into the air, flew to a closed window, and smashed into the glass! He fell limp to the floor and scared the hell out of everybody, especially me! His human guardian said she had never seen him do anything like that before in his life. Thankfully, the parrot was all right, and he stumbled to his feet as the guardian of the tortoise solved the mystery. She told us that when her tortoise was stressed, she would smash her head into the glass of her aquarium over and over, leaving scaly welts on her head. The parrot not only *understood* the questions we were asking the tortoise, he "spoke" to the tortoise about her issue, and then *demonstrated* the tortoise's behavior to the class!

How can we telepath with animals? By the same methods they telepath with each other. In this chapter, we're going to start the exciting adventure of learning how to talk to animals — for real. But first, let's talk about why it works.

COME RESONATE WITH THIS, BABY!

"Phase" and "resonance" are scientific terms that help us understand how we may nonverbally contact other living beings through a quantum process. Dr. Mitchell tells us, the phenomenon of retrieving information nonlocally operates by "phase-conjugate-adaptive-resonance." That's the scientific term. Oof! I like "Resogenesis" better. So for our purposes of communicating with animals, we are going to rename "resonance" as "Resogenesis," meaning to communicate with all life. In *The Way of the Explorer*, Dr. Mitchell explains resonance like this:

> Information is not transferred from one particle to another, but rather the wave aspects of the particles are in some way interconnected non-locally and "resonate" so as to maintain the correlation of their characteristics. They do not behave as particles at all, but rather as *fields*, filling all space, orchestrated and mediated in their properties by a mechanism not yet understood. Because the rules of quantum theory are supposed to apply to all matter, not just subatomic matter, by extension of this ubiquitous, interconnected "resonance," it suggests that *all nature* is in some sense wavelike, fieldlike, and "mindlike."

In other words, we can solicit information from animals by *willing* our consciousness to be mobile and to travel on electromagnetic waves, instead of viewing ourselves as isolated particles in a cold, disconnected universe.

Here's an easier way to understand this: In order for bats to navigate and hunt effectively, they use echolocation, or "biosonar." This means that they emit high-frequency sound waves into the environment. When the sound waves hit something, they bounce back as an echo. The bats hear this echo and can determine not only the location of something but also what it is — maybe a tasty fly for a midnight snack. This biosonar has a unique signature frequency; the waves are distinguished by their "amplitude" and "frequency" — their height and speed. Bats have to establish the frequency and phase relationships in order to get the unique "image picture" of an object, and they can do it *fast* (flies don't dilly-dally around). Not only bats but dolphins and some whales practice biosonar. More broadly, all matter seems to emit a unique signature frequency, not of sound waves but of electromagnetic energy.

With this new ammunition, we can redefine psychic communication as a process that is somewhat akin to biosonar used by bats and dolphins. Apparently, humans have their own brand of "biosonar" that uses electromagnetic waves. We can't bounce this energy off stuff in the environment like a bat can to find our way in the dark, but we can send out and capture thoughts, feelings, impressions, and memories. Some scientists believe this is a latent attribute in the evolution of the human race that is suddenly becoming activated in people all over the world. We're evolving into six-sensory beings. Now, when you think about it . . . that *rocks!*

When your ability to create Resogenesis is discovered and honed, its usage becomes a *learned skill* — not a fluke or synchronicity you experience by accident once in a lifetime, but an action you can *choose* to engage in and practice on a daily basis until your new "vision" clears and your sense of "second sight" becomes sharp and reliable. With diligence, discipline, and patience, you can craft your new tools and use them joyfully, without fear. Do you think of your mind as a parked airplane that can never leave the hangar, or as a jet that can take flight? The ability to be psychic is a conscious decision, inextricably woven into our self images and core beliefs about ourselves and our own limitations.

Think of Resogenesis as a cool new toy. If you play with it, your brain capacity will reorganize in order to accommodate the new technology. Another terrific way to view Resogenesis is through a computer analogy: You can bring up two programs on a split screen. That's what you'll do with the animals. You'll run both programs at once and feel the thoughts, emotions, and sensations inside both your bodies at the same time. Most humans don't view animals as psychologically complicated beings, with complex emotional lives and comprehensive thought processes. They are conditioned to see them as two-dimensional cardboard cutouts with limited brain capacity. Well, you're in for a wonderful surprise. When we start seeing them as three-dimensional and when we honor the fact that although they are designed differently from us, they are no more shallow than their hairless primate captors, our worldview begins to change. When we commit to the intention of seeing the consciousness inside animals, we invite the "ghost in the machine" to come forth and introduce itself. This "ghost" may or may not express itself in words.

ANIMALOGOS

Recall that psychic communication comes in several forms. Sometimes Q-forms are heard in spoken words, be that in your own mind's voice or in a voice that sounds "foreign" to you or as if it's coming from the "outside"; this ability is called clairaudience ("clear-hearing" in Latin). But I don't know of a term for the phenomenon itself, for the "voices" we may hear when we "tune in" to animals. So I've created the word "Animalogos." If a parrot yells "orange stick" at you, you're hearing a particular Animalogos. The Greek word *Logos* refers to the great creative Word, the divine manifest in creation.

Remember, the human's mind, not the animal's mind, is creating the actual words. In this way, the human brain is interpreting the animal's thoughts by expressing them in language or pictures or sounds. The way you receive intuitive information depends on the development of your brain.

Your skills and aptitudes are stored in neuronets in your brain, which look like trees of sparkling synapses. If you are an artist, the neuronets that hold visual information may be more developed than those that house, say, verbal skills. If you're a writer, the opposite may be true. So an artist may be more more likely to "see" the animals thoughts as "pictures" whereas a writer or musician may be more likely to "hear" words. If you are a therapist or nurse, you may be more apt to pick up the feelings of the animals, and if you are an athlete or dancer, your forte may be medical gestalt where you can actually feel the sensations in the animal's body. Further, if you are a doctor, vet, scientist, or psychiatrist, you will have a wealth of cerebral data to draw on that will help you identify the conditions you perceive and feel.

Thus you may "hear" a word and not see the object mentioned, or you may "see" an object and not hear its verbal counterpart. You may be hit with a flood of emotion, like frustration or sadness or fear, without receiving any words to explain the feelings. These changes in consciousness are your benchmark to assure you that you have "tuned in." And if several of your neuronets are developed, you may be bombarded with data and feel as if you're multitasking. As I'm working, I get a flurry of impressions that all express themselves in different ways. I see, hear, feel emotion and sensation, all in a dancing circus of stimuli. This is because I've practiced an eclectic array of skills: I write, speak, dance, paint, draw, act, play piano, and work as a counselor. Because my neuronets are all equally developed, the data have many "tunnels" to choose from as the frequencies pour into my brain. Many of you will have a similar experience, but some of you will find that your intuition favors a particular neuronet that is more developed than the others.

That, in essence, is the first paradigm shift we must embrace — the new view of mental chemistry that allows us to perceive the human mind not just as a radio station but as a shortwave radio that can both send and receive messages. The more aware we become of taking in intuitive data from the world around us, the more likely we are to be able to develop a new technology that allows us to use it deliberately.

The second paradigm shift involves our view of animals themselves. When you establish Resogenesis for the first time and connect with the animal you wish to talk to, you're in for a *big* surprise! Most animals are fiercely intelligent beings who experience the entire spectrum of emotions we call "human" and have complex emotional relationships that rival our own. "Turtles, too, Amelia?" you may ask. Yes, turtles, too. "Snakes, too, Amelia?" Yes, snakes, too. "Fish, too?" Yes, fish, too. "Butterflies, too?" Yes, insects, too. Reptiles, fish, and tarantulas have all functioned as guest teachers in my workshops, where they've poured out a shocking amount of information about their lives into my astonished students. Welcome to the new world.

When we marshal our energy to travel in mental waves, we can merge with other species and discover how contemplative they really are. Think of Mr. Spock and his Vulcan mind-meld. The mind-meld goes both ways, and animals are far better at it than most of us are. For instance, all "pets" know what their human guardians are thinking and feeling. They often describe not only their own medical conditions and emotional challenges, but those of their "owners" as well. I listen to them all day!

And now you can, too! Let's abandon the harsh, outdated laws of the "civilized" world. Let's leave behind the peasant village, with all its medieval politics and misconceptions. Come join me in the woods, where the outlaws play.

AN EXERCISE IN RESOGENESIS:
READING PHOTOGRAPHS

Believe it or not, in teaching you to speak with animals, I am not going to have you start with a live animal. I want you to try this for the first time with a photograph of an animal. And I suggest that you start to learn this process with animals you don't know at all because you may have preconceived notions about your own animals, or fears and emotional blockages that keep you from getting accurate information. This is our starting point, but keep in mind that the work will evolve until you can talk to your own animals. If the animal is on the Other Side, you may still be able to establish a connection. My belief is that all spirits survive the grave, whereas Dr. Mitchell believes that the animals simply leave a holographic record in the ZP field, and that you are not actually contacting a departed spirit, but reading the memories of the spirit's life on earth. No matter which belief system you adopt, the results remain the same. Almost every student I've ever had was successful in reaching through the gates of heaven and communing with "angels." There is no better way to learn this than through practicing with photographs.

Choose a human partner who is compassionate and willing to hear whatever you have to say, even if the information is uncomfortable. Invite your partner to jot down a series of easy questions, ones that have brass-tacks answers, like: "What's your favorite food? What color is your bed? What color is your food bowl?" The final few questions might be mysteries that need to be solved.

You may want to work with a selection of photos, so that you can choose the one that "speaks" to you the loudest. You will need to be able to see clearly into the animal's eyes. The eyes really are the window of the soul, and this holds true even when establishing Resogenesis with an animal in a photograph. Have a pen and notebook handy to write down your thoughts and answer the list of questions.

I should point out that the ability to commune with other living beings nonlocally does not rely on having a photograph of the subject, but the photograph is helpful in that it creates the first portal in the journey across the web of light, the ZP field (remember the ZP field?). Think of the photograph as a "coordinate" in space that you will use to focus your attention. The photograph is your e-ticket, your ability to concentrate that creates a threshold, and your intention launches you across the threshold into the universal library. Think of the ZP field as a spiderweb that wraps around the earth, an electric field buzzing with information. In order to enter the system, you must play connect-the-dots between these silver intersections.

The first step is to prepare your consciousness. You might read this section through once, and then have your partner read it out loud so that you can concentrate on my words. Acknowledge that individuals are separated only by flesh; our energy, our "inside" world, is all swimming together in an ocean of light, the "Implicate Order." Implicate Order is not available to you when you are focused on Explicate Order, the domain where your ego resides in time and space, consumed with thoughts of the past and future, present worries, and preoccupation with the contents of your mind. Implicate Order is only available when you shift your state of consciousness into the inner, tranquil core of your being, where your mind can relax and become silent, humble, still, and grateful and where you can focus only on love. The key word here is "still."

If you are thinking right now, you are locked in Explicate Order. The only way to stop thinking is to drop your focus down into your heart. Let's take your consciousness — this sense of identity may feel like a buzzing in your head — and lower your attention into your lungs. Now imagine the you-you-know-yourself-to-be as a silver ball of light right between your shoulder blades. Imagine you can feel your own spinal fluid floating up and down your spine, sparkling with information about you that travels on tiny points of light. Just the thought of this will bring you back to "center." Here in your own spine, you will feel your own signature frequency. Identify what it feels like to be you, unique from every other being on earth.

Now imagine a lightning bolt rising up out of center of the earth and into the bottom of your feet. This ray of light reaches up into your calves, up the backs of your legs, into your spine, your neck, and out the top of your head. This is the gift of life the Goddess Mother Earth gives us. Now envision a ray of silver light reaching down from the stars and into the top of your head. As it glides down the back of your neck, it spirals around the other bolt of lightning, gently swirling like the dance of DNA. It moves like a laser beam down your legs and shoots out the bottoms of your feet. Tendrils of light reach deep into the ground and into the center of the earth. This is the gift we give back to the Goddess Mother Earth. Now we are "grounded," anchored safely between the earth and the stars. Your intention is to feel your energy, connected to the earth through your feet, almost like the roots of a plant, but with frequencies moving through you in two directions, up and down the stem of your spine like the currents of a battery.

Let's bring our attention back to that silver ball of light in your chest. With every breath, add fuel to the flame so that the sphere glows brighter. See spokes of light reaching out from this fire, like the rays of a star. This is your signature frequency, shining out into the world around you, offering quantum information about yourself and seeking signals from others. Once you can picture the rays of light, you're ready to establish Resogenesis.

Open your eyes and look at the photo of the animal you wish to contact. We are going to create a standing wave. Envision a silver wave of light coming out of your heart and connecting to the heart of the animal. The wave, your "Lumensilta" (bridge of light), curves through space like a shimmering lariat and connects to the animal in the photo. Although this is mental imagery, the wave that you're forming is *real*, and holographic information will travel back and forth along this wave of light. As the wave reaches the animal's heart, feel the joyous jolt of contact, like a plug locking snugly into a socket, and acknowledge that electromagnetic impulses will be exchanged between the two of you.

Send the first frequency: Love. Look into the animal's eyes and project love from your heart, like water coursing through a hose. Mentally tell the animal how much you love him and ask his permission to talk to you. A "yes" answer will feel like a wave of bliss or tranquility. A "no" answer will make you antsy, nervous, sad, or empty. (It is so very rare that you will ever be denied contact with an animal.) A simple feeling of peace may be all you need to interpret it as a "yes." Remember, this is subtle work.

Send the second frequency: Reverence. Mentally tell the animal how beautiful you think he is. Flattery will get you everywhere.

Send the third frequency: Gratitude. Tell him how much you value him, and if he's passed way, thank him for the lessons he taught to his people here on earth. Again, just simply think these thoughts in your mind as if the animal could hear you. Tell him that you appreciate the time he spent on earth and that you are thrilled to have this opportunity to talk to him.

Send the fourth frequency: Humility. Ask for the animal's help. Invite the animal to teach you how to hear him speak, how to see these Q-forms. Remember, all animals know how to perceive this information.

Now check your body. If you feel exceptionally calm, that is a good indication that something about your normal processes has shifted. Excitement and elation are the physical indicators to show that you've "tuned in," but if your eyes mist over with tears and you suddenly feel some odd emotion that is not your own, you know that you have successfully established Resogenesis.

Next ask the series of questions, and have your partner jot down the answers as you give them, one by one, without giving your mind time to edit the information. Let's start with simple questions that can be easily verified by the animal's guardian. In addition to the few questions I've already mentioned, your list of questions could look like this:

- What is your favorite place to sleep in the house?
- Are there other animals at home?

- What species are they?
- What color are they?
- What do you call them?
- How do you feel about them?
- How are you feeling emotionally?
- Are you lonely or grieving the loss of anyone?
- Are you happy and satisfied with your diet?
- What is your favorite activity?
- What does your favorite toy look like?
- Who is your other favorite person other than your guardian?
- What does this person look like?
- How often do you see this person?
- What do you do together?
- Are you in love?
- Have you ever been in love?
- How do you feel about the other animals at home?
- Do you have a job?
- What could your guardian or family change about your life to make you happier?
- How does your body feel?
- Are you in any pain?
- Is there anything you'd like me to tell your guardian?

If the animal has died and is now in heaven, you'll need to tailor your questions accordingly. A few sample questions might be:

- Who are you with now?
- How did you feel about your final days of life on earth?

- Can you tell me how you died?
- Did your guardian let you go too soon?
- Did your guardian keep you on earth too long?
- What other animals are with you?
- What does your world look like now?
- How do you spend the majority of your time?
- Do you have a job?
- What was the purpose of your lifetime on earth?
- What was your favorite activity when you were on earth?
- What lessons were you trying to teach the people who loved you?
- Are you planning to come back?
- When?
- What will your body look like?
- Do you have a message for your guardian?
- Do you visit your guardian often and if so, when?
- How can your guardian better learn to perceive your presence?
- Do you have advice about the treatment of the animals still on earth?
- What can you teach us about life and death?

Again, don't give yourself time to "think." As you answer these questions, write down or tell your partner the first thing that comes into your mind. Strong emotions or sensations will be your indication that you have established Resogenesis. Another validation is the speed at which you receive the impressions. If thoughts come into your mind at warp speed, even with images jumbled on top of each other, or if you have the feeling that ideas are coming from "left field" (if they surprise you), that is a good indication that the Q-forms are flowing in from the animal and are not of your own making.

When you feel that your conversation is complete, thank the animal for sharing his wisdom with you and bring your focus back into your body. See the silver cord dissolve and in its place, envision a waterfall of stars pouring down over the animal, breaking the resonance between you and bringing the animal back safely into his own signature frequency. After you break contact, picture a cascade of stars falling down over your own body, surrounding you with a blanket of protection. Go over your answers with your partner and when you can, confirm the Q-forms you received with the animal's guardian.

MONKEY CHATTER

Okay, did you try it? Did you feel successful? If not, what got in your way? Did you find out what thoughts rule your mind? These are often the pesky attention grabbers that ruin your cerebral office party with tacky lampshades on their heads: other people's opinions, emotions, and demands; your own emotions, fears, or guilt. When we can't quiet our minds and our intuition gets drown out by a flood of busy thoughts, I call this stream of dribble "Monkey Chatter."

Are other people's opinions dominating your thought processes? One of my best students said that as soon as she tries to "talk" to her cat and she receives an "answer," the voice that screams "No!" is the loudest voice in her mind. I hear this a lot. Why? Why can't the new voice say, "I am intuitive!" Is it because the voice of the child you once were was not allowed to say, "But Mom, it worked once . . . really!"? Can we learn to give our own authentic inner voice equal treatment?

My mentor and dear friend Dr. Bernie Siegel has coined the phrase "exceptional cancer patient" to honor patients who defy all statistics and live to heal themselves despite all odds. This is also true of learning to hone your intuition. The one time you were magically right gets ruled out by the hundreds of times you were wrong. Why? Odds are not our friends. And the imprint of success on the brain never really has a chance. Some scientists believe we must create a new groove, a new chemical pathway, in the brain in order to learn something new. This is the passageway through which electromagnetic impulses (and intuitive information) travel. Like little tiny avalanches of snow, the impulses go flurrying downhill and follow the same path until the cranial landscape changes.

Are your thoughts like bowling balls that consistently find the gutter? Repatterning the brain takes diligence. Can you find the grace in your stride? Or are you afraid to move? Remember, it takes consistent practice and confidence. The true test will be whether you can be fearless enough to let other people's laughter roll off you like water off a duck's tookus — *and still keep trying.* The animals are worth it. Granted, you will need a fair measure of energy and devotion to develop these new skills, but heck, you're already expending precious energy in ignoring your intuition. That takes energy, too! And we're at a place now in human evolution where ignoring the development of intuition is not only archaic, it's just plain dumb.

Let's create a new imprint with your brain chemistry that allows the neurons to find their way through the dark consistently. We're going to plant tiny nightlights in the hallways of your brain so that your neurons can get up in the middle of the night and find their way to the bathroom.

People will goad you in the beginning: "But you were wrong about this, that, and the other!" That's like saying, "You threw eight gutter balls. You'll never learn how to bowl." Well, your ninth ball may hit two pins and your tenth may be a strike. When you hit the strike, memorize everything you did to lead up to it. Asking the following questions when you get something right will help you get it right again.

AN EXERCISE IN MEMORIZING SUCCESS

When you make some progress in your attempts to connect with an animal, ask yourself the following questions about the experience:

- How did your body feel at the time? Relaxed or tense?
- What were you thinking about just before the miracle hit?

- Did the Q-form seem to come in quicker than your normal thinking process?

- Did it startle you?

- Was it easier than you thought?

- Did the thought come in with a surefire sense of "knowingness," or was it quiet or hazy?

- How long before had you last eaten?

- What did you eat that day?

- What position were you in? Sitting, standing, or lying down?

- Were you listening to music?

- Was it evening? Were you about to doze off to sleep?

- Was it first thing in the morning before you had contact with any other humans? Were you touching the animal?

- Was the animal in the room?

- Did you have a picture of the animal, or were you just thinking about the animal?

- Were you distracted, concentrating on something else, letting your mind wander laterally? "Just floating?" Or were you in an intense state of concentration?

- Did you pray before you asked the question?

- Did you say, "I love you" to the animal who communed with you?

- Where was your internal focus? In your heart? Your third eye? Your stomach?

- What did the information look like? Was it a picture?

- Was it clear, or blurry?

- Did the image feel like you were "making it up," or did it feel like it came in from "left field?"

- Does this thinking process feel different from your normal thinking process?

- Did you hear a voice? If so, was it your own voice or a "foreign" voice in your head?

- Was it male or female? Did it have an accent?

- Did you feel any emotion?

- Were the sensations in your heart or stomach?

- Did these emotions feel familiar to you, or were they distinctly different from your usual emotions?

- Did you feel any sensations in your body?

- Were they subtle or strong? Had you ever felt anything like this before?

STAY OFF THE PATH

As you learn how to communicate with your animal, notice everything. Record everything. Memorize every detail. You have journeyed to a new state of consciousness and I want you to be able to *get back*. Think of your answers to the questions above as the crumbs Hansel and Gretel left as they braved their way into the woods, except with a unique twist. The woods *are* your home. The wilderness of Implicate Order is your true home. The peasant village is a big snore. So let's figure out how to pack up our bags and move into the woods where life will be more exciting and animal-filled.

The information you just discovered was always there, just shrouded in the trappings of the "civilized" world. Now this information is shining and available. You've found a new location inside your brain and chartered this new territory as your own. Whatever you do at this point, celebrate and applaud yourself. When you hit a psychic strike, you did something right. Figure out what it was and record it.

Now you can practice recreating the line of action or thought that led you to the revelation. For this exercise, let's think about the revelation not as an action, but as a locale, a new state of consciousness within your brain or psyche where you can establish dominion. Stick a flag in the ground and do a little dance. You will master the ability to travel from your normal state of consciousness to this slightly altered state — this more expanded state of knowledge within you. From here on out you'll have a change in perspective.

For your success to be a fluke would require the information to have entered from the outside, randomly. But there's no such thing. *You* moved. Karl Gnass, one of the world's most magnificent art teachers, once said there are two ways to achieve a different perspective: (1) move the light and (2) get up and move yourself.

When you move the light source, the model changes and you have an entirely different painting. What was in the dark is now light, and what was in the light is now in shadow. Our other method of obtaining a different perspective is to move our position. A problem can't be solved from the same state of mind that created it. If you want to know what's wrong with your horse, you have to move, to mentally *become* our horse. From this perspective, it would be impossible not to know what was wrong with your horse.

LEARN TO LIVE WITHOUT OBJECTION

"I AM PSYCHIC! I knew something I shouldn't have known. The magic works! It really does, Mommy!"

Who said that? You did. Once upon a time. Once upon a time, somewhere in your past, your voice got squelched and overruled by some authority figure who was much larger than you, knew better than you, and could even punish you and control your food intake! Yikes! You depended on that person for your survival and your education. They had a voice that could say, "Because I said so!" They could overrule any independent thinking process you might have been exploring.

Eventually, the part of you that could communicate with animals and see spirits got beaten into submission. The critical parent voice may have become *your* voice, or so you may inadvertently believe. But any voice that says you are *not* intuitive is not *your* voice. Any voice that says you can't telepath with animals is not your voice. All children are born knowing the truth. It is our birthright as human beings to be telepathic. It is as intrinsically human and available as any of our outer five senses.

How does the child stand up to the misinformed inner parent? How do we battle these vintage belief systems? With big mouths. By identifying with the truth and affirming it loudly in the face of the inner critical parent. Try this, the next time that harping voice in your head tells you that you can't really hear the thoughts or feel the feelings of your beloved animals. Declare: "You are *not* going to stop me from being who I am!!! I own my intuition!"

I recently taught a seminar in Rhode Island where I asked my students to write down the name of the one person they most needed to forgive, then I collected the papers in order to pray over their answers and help them with their emotional blocks. Of course, I expected to find a list that included mothers, fathers, and ex-husbands. I was stunned to find that almost everyone in the room had written the word "myself." How very sad that our greatest enemy is so often ourselves.

MEET YOUR TROLL

WHEN YOU DELVE out into the psychic woods to make contact with the animals, you will find a troll under your bridge. It will come out of hiding and demand payment. You will have to discover what currency your particular troll demands. You must load the intuitive inner child with as much ammunition possible to eloquently fight her case against the trolls of the past. Eventually, "You can't do it because I said so!" will cease to be so intimidating and the voice inside your head that says "It's impossible!" will start to sound just plain silly. When the troll pipes up, out-think it, out-reason it, out-"adult" it, until the child becomes the loquacious one.

Let's say your troll is your mother. You could try to outsmart her with something like, "I'm just establishing phase-conjugate-adaptive-resonance with the animals and perceiving their quantum holography, Mom." That oughta shut her up. Or you could attack the troll's tactics. "What makes your opinion more important than mine? Who taught you your belief systems? Where did you learn to be a bully? Bullying me doesn't work."

Or let's say you've had lots of Jungian therapy. You could try some fancy footwork like this: "I hear you. I acknowledge your feelings. And what I think I hear you say is that you are all-knowing and that I have no right to try something different from the belief system you learned as a child and went on to teach your children." Then go ahead and telepath with the animal, anyway. The troll may not surrender, but you two may learn to coexist.

If you consistently identify with the child, not the troll, soon you and the booming voice will be in a less one-sided relationship. Believe me when I tell you even I have a troll, and she rarely sleeps. I now acknowledge my self-doubt because I know it will always be there. When I'm having a bad day, my troll stirs from her sleep and starts thumping on the bottom of the bridge. I say to her, "I hear you. I understand you're doubting my process, but this animal needs my help, and I'm going to proceed with this anyway. In the off-chance that I'm right, this animal will benefit, and it's worth it to me to risk being wrong." Eventually, the troll will simply have to take a seat and do something else while the child plays.

With practice, you will be able to turn your invisible critical parent (troll) into a cheerleader, and she will offer up terrific advice. But this comes later in the process, where you're analyzing your imagery. If you can appease the critical parent and allow her to work in tandem with you, she might help guide you through your intuitive process more thoroughly. After many years of inner dialogue with my self-doubt, I've finally reached the point where I can ask my troll to come out and dance. In fact, my troll has become my choreographer. She's a sharp judge, and yours is, too.

It will be your troll who guides you through a body scan with instructions like, "Check the forepaw again. You missed something. Look at the kidneys. Check the teeth again." When you give her a job to do rather than just battling her or trying to tune her out, you might find that you'll get more comprehensive data with her cooperation. She gives voice to the part of you that nitpicks. And there are times when meticulousness is a great virtue. These are among the blessings that are born of abuse.

We have to be tough. The abusive, critical parent inside us is counterproductive to our growth. But before we can fight social injustice, ignorance, corporate America, and all those who would harm our animals, we must first fight the biggest, scariest adversary we've got: ourselves. (There's a saying from the old comic strip Pogo: "We have met the enemy and he is us.") All interior structures of old negative patterns need to dissolve.

Let's light up all the dark corridors inside us and think back to a time before any of this damage was incurred, an age when we were all fresh and new. Let's go back to the original woods. Eden Consciousness starts inside you.

GIVE GOD A PEANUT

I WAS FOUR YEARS OLD. It must have been winter, because I remember the white froth of my breath as I panted expectantly, gazing over the fence, perched on cold tip-toes. I was at a zoo in Fort Worth, Texas. I remember human arms wrapping around my snug coat from behind and lifting me up, but I don't remember whose they were — father, mother, or grandmother — so intent was I on my mission: to deliver the peanut to the elephant's nose. (This was in the early 1970s, long before today's high-security prison-like enclosures, designed to isolate "dangerous" elephants from innocent children.)

I'll never forget the feeling — the spontaneous squeal that escaped my lips when the warm, wet sea-anemone of a nose reached out and wrapped around my small trembling fingers to take my offering. When that solicitous tube came my way, rough and wrinkled on the outside but muscular and soft on the inside, I popped the peanut into the snoot, like I was feeding a bullet into the barrel of a velvet shotgun.

I have many other memories of being four years old and younger, of tulips, of snow, of jumping naked on my bed, but this memory remains an indelible hologram — a moment frozen in time and space — my first experience of awe, reverence, and unspeakable delight. It was the moment my life began. That was the day I had been chosen. The elephant deliberately came to me, over all the other groping, sticky, crayon-sized fingers in the crowd. In that moment, I was signed, sealed, and delivered into the arms of Ganesha, the elephant god. For I had indeed touched the face of God.

I've spent the rest of my life trying to recreate the opportunity to give God another peanut. And my life's work has become to try to help preserve these glorious animals so that other four-year-olds might share in the splendor and glory of God's most magical wild creations. Will you help me create visions of a future that can sustain that fragile happiness?

In each of the following chapters, I'm going to share with you my pride and joy, the success stories of my students that pertain to each subject, just to show you that I'm not the only one who can do this. Thousands of people all over the world are succeeding, too. (A contact list of all the professional animal communicators I've trained can be found in the back of this book.)

This first example comes from a first-time student named Julie Barone, a novice who took an introductory animal communication class with me last summer at the Omega Institute in New York. When Julie "read" a picture of a cat for the first time, not only did she knock the owner's socks off but she also blew her own mind. Mine, too! After she shared her shocking success story with the class, she showed me the floor plan of the house she's drawn *from the cat's perspective*, complete with all the furniture and windows in place! I asked Julie how she knew she was "in" the body of the cat. She said, "I had whiskers!"

Looking Out the Cat's Eyes

I started the class without any expectations of learning. I assumed Amelia had a gift and that we would get to see some great demonstrations and hear about her technique, but I didn't think we'd be able to communicate ourselves after two days. I thought there might be a marketing catch at the end of the weekend to get us to sign up for a longer course in order to really learn how to communicate.

I was attending the class as a horse handler — the animals from Catskill Animal Sanctuary were the demonstration animals for the weekend. All of Saturday I felt like I wasn't getting anything out of the class, especially since I knew the histories and personalities of the animals we worked with. I was so disappointed that I skipped the afternoon session on Saturday and spent it outside with the horses (which turned out to be a great bonding session for Dino and me, and it was lucky for Chester, who got tangled in his lead and could have broken a leg if no one was around).

On Sunday afternoon things started to change for me. We did a meditation on connecting with our animal spirit guides. I usually can't quiet my mind enough to meditate, but somehow it worked this time. My spirit guide appeared in the forest as a mythical creature with the body of a deer and a head that was a cross between a moose and a ram. He gave me a blue orb of light to help me connect with the animals. After the meditation, we did an exercise where Amelia wanted us to talk to animals by looking at a photograph. I traded pictures with the lady next to me. I was looking at Sergio the cat. I concentrated on his face and closed my eyes. I imagined giving the blue orb of light to Sergio. Suddenly, I could see into a room as if I were looking out of Sergio's eyes! I had a feeling that I *had* whiskers! I could clearly see whatever Sergio looked at as he turned his head.

I asked him if there was anything bothering him, and he showed me a piano with a white cloth laid across the top. I asked him if it was the sound from the piano he didn't like, and he said, "No, it's the cloth. It's too slippery when I jump on top of the piano." I asked him what he would like to eat. "More little yellow birds," he replied, "and more canned cat food. The crunchy stuff hurts my teeth." I asked if he was missing anyone, and I got a sense that an orange cat was missing from his life. He also said he wanted to go outside more often like he used to. It was too boring inside.

I reported all this back to my partner, and it turns out it was all true! Sergio used to go outside to eat yellow finches until his owner built an enclosure to keep the cats away from the birds. And she did have a piano with a white cloth on it! The cloth was often on the floor when she came home, and Sergio loved to sit up there on the piano. The orange cat was his brother, who had been ignoring him for a few weeks in favor of other cats in the house.

I told her I thought I could draw a picture of her house. So I did. And I got everything in the right place! The big, chunky, floral print couch across the room from the piano, the window seat (Sergio's perch while I was looking through his eyes), blue-gray carpet, a picture window in the dining room, bookshelves between the dining room and kitchen doorways, and lots of yellow in the kitchen. Everything was accurate! It was amazing!

LOVE'S PARADISE

THINK OF ONE THING YOU'RE GRATEFUL FOR. Now think of the one person you love more than any other person on earth. Now think of the one animal you love more that any other animal in your life. Now think of the animal, in heaven or on earth, that you've loved more than any animal you've ever loved. You will love them for all time. No one can ever take that away from you.

Now, if you can send *that* much love to every animal you meet, you will learn to see and hear their thoughts. You'll enter the realm where the sticky elephant snout is such a religious experience that something inside you explodes. The love is so huge you can actually tune out the world of outer distractions and surf in that sacred silence where there is nothing but awe and grace and gratitude. For a holy instant, you're in awe that we can live on a planet aside such beauty.

Then it happens. You hear their thoughts. Moses taught that we should not bow down to graven images. But our society has become so "form" oriented, so object worshipping, that we've neglected the precious things, the things that purr and trumpet and lick your face. All we need do is put our focus back on what matters, and the magic will sweep us up in its timeless embrace.

Don't get me wrong. I dig my fast car, my miniskirts, go-go boots, and collection of fake furs. I spend a fortune at my hairdresser on my blonde weave, and I spare no expense on my rhinestoned, high-heeled salsa sandals. I'm a girly girl and probably have the largest collection of pink lipsticks on earth. But the second I see an animal, I'm so hypnotized that I lose all sense of the world around me — my heart almost shatters as I fall into its eyes.

The world responds to you by corresponding to your thought. Put your thought on the elephant, and with concentration you will "become" the elephant. Only by getting inside the elephant can you hear his thoughts, feelings, and sense the feelings inside his body.

Here are some wonderful words from my teacher's teacher, the legendary Dr. Raymond Charles Barker, who trained Dr. Tom Johnson, my minister. In *The Power of Decision*, this king of the big cheeses tells us: "Modern thinkers would like us to believe that God has gone out of business. This is an impossibility. The Infinite Mind has to be an Infinite Process."

When you touch that gooey elephant nose and surrender to the mystery of that animal's mind, you leave Explicate Order for Implicate Order, where you and the animal are one. That is Love's Paradise, where heaven and earth meet, and infinite process is in full motion. Once you step out of your head and establish Resogenesis, you have just leaped off into eternity. The love where you commune with and hear animals is so profound, it defies all space and time.

In the next chapter we explore how to put that love to work for us so that you can learn the difference between fear and intuition, and even learn how to read the thoughts of your own animals at home.

CHAPTER THREE

Resogenesis That Knows

It is only those who see the invisible who can do the impossible.

— DR. ERNEST HOLMES, FOUNDER OF THE SCIENCE OF MIND

THE DIFFERENCE BETWEEN FEAR AND INTUITION

"WHAT ARE YA, MORMON?" That's what I asked my chiropractor when I first met him and saw a picture of him with his *five* sons.

"Actually, I am!" he said with a chuckle. "Most people ask me if I'm Catholic."

"Do all your kids get along?" I asked.

"Of course not!" he said. "They're not *supposed* to!"

It was the first time I'd ever heard a parent blatantly admit that fact, and it cracked me up. His answer has been a big help in my workshops, during which someone invariably stands up and yells, "But *your* cats get along, don't they, Amelia?"

Now I can tell the truth. "Of course not!" I'll answer. They're not sup-posed to! They're *cats!*"

Indeed, I had a famous feud on my hands." My two old-lady felines despised each other. They couldn't stand to be in the same room. I'd jok-ingly call Florabelle Beasley "the Queen of Austria" and Emma Curtis

Hopkins "the Queen of France." The girls were as different as any two women could be. Hopkins was born long-haired and luxuriant. If she were human she would have been a Carmen Miranda, but only if Carmen Miranda were fat, French, flamboyant, and perpetually flustered. Flo was her exact opposite. A short-haired, short-tempered, no-nonsense model, Flo was born in drag. Her svelte tuxedo was tailored and trim. When you looked at her tiny black and white face, you would get the same view as if you'd just bitten into an Oreo cookie, and her personality was every bit as crisp. If Flo were human, she'd be a Bette Davis. For those of you who've read Susan Chernak McElroy's groundbreaking bestseller *Animals as Teachers and Healers*, you've found an entire chapter on infamous Flo. She was Susan's compatriot for fifteen years before Susan developed an allergy to her and gifted the unsinkable old broad to me. Once I got Florabelle home, I discovered why sneaky Susan was willing to part with the feline love of her life. This was no kitty-cat. This was a 10-pound can of whoop-ass.

Flo hated Hopkins, and rightly so. Neither one had put an ad in the paper for a roommate. I brought acerbic Flo home to live with the most resplendently beautiful and flamboyant cat on earth, and living with Carmen Miranda and her maracas and fruited head must have made Flo feel an old shrew. Ol' Aunt Flo is still with me today, raising hell and ruling the world, but Hopkins died in my arms last summer.

Little Hopkins, the Queen of France, was a vision — a rescued Maine coon who spent her first eight years in a crack house. She was the pièce de résistance in God's cat-painting factory: Her markings made her look like she'd run through an explosion at Baskin Robbins — swirls of mocha fudge and dots of caramel on a spill of pumpkin ice cream; then to top it all off, she'd waded through a puddle of marshmallow crème on the way out the door. The minute I saw her, she literally took my breath. "Oh my God, I gotta have her!" was all I could say. I fell madly in love with her and slept every night with her paw in my hand, gently caressing the white tufts of fluff between her toes.

Two and a half years later, I reached down one morning to pick her up, and I felt a knot on her tummy under my finger. Here it was, dear readers, the awful moment I'd *not* been waiting for. The instant my hand touched that tumor I *knew* it was cancer, and I knew my little girl was going to die. But I was not afraid. If you learn one thing from this book, learn this: Intuition is *knowing*, and there's no fear in it. There's peace in knowing, even when the knowledge is the worst possible news God could ever tell you. Fear is a fluctuating frequency, an oscillating mass of chaos. You feel your mind bouncing back and forth between what you *know* and what you *want* to know. But that happens as a *reaction* to intuition, which is your first and true reaction. Your true reaction hits you in the *gut*.

The second my finger touched that tumor, I felt a warm wave of peace wash over me. Time stopped, and for what seemed like an eternity, I was weightless, floating in a sea of silence. Like a nuclear blast, everything around me disappeared and went white.

When I "came back," the fear hit me and I started bartering with God: "Please God, don't let this be... don't let this be..." Then the denial kicked in: "No, no, it isn't! It can't be! It's just a benign tumor! I'm over-reacting! It's nothing! Just a fatty tumor!"

It was too late. I already knew. My mind was arguing because my heart had already told me the truth. I think that's what we do, and perhaps that's what fear is: the fluctuation of energy when your mind is battling your heart. Our goal is to act on our first impulse, on the authentic information we receive with lightning speed. Every cell in my body knew I was touching cancer. I had never touched a cancerous tumor before, but my body could identify it more quickly and accurately than my mind.

Cancer carries with it a sickening sinking feeling. To me, its signature frequency has a sad, slipping-away sensation, like wet sand on the beach getting siphoned out from under your feet when the tide goes out. But each and every one of you will have a different response to cancer's signature frequency. Over time, as you find yourself exposed to humans or animals who have cancer, you will memorize the *feeling* of cancer and how your own unique body and emotions react. You will learn what being in the presence of cancer *feels* like, and the next time you encounter it, you will recognize it, even if you're merely looking at a photograph of an animal and you "see" it in the animal's eyes.

The moment I came back from that timeless place of knowing, I sat down with Hopkins in my lap and burst into tears. It is in these moments — when our emotions ravage us and we're engulfed in fear — that we can't seem to make our intuition work. I encourage you all to partner off with other animal communication students so that in a crisis like this, you can pick up the phone and call your partner for guidance. When our fear engages, it is very difficult to get a clear answer. I went for it anyway; even as I was shaking and heaving with tears, I literally forced my clairaudience to work.

"Hopkins, is this cancer?" I asked.

"Yes, Mommy. I'm going to die now," I heard the words in my head. She wasn't remotely afraid, but my heart was utterly broken. For the next year, she endured a series of surgeries as she bravely battled what is the equivalent to human breast cancer. She spent her every waking moment purring ... and loving me. That's all she knew how to do.

My glorious vet, Dr. Karen Martin, put Hopkins to sleep in my embrace, and I've never witnessed such a graceful voyage to heaven. I held Hopkins against my heart and ushered her safely into the arms of her angels. She not only purred until she took her last breath, but she polished off her life with a supernatural surprise! Karen came back into the room long after she'd given Hopkins the last injection, and I said, "I know they aren't supposed to be able to purr after their hearts stop beating ... but her heart stopped fifteen minutes ago ... and she's *still purring!*" Warm and buzzing, she continued to purr for what was almost twenty minutes. Wouldn'cha know? Even her last moment was a miracle. There's a saying, "Life is not measured by the breaths we take, but by the moments that take our breath." That impossible purring was proof that love is not the slave even of breath.

WHEN IN DOUBT, ASK!

EVEN THOUGH IN THIS SAD SITUATION, my intuition told me Hopkins was going to die, the opposite scenario can joyously happen. Every one, even the vet, might tell you that your animal is going to die, and in your heart of hearts you know this just isn't true. I had a horrible scare with Ol' Aunt Flo the summer before last. Already sixteen years old, she came down with the most hideous kidney infection I've ever seen. Two specialists gave her the miserable prognoses of liver and kidney failure. For eleven days I stayed up all night, crying hysterically, sticking needles in her back and giving her intravenous fluids. Every single time I left the house to go to the market for twenty minutes, I was terrified that I'd come home and find her gone.

Now, the wonderful part about writing a second book is that I can show you how I've changed my tune. In my last book, I harped and harped about allowing your animals to have a safe and peaceful passage to heaven when *they* are ready to go, not when *you* are ready to release them. I've raved about how many animals hang on and suffer needlessly for months or even years after the time they should make their ascension just because their human guardians are not ready to let them go. They stay and suffer for *us*. So many times, after an animal has languished for years, all I have to do is visit them, council their guardian until the person is ready to let the animal go, then the animal will die that night, peacefully, with no assistance. I've often ushered them into the Light all by myself; they die on the spot, in my arms with no drugs and no vets. I simply function as a puppy priest, willing to guide them into the gates of heaven.

If I had a nickel for every time I've told my students *not* to fight their animal's death, I'd have a pile of coins from here to the moon. (Okay, maybe not to the moon, but definitely around the block.) So when Flo got sick, I took my own advice and said to her, "If you need to go, I totally understand. You have my blessing. I'll help you leave any way I can."

There are these terrible death-poses cats get into when they're about to die. I had seen it earlier with my cat Rodney in his final forty-eight hours. Beautiful Flora started twisting herself into these wretched poses, the worst of which, comically tragic as it may sound, was simply sitting in a bun, with her head fallen so far forward that her beautiful little forehead was touching the ground. She couldn't hold her tiny head up any longer. I had seen Rodney do this on the last day of his life, and when I recognized that pose, I knew it was all over.

But she endured. For eleven days, she was sicker than any kitty I've ever seen in my life, and everyday I just kept telling her she could die with my blessing whenever she wanted. I wasn't about to resist her voyage when I had spent a decade encouraging my students to help their animals die. But on the night of the eleventh day, everything changed.

I was holding her on my chest in bed, crying softly and listening to her labored breath. She was finally leaving. Just above my head, a "doorway" opened in space, and the sparkling light of heaven came streaming through. I "saw" my grandmother, Rheua-Nell, appear and urgently reach out her hands to take Flora as she had once taken Rodney. Other angels flanked her, and my childhood dogs, Gus and Gretel, came bounding out of the tunnel of light. But this time, I didn't cooperate as I had done years before with Rodney. I started screaming, "No! No! You can't have her! No! Go away! Not yet! I won't let you take her! Noooo!!!!"

Well, not only did I probably scare half the neighbors in my building and a few of the bagmen in the alley out back, but I even howled loud enough to scare off my own angels. Rheau-Nell turned around and walked back into the light. The two scrambling dogs followed, and the doorway snapped shut. There in the darkness, Flo and I slept through another night.

Now, this cat hadn't moved for thirteen days. I'd been carrying her to her litter box because she couldn't walk. Toward the end of our final hell-week, she couldn't even stand up. Eating or drinking was utterly out of the question. She hadn't gone anywhere near her food bowl for over two weeks. I'd been force-feeding her liquid vitamins while my tears dripped on her face.

The next morning, I got up to find Flo sauntering across the living room into the kitchen, completely nonplused. She looked absolutely healthy and normal, as if nothing had ever happened. In fact, she looked five years younger! She walked briskly over to her empty food bowl, sniffed it, and then glared over her shoulder at me with a look of utter dismay.

"*Flo!*" I screamed. "You're alive!"

"What are you looking at?" she snapped. "And where's my food!?"

Flo was back with a vengeance. Mean, cantankerous Ol' Flo had dodged the grim reaper once again and popped him in the nose. Maybe she had just needed to know I loved her enough to fight for her life.

Now, the lesson in this story can be excavated from the fact that I had *not* bothered to ask Flo if she was going to die. I had asked Hopkins and she answered me instantly, but I had just *assumed* Flo was going to leave this world because she was already fifteen years old and all the vets told me she was not going to make it. If I had merely asked her instead, I wouldn't have had to go through two weeks of emotional hell. I could have just asked, "Flo, are you going to die?" And she would have yelled, "*No! Are you!?*"

I know now that a decision had been made on my behalf. Two years later, because I'm still in contact with Hopkins — and because Florabelle single-handedly monopolizes my heart and my home — I realize the two women had made an unspoken agreement. Hopkins, the little Venus, had been bestowed with the luxury of going "over the rainbow" to join my dearly departed Maine coon, Mr. Jones, so that she could experience true love and get some rest. Meanwhile, Ol' Aunt Flo, the little terror, decided she would stay here on earth with me because she was the stronger of the two cats. Her job is to protect me, to teach me how to set boundaries, express my anger (say "No!" loudly and often), and to take long naps, and she does this job extremely well.

HOW DO I SURVIVE THE PAIN?

MOST OF MY STUDENTS these days don't ask me, "How do I learn to talk to animals?" They're already doing it. The most common question is, "How do I survive the pain of communicating with an animal who is suffering?" Here's an interesting way of looking at it. This comes again from Dr. Raymond Charles Barker in his book, *The Power of Decision*:

> You project yourself onto the screen of life. You are the cause of your own experience. Situations, events, and things proceed from your consciousness to appear on the screen of life. The screen of life is as impersonal as the motion picture screen in a theatre. One week a

tragedy may appear on the screen and the next week a comedy may be shown. The screen does not know what it is showing to the audience. It only knows how to show it. A motion picture scene wherein a man is shot puts no hole in the screen. It remains what it is. In your own life, you are the projector of your consciousness on the screen of experience.

I'm going to translate this passage to include the idea that every animal's pain is also being projected onto the screen of life. The pain isn't *you*. Dr. Barker takes it so far as to infer that not only is the animal's pain not your own, but your *own* pain is not your own. When we can differentiate between the screen (our outer experience) and the film rolling through the projector (our intentionality) and even the light pouring through the film (our consciousness), we are no longer a slave to space and time. Dr. Deepak Chopra uses a couple of terms that serve us really well: "silent witness" defines the "other you" that appears in your mind when you are arguing with yourself, the "you" that knows better. This is the aspect of you that houses your soul and intuition. Within this inner sanctum, we can stand back — detached from our emotions — and identify that we are not our thoughts.

Deepak speaks of the "space between the thoughts" and refers to this realm of meditative mastery as "virtual domain." It is here in this space that we can remove our thoughts and emotions from our mind in order to hear the thoughts of animals. If you can't attain this distance from your own physical machinery, you're going to be a hysterical basket case when you tune into animals. If you think you *are* your thought and feelings, you're screwed.

Meditation and emotional distance require a huge amount of discipline; I don't mean to be glib about any of this. The trigger that tells me I'm "tuned in" to an animal is the fact that my eyes fill up with tears. I cry through almost every contact I make with an animal. You can't learn to feel their pain without feeling their pain. If you're concerned with your own comfort, I urge you to think before you learn the techniques in this book. None of this will be comfortable. We're ripping the fabric off the universe as you know it. It may be thrilling, it may be life-changing, it may be searingly painful, but it will not let you exist in your current comfort zone. Our goals here are to focus on content and meaning instead of form, on motion and process instead of stasis. I can't tell you it's not going to hurt, but I can tell you that it will be *worth it!*

SLOW DOWN!

IF YOU WANT A PIECE OF INFORMATION from an animal, send them a wave of love together with a sense of patience, which they've probably never felt from a human being before. Human beings are in a terrible rush. Most of us are a bunch of clumsy fusspots, racing around like chickens with their heads cut off. Our animals can tell us something over and over and over but we're so busy being flusterbudgets and filling our lives with nonsense that we can't hear them, so they eventually give up. When you're having trouble downloading a piece of information, or when you're calling your cat to come in for the evening, send this thought, "I will wait here forever. You don't think I'm that stubborn, but I am. I will wait right here for hours and stand in silence until you answer me or come home." This shows that you expect to get what you want. I'm not saying it will always work, but you'll be amazed at how often it does.

I don't give up easily. That may be one of the primary reasons I've succeeded with animal communication. One of the most remarkable art teachers in the world, Glen Villpu, said, "I'm not more talented than anyone else. I'm just more patient." He'll spend hours or even days on a drawing that the rest of us would abandon and crumple up in five minutes. So it is with animal communication, as well. There's a saying, "The longest journey you'll ever take is from your head to your heart." Well if we've got a long walk ahead of us, let's get going, okay?

THE HEART OF THE MATTER

REMEMBER THAT TO PRACTICE Resogenesis is to vibrate on the same frequency as an animal. In achieving Resogenesis, you may feel as if your body were a radio and the transmissions from the animals or other humans were a radio program you're listening in on. Most of my students find that it is more comfortable for them to "stay inside their own bodies" and ask questions of the animal. But if you take it a step further, you can establish what I call "Unimorphosis." In this remarkable shift, you feel as if you are *inside* the animal's body, looking out *his* eyes. This consciousness-merger might be an attribute of the phase-relationships between frequencies aligning in perfect unison. This can be scary for some students, who would prefer to just listen to the radio program, not become the radio. I do both techniques and enjoy both tremendously, but that enjoyment comes only with practice.

In order to make either of these processes work, we must *will* our consciousness to be mobile and travel on waves, instead of viewing ourselves as isolated particles in a cold, disconnected universe. The fire that lights the fuse of intentionality is not in the head but in the heart. Intentionality is not put in motion by grasping these scientific concepts or by the ability to comprehend and measure the world around us with our heads. The mysteries of interconnection are solved in the *heart*, and the only prerequisite for establishing intentionality and achieving communion with nonhuman animals is loving desire. We don't "cohere" with our *thoughts*, per se, but with our *feelings*. Your emotions establish who you will connect with and who you won't. The intentionality that comes into play is not a mere act of will, but a commitment to be loving, and learning to love like that takes discipline.

I'd like to share with you now a miracle story from one of our youngest teachers. There's a little fairy-tale paradise way out in the ocean between England and Scotland called the Isle of Man. When I arrive there every June, the island is covered with nothing but green rolling hills graced with baby lambs who have just joined the world. The Isle of Man is actually the place that produced the famous tailless Manx cats ("Manx" meaning "things-that-come-from-the-Isle-of-Man"). The facility there where I teach annually, Brightlife, has inadvertently become the meeting place of aspiring animal communicators from countries all over the world. But this story comes from one of my only students who actually live on the island. The Brightlife manager's son, Matthew Collister, was nine when he first started studying with me, and he wrote this story when he was eleven.

Who better than a little boy could explain to us how easy it is to connect with the power of love inside your own heart?

"Just Ask Him Where He Left It!"

One fine Manx winter's morning (in other words, one day when it was pouring with rain), my mum and I went to check on Buzz, my horse, who had been wintered out for a much-deserved holiday. We called him over, and as he trotted up to us, we noticed that he did not have his head collar on. This immediately went down as "new head collar for Buzz" on his Christmas list! Mum decided to search the six-acre field of long grass for his head collar. While my mum was looking, without success, I gave Buzz some treats, and then something in me went "Click!" I remembered my animal telepathy, and this is how I did it: First, I closed my eyes and went down into my heart and sent a beam of light that connected my heart to his, and I traveled along this beam of light, sending love at the same time, and then, I *was* the horse. When I was in him, I felt the need to take the head collar off, as it was too loose and it was irritating me. So I went down to roll and finally I got it off, then I looked around.

With that, I opened my eyes and said to Buzz, "Thank you." I went off to the spot that he had rolled in. As I got there I looked around but could not see it, so I went up a bit and something caught my eye — the head collar was lying right in front of me! I was amazed! I went running to my mum with it in my hand. When I went back to thank Buzz again, I found it difficult to believe that it had happened and wanted to put it down as a fluke, but as time has passed, I have learned to trust and go with what the animal tells me.

Matthew has found two other missing objects since this incident, and his little sister has now mastered the skill. When his mother, Jane, relayed one of the latest incidents to me, she said she'd gotten flustered because one of the horses had lost a shoe. Matthew looked at her with utter dismay and said, exasperated, "Mum! Just ask him where he *left* it!" (Ouch! Nothing like a psychic eleven-year-old to make you feel like an idiot.)

Now let's take a closer look at this. When Matthew tells us he's "traveling along a beam of light," he's referencing an exercise I wrote in *Straight from the Horse's Mouth*. At that time, I knew how to make this quantum process work, but I didn't know what the Sam Hill to call it.

Matthew calls it "building the bridge." (Our word for this wave of loving energy is now "Lumensilta," from the Latin root *lumen*, meaning "light," and the Finnish word *silta*, meaning "bridge.")

Matthew "travels" along the Lumensilta by allowing his mind to function in the "wave" aspect, not in the "particle" consciousness where most of us spend our waking hours. Let's take a brief look at what the particle-wave theory is all about, because this is the simplest, most effective way to explain the different modes of operation whereby your consciousness can learn to fly.

THE PARTICLE-WAVE THEORY

ALBERT EINSTEIN SHOWED definitively that matter is composed of particles. A physicist named Thomas Young had a century earlier proposed the particle-wave theory after his discovery of a phenomenon called interference. Bestselling author Gary Zukav describes this beautifully. In Gary's book *The Dancing Wu Li Masters*, he tells us:

> Young's double-slit experiment showed that light must be wave-like because only waves can create interference patterns. The situation, then, was as follows: Einstein, using photoelectric effect, "proved" that light is particle-like, and Young, using the phenomenon of interference, "proved" that light is wave-like. But a wave cannot be a particle and a particle cannot be a wave. The wave-particle duality was (is) one of the thorniest problems in quantum mechanics. Physicists like to have tidy theories which explain everything, and if they are not able to do that, they like to have tidy theories about why they can't. The wave-particle duality is not a tidy situation. In fact, its untidiness has forced physicists into radical new ways of perceiving physical reality. These new perceptual frames are considerably more compatible with the nature of personal experience than were the old.

For most of us, life is seldom black and white. The wave-particle duality marked the end of the "Either-Or" way of looking at the world.

Most "muggles" (that's Harry Potter's term for a nonmagical person) are what I would call "separatists." Separatists are antimystic and adamant that their consciousness is contained within their own body, like water frozen into an ice cube in a tray. You might say the primary difference between a psychic, which you are now becoming, and a separatist is that psychics ride the waves, whereas separatists count the particles. When we think of ourselves as waves — as water, not ice — any two drops in this big ocean of human and animal energy can join at any point and flow together in harmony. Our bodies and minds are separate from one another, *and* yet they are not. The nature of reality and the existence of matter therein is not dualistic. It is holographic, meaning more than one definition of physical reality is correct at any one time.

Water makes a splendid analogy for consciousness. Water has three forms, but only one essence. The building block, H_2O, remains the same even if the water has taken the form of ice or steam. The same is true of your mind. I would liken Resogenesis to flowing water; in Resogenesis you're allowing your awareness to travel on a wave of energy in order to connect with an animal or another human being. In its "steam" form, consciousness might be like an even more refined wave, one that enables you to take flight in your own mind and "track" lost animals or "see" departed souls through the veils of heaven.

A skeptic has a mind like a chunk of ice. You don't. You can make choices. Your view of the universe has everything to do with your perspective, and your perspective is determined by how you *choose* to operate your own mind. Water responds to outer elements. Your consciousness also responds to outer stimuli, but you can train it to respond to inner stimuli as well, depending on the challenge. You can reconfigure your thinking processes so that your inner skills are multidimensional, adapting to address the need at hand, just as a wave can be a particle and a particle can be a wave, depending on the circumstances.

Okay, here are some eye-opening stories that illustrate how one of my best students chooses to activate her mental powers in order to help animals. Heidi is a retired cop, who now practices as a professional animal communicator in Northern California.

Secrets of a Psychic Peace Officer

When I joined the California Highway Patrol, I became a road patrol officer assigned to the Hayward area, south of Oakland, California. I regularly patrolled the unincorporated county areas and became quite active in drug enforcement. I became trained as a drug recognition expert (DRE) and studied search and seizure laws in order to make good arrests.

From the beginning of my training as an officer, I was encouraged, as all officers are, to "listen to gut feelings." Actively listening to that "little voice" not only saved my life, it became rather convenient in my day-to-day work. I began to ask my "little voice" other advice, like whether or not a person was armed or had drugs. After a few years of cultivating this friendship with my little voice, I began secretly using it on a regular basis. I would "search" vehicles and persons by "touching" them, or physically extending my hand like a wand. I would ask questions and see in my mind's eye the true answers about weapons and drugs, in contradiction to spoken denials. I would touch cars at an accident scene, and see a little replay of the crash. It made it very easy to understand witnesses and write the reports. When I got caught by fellow officers, I would smile, say I was "using the force" and then change the subject quickly, as I knew these cynical cops would think I was nuts if I told them I really *was* "using the force." I began keeping a squeaky pig toy (named Edna) on the dashboard of my patrol car that I had dressed in CHP blue and gold. If anyone questioned me too specifically about how I had found things, I would say, "Oh, Edna told me."

Only now do I openly admit being psychic and that I used that skill in police work. Now I am retired and don't have to worry what other cops will think. When I heard Amelia was coming to Northern California, I made a beeline to her workshop, because I had always wanted to extend these abilities to animals. Amelia made quite a fuss over me in the workshop, and every time I was right about one of the animals, Amelia and I both shared many happy tears. She started referring clients to me immediately and encouraged my new career. Here are two stories of the miracles that have happened since I studied with her.

South African Temper Tantrum

I received an email from a lady in South Africa who wanted help with her horses. She said she found me by doing an Internet search, as I am listed as an animal communicator on www.infohorse.com and a few other sites. She emailed me photos of the horses and a list of questions. I was a bit nervous, as I had not done a reading completely by email, but I decided to give it my best. I still don't know how this works, but it definitely does work.

One of her horses was behaving oddly. She said that when she approached the barn, the horse, a tall chestnut American saddle horse named Guy Fawkes, would put his head down and bite at his own forelegs (leaving marks). Then, while biting himself, he would buck and kick with his hind legs, kicking the wall of the stall. Having known several horses and worked with them for over five years, I knew not only that this was very odd, but that the horse could seriously injure himself. I had never heard of a horse biting itself.

When I contacted the horse it seemed like he was a jealous little kid wanting Mommy to hold him first, and longer, than the other kids. He said this behavior always got him the attention he wanted.

While trying to think of a solution, I remembered discussing positive and negative attention with my own son when he was a toddler. (I really have no patience for tantrums, ever.) I remembered that I simply told my son to ask for attention. It worked. He would toddle over and say, "Mommy, I need 'tention." I would answer him and give him attention as soon as I could. I did not know what else to do to modify the horse's behavior, so I suggested to the horse that he ask for attention by whinnying. I told him his tantrum may get him hurt.

Before I could report back to the client, I received an email from her expressing concern because the horse had stopped bucking in his stall, but now was whinnying all the time. She was constantly going out to the barn to check him. I admitted that it had been my suggestion and promised to further negotiate now that he was willing to try something new. He finally agreed to only whinny during daylight so everyone could get some sleep.

Where Are My Ducks?

When my son, Trevenen, was ten years old, he wanted some pet ducks and purchased some ducklings from the local feed store. He hand-fed them and cuddled them twice a day. There were five Khaki Campbells and two white Pekings. When the ducks got big enough (too big to be picked up by eagles or hawks), they were set loose to free range. Each day they were still hand-fed. Trev had named them all and cared for them like a mother hen.

As spring turned to summer and the ducks matured, it became clear that out of the seven ducks, there were only three females. When the Khaki Campbell males grew up, they had dark brown hoods on their heads, brown bodies with white at the edges of their wings, dark brown tail feathers to match the hoods, and orange feet. The females were a uniform brown with gray feet, the better to camouflage themselves and their nests. The white Pekings grew up to be all white with orange feet and bills. The two Pekings were male and female and paired up quickly, but that left too many brown bachelors.

One morning, Trev came to me and said, "Mom, I can't find Thrasher and Dasher" (the Peking ducks). "Would you tell me if they are dead? Did a coyote get them last night?"

I knew my son was trying to be brave, but all I could see was my little boy's heart breaking. I reached out with my mind and called to Thrasher and Dasher. I instantly felt Dasher's presence. I asked her if she was all right, and she said she was. I asked, "Where are you?"

"Hiding."

"Why are you hiding?"

"*They* won't leave me alone!"

I got the image of three of the bachelors trying to mate her and nearly drowning her. I relayed the information to Trev, but he was not satisfied.

He wanted to see them. I tried again, but she refused to tell me where she was. I slipped in the question, "Well, will you show me where you are?" For a split second, I got an image of what looked like very tall green grass, then silence. She literally was refusing to talk or show me anything. It was as if she shut her eyes tight and clamped her bill shut. I tried asking her mate, but he would not tell, either. While Trev felt better knowing they were alive, he would not quit. We could not think of anywhere nearby where there was tall green grass. About this time, the three bachelor ducks came waddling by, single file, and my son wanted me to ask them if they had seen the Pekings.

Before I even got the question out, I heard, in a bit of a threatening tone, "Don't say anything!" It seemed to be coming from the leading duck. The one in the rear of the line meekly chimed in, "I'm gonna tell!"

Then, like street thugs, the two leading ducks stopped and turned on the last duck. They began threatening to hurt him if he talked. I felt there was some bullying on the part of the two, and some jealousy from the one wanting to tell. The two ducks began pushing at the third, but he stood his ground during the argument. Finally, after rapid-fire exchanges of threats to shut up and threats of telling (all the while the trio were bumping chests), the third duck blurted out, "She's in the ditch! They would not leave her alone so she's hiding!!" I saw a high-speed film in my mind of the two ducks trying mercilessly to mate the missing Peking hen, and the third duck not getting any action. As soon as the third duck said this, the two guilty ones ducked under the fence and ran away into the orchard, followed slowly by the tattletale.

When I hear the animals, I rarely hear a specific voice. It is usually just as if I am talking to myself in my own mind, but the energy is different. It is as if I am doing different character voices myself. It also has directionality, which helps me know where it comes from. It is like having a conversation with myself, but the other voice is coming from another room. It comes very fast, and often questions are answered before I finish asking them. The speed, direction, and characters let me know it is not coming from me, that it is not just my imagination.

After a good chuckle, I told my son what had been said. I started to head into the house when he gently took me by the hand and asked, "Mommy, would you please help me look for them?" He only calls me "Mommy" when it can be said privately and he really wants something. His pleading blue eyes won out. We looked for them again. Finally, when we were just about to give up, I spotted the two MIAs and called Trev. The white Peking female, Dasher, was hiding in the tall reed-like plants in the ditch. That confirmed the split-second image I had gotten of tall green "grass." The greenery was so dense that she could hide and only be seen from a certain viewpoint.

Her mate, Thrasher, was with her. When we made eye contact, I heard, "Don't tell them where I am, okay?" I promised not to tell. My son asked me to warn the bachelors that they would be penned up if they did not leave her alone. The guilty bachelors stayed out of sight until the evening feeding.

Later that morning, after the Pekings had finished their swim and emerged from the irrigation ditch, Trev hand-fed them, then ushered them back into a secure pen. He left them there for several days so the female could start a nest if she wished and could get a break from the persistent bachelors.

THREE KEYS TO COMMUNICATION

WELL, BY NOW I'LL BET you're champing at the bit to learn how to do this for yourself. If Heidi can actually hear what a bunch of ducks are saying about each other, I'll bet you can learn how to hear one animal at a time. But let's first take note of some of Heidi's wisdom. She told us that although this type of telepathic communication feels like she's having a conversation with herself, there are slight differences in the nature of the incoming data. She gave us three keys to help us understand the subtle nuances in information you'll receive from animals.

1. Speed: The biggest flag that your intuition is working is the speed at which the info comes in. As you employ your thinking process, your thoughts have a certain rhythm. One of the ways you know that information is coming in from the outside is that the answers come in like lightning. When you ask the animals a list of questions, they often answer you in rapid fire, even *before* you've finished asking the questions. When I telepath with an animal, the process happens so fast it almost hurts. It takes a huge amount of concentration to allow your mind to move that quickly.

2. Direction: Heidi said the voices sound like they're coming in from the next room. This is a subtle distinction, but the Animalogos (voices) seem to have a "coming-out-of-left-field" quality. When the animal's answers surprise you and they say something you never would have thought of on your own, you know you're "doing it." These answers may startle you and make you laugh, or they may come in with strong emotion. If you get hit with a wave of sorrow or a blast of anger that absolutely shocks you, you know you've made contact.

3. Character: Not all of you will hear strange voices or accents that sound different from your own thinking process. Many of you will, but some will simply receive information in what feels like your own "mind's voice." The clearest way to test your own process is to "talk" to more than one animal at a time and see if their Animalogos sound different. Even if you are one of the people who hears animals in your own mind's voice, you may feel the difference in their personalities. If you are talking to one animal at a time, you may not be able to differentiate their "voices" from your own thinking process, but when you have more than one, their vibrations will calibrate at different speeds. A cat "sounds" nothing like a dog, and more importantly, they will not *feel* the same.

   When my students swap photos and read each other's animals, one of the triumphs I observe regularly is the ability to get the character traits of that particular animal. I've had some students report that their partner may not have gotten all the nitpicky answers right, but they simply nailed the *personality* of that particular animal. In many respects, this is much more important.

Let's put these ideas to work now and get the ball rolling. I suggest you try this exercise with someone else's animal. In fact, I'd like you to try this with an animal that you don't know very well. If you start with your own animals, you may have preconceived notions about their answers, and your emotional ties to them may be so strong that you can't get a detached perspective. If the animal's guardian would like to make out a list of questions about topics they can confirm, that would be helpful. But I've created some sample questions below for your first live telepathic encounter. Please jot the questions down in a notebook, and I encourage you to write down the answers as well. Writing sometimes circumvents the critical mind, and if you allow yourself to free-associate — write any thoughts, names, tastes, colors, smells, and textures that come to you as you go along — you may find that writing opens up your creative channels to better hear the animals.

And finally, please be aware that when we activate our Lumensonar, we are not sending only waves of light. Think of a dolphin. The sonar has to bounce off something to come back with its data. For our purposes, the frequency you'll send is a particular emotion. This is how we ask questions. If you send a wave of fear, you'll identify the holograms that "match up" with the frequency of fear. For instance, we always start with love because that's what established the connection and builds trust between you and your animal friend. After that we can explore more negative emotions in order to get information. If you're communicating with a dog and you send a wave of fear, you might suddenly hear thunder and want to go hide under the bed. Or worse, if you ask questions about prior abuse, you might even hear shouting and feel the pain of being struck.

If you send a wave of energy and nothing comes back, that's a "no" answer. The Lumensonar will have nothing to identify, and it will just fade away. A "yes" answer comes back with an amplified sensation of whatever emotion you sent. With this you may see mental pictures or even what Heidi called a "high-speed film" clip. But enough explanation. Let's get going!

AN EXERCISE IN RESOGENESIS: HOW TO LEARN TO LISTEN

Sit quietly with your chosen animal, with your notebook in your lap and your pen in your hand. I open every communication with a prayer, so here I will quote my favorite one. In my last book, we addressed this prayer to Sekhmet, the lion-headed goddess of ancient Egypt, but now I'd like to address it to Archangel Raphael, who is the archangel of both animals and healing. You may address it to whomever you wish. For instance, in the Catholic tradition, our patron is Saint Francis, and in the Buddhist tradition, the goddess of the animals is Quan Yin, the female aspect of the Buddha. In the Hindu tradition, Lord Ganesha is the remover of obstacles and keeper of the animals. Tailor this prayer to your own Higher Power, or you may join me in honoring Archangel Raphael. Sit quietly with your animal friend and say silently along with me:

Archangel Raphael,
Gently take us by the hand
And lead us up the little path,
Through the narrow gates,
And into the Holy of Holies, where all is righteousness.
For it is here that we are one with the Father.
And we thank thee, Father, for hearing us
(Thou hearest us always.)
And for leading us into the way of the truth that frees,
The perfect love that casts out all fear,
The peace that passeth all understanding,
And the way of eternal life. Amen.

Now focus on your breath. We're going to take three deep breaths with three normal breaths in between. Hold each deep breath for a count of ten. Take a deep breath in — inhaling a golden ball of light into your lungs — and count silently along with me — one, two, three, four, five, six, seven, eight, nine, ten. And blow it out. Now take a normal breath in, and then exhale.

Inhale your second deep breath, and with this, you'll feel your shoulders relax. Savor the breath, then as you exhale, release any tension, aches and pains, fear, anger, worry, anxiety, or doubts about the process.

Take a normal breath in, feeling your stomach soften as your chest fills with warm, life-giving air. With this breath, we're inhaling all good things: joy, peace, comfort, love, tranquility, happiness, triumph, excitement. And gently blow it out.

Resting your focus in your lungs, think of something you're grateful for. Now think of something else you're grateful for, and take a moment to thank God for this blessing. Now think of the person you love more than any other person on earth. Next, think of the animal you love more than any other animal in your life. You might feel the corners of your mouth start to lift into a smile. Keep your mind quiet as you breathe deeply and center your attention in your heart. Now think of an animal you've loved that has flown over the rainbow and is now in heaven. Let the gratitude fill you as you silently thank God for the precious moments you shared with this being you loved so much. If your eyes mist over, you know you've entered the magical trance where I need you to go.

Think of your heart as a silver star shining in space. Your "mind" is no longer located in your head, but has moved down into your heart. If we took your body away, this is all that would be left — a dazzling silver star shining its light. With every breath, this star that you are grows brighter and larger. Silver spokes of light are reaching out of you in every direction, and with your intentionality, you can "will" them to fly anywhere you wish.

Now open your eyes and look at the animal you'd like to contact.

Send a ray of light out from your heart to form a bridge with the animal. I want you to love this animal as much as you've ever loved one of your own animals. I want you to love this animal as much as you've ever loved a human being. In this moment, I want you to love this animal more than you've ever loved anything. Look at how stunningly beautiful she is. Look at her markings. Look at her design. Look at her majesty. I want you to feel her beauty as if you're looking at her — I mean really "seeing" her — for the first time. You may touch her if you wish and pet her gently as you tell them softly these words: "I love you. I love you. I love you. I'm not going to try to change you. I'm not going to try to control you. I won't use your secrets against you. I'm not here to manipulate you. You can trust me. I can hear anything. I am an attorney for the defense, not the prosecution. I'm here for *you* and you alone. I will voice your wishes and defend your needs no matter what your human guardian thinks. I promise to listen. I can hear you, now. Will you please share your thoughts?"

Here are some possible questions for animals but feel free to tailor the questions to the animal's specific needs. If the animal's human guardian can absolutely verify the answers, you can easily track your own progress. Take your pen in your hand and jot down the first thing that comes to mind as you ask these questions.

Questions for a Dog

1. *What's your favorite food?* Picture the animal hungry. Pretend you are her, inside her body. Your stomach grumbles. You start to salivate. A dish in front of you is filled with your favorite food. What is it? What color is it? What texture? How does it smell?

2. *What is your favorite treat?* In a slightly different context, picture yourself in the body of the dog, looking out her eyes. You see a human hand coming toward you, holding your favorite treat. This is something delectable that you don't get very often. What is it?

3. *What does your favorite toy look like?* See something right in front of your nose that you pick up with your mouth. Remember, you can't use your arms. Almost your entire world is experienced through your nose and mouth. What color is this toy? What do you do with it? Do people throw it at you so that you can catch it midair? Do you tug on it? Do you hide it? Is it a "dog-toy," or did you steal it from the humans? Do you think that's funny?

4. *Is there another dog at home?* Envision you are in this dog's body and you're looking around the house. Do you see another dog? Send the present dog a huge ball of raw creative energy. You are manufacturing a cloud of atoms next to this dog that will suddenly organize and take shape. I like to call this a "probability cloud" because you don't know what the energy will reveal until your intuition organizes it. If the energy begins to "cohere" and you "see" a shadowy shape next to the dog, that's a "yes" answer.

5. *If so, what does this other dog look like? What color is it? What size? What shape? What breed? Is it larger? Smaller? Male? Female? What does it smell like?* If you already know the answer to this question, ask instead:

6. *How do you feel about this other dog?* From within the body of the dog you are communicating with, you see the other dog approaching you. How do you feel emotionally? Warm? Excited? Happy? Annoyed? Jealous? Threatened? Ask your friend to show you the emotional dynamics of their relationship. Is your friend protective of the other dog? If so, why? Intimidated? If so, why? Ask her to elaborate: *When this other dog "talks" to you, what does it say? What is his attitude toward you? How do you feel about him?*

7. *If there is not another dog, would you like to have a partner?* Again we send the probability cloud to "form" the body of a dog. See this spirit-animal walking beside, playing with, sleeping with, and eating alongside this dog. How does this dog feel about that?

8. *Are you missing anyone?* Send the frequency of loneliness. The feeling will travel via Lumensonar and "match up" with the Q-forms that align with that emotion. They'll boomerang back to you, and you'll see the pictures in your mind of whom this dog misses.

9. *Are you showing me the memory of a dog?* Send the probability cloud and see what shape it takes. Memories are fuzzier, duller, and more subtle than the crisp edges of an image of a living creature. The spirit of a dog that has passed away may also take a softer image.

10. *Are you in love with another dog?* Send the frequency of love and see what images come back.

11. *What does this dog look like?* Hold the frequency of love in your body and see how clearly you can envision this other dog. Use all your senses: sight, taste, hearing, sensation, and most of all, smell!

12. *Where do you see this other dog?* Visualize that you are in the body of this dog and that your beloved dog-friend is approaching you. Now look at the terrain around you. Where are you? Inside someone's house? In the park? On the sidewalk? What do you see? What temperature is it? What time of day is it? Are you going for a walk? Is there a lead tugging on your neck?

13. *Do you see him/her often enough? How often do your encounters take place?* Do you feel satisfied when you make the connection to the other dog or is there a sense of longing attached to this vision?

14. *How do you feel about cats?* Envision you are approaching a cat and smelling its delicious perfume. Bury your nose into its fur. How do you feel?

15. *Is there a cat at home?* Picture you are in the dog's body at the appropriate height off the floor. Now look up. Chances are if there is a cat, it will be on a chair or perch over your head.

16. *If so, is it in your house or outside of your house?* From the dog's perspective, search the house. If you don't find a cat there, look out in the back yard, up high, perhaps on the fence. Then look out in the front yard.

17. *What color is this cat?* Try to see it clearly and notice the distinctions in color. Are its paws a different color from its body? What breed is it? How long is its fur?

18. *What do you call this cat?* Don't be scared. Just free-associate and jot down the first thing that comes to mind.

19. *What's your favorite activity?* Envision that you're in the dog's body and you're insanely happy. What are you doing? Use your five senses. What's under your feet? What do you taste? What do you smell? Are you outside or inside? In water? In a car? What do you hear? What time of the day is it? Are there other animals with you?

20. *Do you get to engage in this activity often enough?* Feel the bliss of engaging in your favorite activity. Now send the frequency of longing. If the longing is "matched" and comes back twice as strong, that's a "yes" answer. It means the dog misses doing what he loves to do.

21. *What color is your bed?* From inside the dog's body, feel yourself getting sleepy and climbing into your bed. Now look down. What color is the cushion or blanket under your paws.

22. *Where's your favorite place to sleep in the house?* Imagine you're settling into your favorite spot. Is it a "dog bed," or are you on a piece of the human's furniture? What room are you in? Where is the kitchen from this perspective? (Dogs will always mention how far they are from the good smells.) How far are you from the nearest heater or stove? How much light is there in this room? What do you see from this spot, and why do you like it so much? From this vantage point, can you see out the window? Can you see the front door? Can you see people cooking in the

kitchen? Are you sleeping on your human's bed? Are there stairs in the house?

23. *Do you have a job?* Now, as the dog, you are filled with a sense of purpose. What is it that is the most important activity in your life? You may ask more specific questions by sending the mental pictures of the dog performing search and rescue or working with children or elderly people in pet-assisted therapy. If you're working with a police dog or a seeing eye dog, you can ask him about any aspect of his work by sending a specific stream of Q-forms.

24. *What is your relationship to your guardian?* From the dog's perspective, look up and see your human approaching you. How do you feel?

25. *What does your guardian do that irritates you?* From inside the dog's body, manufacture the feeling of frustration. What do you want that you're not getting? What is the person making you do that you don't like? If you could speak to this person and set them straight, what would you say?

All right, I think you've gotten the hang of how to ask questions. Here is a list of more possible questions you might ask your dog friend. The only one I'm going to elaborate on is how to ask about pregnancy.

1. *Are you in love with an animal that is not a dog?*

2. *What does this animal or human look like?*

3. *What do you call them?*

4. *What does your human guardian do for a living?*

5. *Who is your favorite human other than your guardian?*

6. *How old is this person?*

7. *What color is this person's hair?*

8. *How do you feel about children?*

9. *Have you ever had puppies?* Feel the heaviness in your abdomen. The way you can distinguish if the dog has actually had puppies or just wants to have puppies is by sending the pain of childbirth. If the condition existed, the pain of delivery will have made a strong impression. Now look around your feet just after you've delivered. How many puppies do you see? How many litters have you had?

10. *Would you like to have puppies or a substitute for puppies (like cats or stuffed animals)?* Picture you are in the dog's body and looking at your own puppies through your own eyes. How do you feel about them? Now imagine you are carrying stuffed animals around in your mouth, herding your toy puppies. Now picture you have cats to take care of instead of puppies of your own. Are you feeling like a good mother? Are the cats safe in your care?

11. *What do you see on your favorite walk?*

12. *How does your guardian feel about the way you interact with other dogs?*

13. *What makes you angry?*

14. *What scares you?*

15. *Are you in pain?* (We'll explore medical gestalt in depth in future chapters.)

Questions for a Cat

1. *What is the purpose of life on earth?* Could you give a brief overview of the feline's participation in human evolution? (Just kidding.)

2. *What's your favorite food?* Picture the cat eating something that tastes absolutely delicious to him even if it might be out of context for you. Remember that if you find yourself crunching on the bones of a delicious mouse or sparrow, this is the best confirmation in the world to prove that you have successfully formed a connection with your cat. The fact that the point of

view is drastically different from your own establishes the level of your success.

3. *Do you go outside?* Envision you are out climbing trees, chasing bugs, sneaking through gardens, and jumping on walls. Are there stars over your head at night, or are you enclosed in a house? Is there grass under your feet or carpet? Is there sunshine on your back or artificial light? If you are outside you will feel the wind in your whiskers, smell the roses, the pine trees, and see the butterflies. You will be in a heavenly paradise of birds, insects, and maybe even rodents to chase.

4. *If you don't go outside, would you like to?* Again, send the temptations of the outside world as opposed to a safe life of merely sleeping on a bed or couch.

5. *Do you hunt?* The wild and wonderful world of a hunting feline is one of constant adventure and anticipation. Even if you have a lap cat named Fluffy who appears to be nothing more than a soft lump of marshmallow fluff, make no mistake. A feline is God's most sophisticated killing machine. The thrill you'll feel if you connect with a hunting cat exceeds any joy a human could ever experience.

6. *What is your favorite animal to hunt (indoors or outdoors)?* There's a big difference between a mouse hunter and a bird hunter, and many cats favor one type of prey over the other. You'll feel the difference because a bird hunter must jump into the air chasing a flying flurry of feathers where a mouse hunter will show you nooks and crannies in wooden molding and floors, or even moles in the garden where the smells of the earth are rich and pungent. Some are consummate hunters who enjoy pursuing both, but like horses who can be divided into categories of "sky" horses and "ground" horses, depending on where they tend to focus their attention, many prefer hunting sky animals over ground animals or vice versa.

7. *Are you the only cat at home?* Look around the house and "see" if there is another cat.

8. *Where is the nearest cat, and what color is it?* Cats are very concerned about other cats. Even if your cat appears to not notice other cats, he will know precisely where the nearest cat lives.

9. *How do you feel about other cats? Would you like to be the only cat?* Send him the thought of having a cat as a companion and see what emotion comes back to you. If you have more than one cat, you can ask each one how he feels about the others by sending him the picture of the other cats, one by one, then gently and carefully monitoring your emotions to see what subtle impressions come in.

10. *What is your favorite activity in your entire world?* Send him the feeling of unadulterated joy. What are you doing that brings you such pleasure?

11. *Is there any pain in your body, and if so, where?* We will cover this in future chapters, where I will talk you through a thorough medical gestalt, but for now, understand that pain in an animal's body will attract your consciousness like a magnet. When you are seeking the sore spots, your mind will be drawn to the part of the body that hurts. When you try to move your attention, it will be perpetually brought back to the body part that is in pain.

12. *What could your handmaiden-slave-guardian do to make you more satisfied?* We all secretly know that dogs have "owners" and cat's have "staff." Felines are completely self-sufficient and don't need human beings. If you are lucky enough to have one living in your house who has chosen you as a life companion, thank your lucky stars. You must be a wonderful person to have earned such an honor. Send your cat the feeling of frustration, then with this, envision a picture of you. Visualize your cat desperately wanting to tell you something that you've always been too oblivious to hear. Silently ask him, "If you could tell me anything I could do to make your life happier, what do you need me to hear?" Then listen. Allow the space for the information to come in. Sit in silence with your beloved cat, quiet your mind, and

pretend he can "speak" to you. He can. Only through the practice of unconditional love and sweet calm silence will you learn
to communicate with cats. They are the quietest of all of God's
creatures. Only if you become quiet will they become loud.

When you've finished your conversation, and this is crucial, see
the bridge of Lumensilta fading away. Picture a waterfall of glitter-
ing white stars pouring down over your animal's head, encasing her
in an energetic snowdrift of protection. Now she is self-contained
and completely separate from your energy field. Next, repeat the
process over your own head, seeing yourself being showered with a
waterfall of crystalline, sparkling energy. It needs to form a sphere
around you so that it has distinct edges, hard as glass. Now you are
protected and sovereign. You will not walk away with that animal's
anxiety or toothache, and she will not walk away with yours. Second, please thank the animal for allowing you to make contact, and
then go out and act on the animal's desire. This is the most essential step. Go immediately and buy her the food she wants or the toy
she asked for. Tell the animal's guardian to make the changes the animal requested immediately. This will encourage the animal to talk
to you more in the future and to understand that humans are not as
stupid or insensitive as she once thought. Your actions will begin to
build that animal's trust in humanity and give her confidence that
she can communicate and actually be heard. This is vital.

And last, keep written records of all your communications and
date the entries in your notebook. Often, the human guardian won't
be able to identify all of your intuitive impressions on the spot, but
they may come back a week, a month, or even a year later to confirm
that "Yes, they found who Christine was!" or "Yes, they x-rayed
the horse and found out the problem was not the hip but the spine."
Circle each one of your correct answers and do a celebration dance
after every confirmation. And most importantly — listen up, because
this is serious stuff — I want you to yell "Hoo-dee-hoo!" every single
time you're right!

In the next chapter, I give you more instruction about how to listen to cats, as well as orangutans, cheetahs, elephants, dogs, and horses, and we'll talk more about learning to differentiate the thoughts and feelings you're generating as opposed to what is actually coming in from the animals.

CHAPTER FOUR

Lumensilta

Listening with Love

Nothing happens until something moves.

— ALBERT EINSTEIN

THE CAT WHO ATE SHEETS

ONE OF MY MOST UNUSUAL READINGS involved two cats, Mavis and Harvey, who lived in the West Hollywood household of two gay men. When one of the human fathers called me for an appointment, I asked him to describe the cats' coloring for me. He said Mavis was black and Harvey was "tawny-buff." I was soon to discover that this was a really an orange tabby — the Honda Civic of cats.

I made advance contact mentally with Mavis as I drove over the canyon to West Hollywood. I used to reach out in advance whenever I was making a house call to see if I could get the animals "online" telepathically before I met them in person. Someone special helped me master this.

He lived at the McCarthy Wildlife Sanctuary in southern Florida, a haven for big cats. The day I went to meet him, *NBC Nightly News* had a camera in my face long before I met any of the tigers in person. I reached out in my mind before we got to the sanctuary and asked the cats what they would like me to tell the news crew. I hadn't even seen photos of these cats; I was working absolutely cold. I had tried this method before, but never under such pressure. I directed my consciousness from cage to cage to see who I would meet there and what I would feel as I tuned in to each one.

The first young tiger told me, "Our eldest tiger just had to have surgery on one of his teeth. I hope it never happens to me." As I moved my focus to each big cat, the story never changed. The level of fear and dread in each cat was nauseating. They were all worried about their king, the alpha male tiger, and the painful problems he was having with his teeth. When I asked one of the younger tigers to show me which tooth, I felt a sharp pain in my upper left molars.

On camera and under stress, I was performing the most mysterious form of aerial propulsion that humans are known to do — flying by the seat of my pants. Nonetheless, I blurted out my diagnosis into the news camera and pointed out which tooth hurt on the upper left side of the old tiger's mouth. When we arrived at the sanctuary, I met all the young tigers first, but I heard the same story again and again from them. Nothing was of more importance to them than the suffering of their magnificent king.

As I finally approached the enclosure of Raja, the eldest male tiger, I could see why they were worried. Here was the most resplendent tiger I've ever seen in my life, but his upper lip was dripping blood. His keeper explained that Raja had had an inoperable cancer tumor in his nasal passage, so his vets had pulled one of his upper left molars in order to try to remove the deadly cancer. Unfortunately for me and all the cats in the world this case might have helped, *NBC Nightly News* never showed the piece, and my beloved Raja eventually succumbed to the cancer before we got to tell his story. I had hoped that this master teacher of a tiger might have been the star of the first American news program where we proved to the world that cats can think and feel and telepathically communicate with humans, but that wish was not granted. Raja joined the angels a year after our meeting. I was utterly devastated. But he taught me the lesson of a lifetime — to trust myself — and his spirit lives on in my heart for all time.

But today I was talking not to tigers but to their miniature cousins, the domestic cats many of us treasure in our households. As I tuned into Mavis, I was in my car on the way to her house in West Hollywood. She was in her house waiting for me to arrive. Her Animalogos sounded like the voice of a sour old actress who had spent her entire life in the theater. She informed me in no uncertain terms that the two men were named "Father" and "Dad." Then she sent me the Q-form of an Italian mother with big, dark curls who dropped by to cook pasta from time to time. I had not connected with Harvey before I arrived at Dad and Father's apartment, so I was not surprised that when I walked in, he ran to hide under the couch. (Animals, no matter how shy, rarely hide if you mentally contact them in advance.) As I settled down onto the couch, Mavis "spoke" while Harvey cowered.

"A blonde man comes over. He's very flamboyant — loud and gregarious — and the music he plays is much too loud!" I repeated this to the man called Father.

"That's our friend who house-sits. He was here for the weekend. He left last night," Father confirmed with a chuckle. "He is a bit loud, and he does play rowdy music." As I continued to tune into Mavis, this is what I heard:

"There's a grandmother who just died. Her spirit visits my house. She was a pianist and she loves this music that my fathers play." (A beautiful New Age tune was playing softly on the stereo.)

"Which one of you had a grandmother who was a pianist?" I asked the two men. "Your grandmother is in the house. Mavis says your grandmother likes your taste in music. When did she pass away?" I asked.

"A year ago," Father said.

"Who else comes over, Mavis?" I mentally asked.

"Lots and lots of children: an older boy and a young girl. She wears flowered dresses with hats. I don't like the boy as much. He wears baggy, funny clothes." (She showed me a girl of four and a boy of seven and a lot of chaos.)

Relaying the message, I asked the men: "Who do all these children belong to?"

"They are my nieces and nephews," Father replied.

Mavis showed me a swarm of children's feet from her perspective. "There are so many of them!" I said.

"Four," Father laughed.

"Tell him I love his mother. I wish she lived here permanently. I never get to see enough of her," Mavis lamented. I aired her complaint.

It took some time for me to coax Harvey out from under the couch. He was gorgeous — a soft butterscotch champagne color, truly *tawny buff*. He had a beautiful, muscular body but was shy and gawky — long-legged and quiet, like a young Jimmy Stewart. I asked him if he needed any medical attention. Mavis interrupted:

"I need more greens. And more oil and butter. I'm too dry. And I want more broccoli." I announced her demands to her guardians and took note that Mavis would not let Harvey answer without butting in.

"I gave her broccoli yesterday!" cried Dad.

Harvey's Animalogos sounded in my head like the voice of a wan British man.

"My iron level is low and I have a calcium deficiency. I do get constipated and I need more greens," Harvey said. I suggested to his fathers that they try giving him fresh meat, cod liver oil, butter, zucchini, peas, and broccoli mixed in with his canned food. The men requested I ask why he was so skittish. Harvey answered:

"I hate the traffic noise in this apartment. I can't even find solace on the balcony because of the cars. In our old home, I could sit on the grass and sniff the flowers, relaxing in the sunshine, where it was quiet. I don't like it here. I don't like the children."

"How long have you lived here?" I asked him.

"Two years." The fathers confirmed that two years was exactly right. Dad wanted to know if Harvey was abused before they got him.

Harvey unveiled the sad memories of leaving his cat-mother too early, of fighting to suckle, of being the runt. He was heartbroken over being wrenched away from his mother and sisters. He displayed a street with busy traffic, absolutely terrifying. Sending a pain in his right hip and the bottom of his back left pad, he told me he may have been hit but he wasn't sure. Children threw things at him and pulled his tail. It was all too painful to remember.

After I shared the bad news, Father verified that this horrible description sounded like his prior home. I recommended a flower box out on the balcony.

Dad asked, "Why do Harvey and Mavis get into such violent fights? They aren't frequent but they almost kill each other."

"Who starts it?" I asked.

"She used to, but now he does," said Dad.

Harvey let me feel the humiliation of being antagonized by Mavis.

"She calls me names," he said.

I told the men, "She provokes him. She may look totally innocent, but when she walks by him, she calls him names."

Suddenly, Mavis couldn't stay out of the conversation and helped prove Harvey's point:

"He's a lazy little wimp. A worthless wuss."

"She's a pushy, overbearing bitch!" Harvey came back.

He tossed me a montage of images: how in their old house their territory was clearly sanctioned; when they moved into the new apartment, she wanted everything for herself and crowded him out; he hid from her in high places, especially the linen closet; if she found him, she screamed for him to get down. This all prompted Dad to ask the million-dollar question:

"Why does he chew holes in our linens? Every few months, we have to buy new sheets. He actually *eats* our sheets and T-shirts! Isn't that bad for him?"

"No wonder he wants butter — to slick 'em down," I laughed. Next, I asked Harvey, "What's up with the sheets?" I checked for more dietary problems because licking wool and plastic can indicate a mineral deficiency. He sent me images of being swaddled in his fathers' linens, like a mummy. I told his fathers:

"It stems from a territorial problem. What do you do with the sheets he ruins?"

"We put them in his bed!" Dad answered, wide-eyed. "We have to, because we can't use them."

"Well, there it is," I chuckled. "If he chews a hole in your sheet, you give him the sheet for his very own, and it's the only territory he has that he doesn't have to share with Mavis. Try giving him the T-shirts and sheets he's already marked; make a special bed out of them, and let him do whatever he wants with them. Tell him, 'These are yours, Harvey.' Then show him the sheets you've bought for the bed and say, 'These are ours, not yours. You have your own.' If you give him some territory of his own, maybe he'll stop trying to steal yours." The men agreed to try this, but then Dad asked:

"How do we keep the cats from fighting? The screaming is awful."

When I asked Harvey about the fights, he sent me Q-forms of Mavis bullying him around. He told me he was terribly henpecked, always bowing down to her, but he never lifted a paw to fight back.

"He's so much bigger than she, he could beat the hell out of her if he wanted to. Tell him to give her one good swat that'll make her back down," I said. I mentally demonstrated to Harvey that he needed to bat Mavis in the face. (No claws extended, just a warning bat.)

"I don't want to hurt her!" Harvey said.

At this point, Mavis stood up from where she was lying and left the room in a huff. Dad said, "Jeez! Mavis didn't like that idea!" I continued to reason with the henpecked cat:

"Harvey, you don't have to hurt her; just make her respect you. You've got to stand up to her and give her a swat when she starts terrorizing you. If you don't, you'll never have any territory." I reinforced the vision of him giving her a quick pop on the nose.

Hoping I had made progress with this problem, I pressed Mavis for any confidential information.

"Father is planning to change careers. Tell him the new job will be much better for him. Tell him not to be afraid. He'll be much more successful." When I shared her prediction, Father almost fell off his chair. He confirmed he'd just received a new job offer.

"He's not appreciated where he works now," Mavis explained. "He has a very domineering female boss who gives him too much trouble." She sent a picture of a big, dark-haired, masculine woman. When I relayed the message, Dad laughed out loud.

"It's a gay man," he said, eyes twinkling. I told him that animals frequently get the two mixed up. The energy reads so similarly.

"There are too many people around him, draining his energy and forcing him to talk," Mavis continued. With this, she showed me his throat and sent the sensation of pain. "Energy is leaking out, causing his voice to get tired. He's not gregarious like Dad. Father is quiet and sensitive. He doesn't need to be working on all those obnoxious people all day." She shows me yappy, vain women sitting in chairs.

I couldn't help but ask Father "What do you do for a living?"

"I'm a hairdresser," he said.

At this point in the conversation, Mavis began to make many predictions about her father's future: career changes and promotions, even indicating a projected time frame.

"By October, the new job will be secured, by January he will get a promotion. This will lead to other offers down the road. He'll be able to direct print ads or commercials in two years." She formulated the image of a tree going up and up, then branching out in many directions.

"Father is more outgoing and talkative than Dad, so he's more suited for this type of work." The men verified this as well.

Mavis continued to make predictions: "Father will be brought into Dad's career also, doing hair for commercials or TV shows."

Father was delighted with this news. "That would be wonderful! I've always wanted to do that."

I thanked Mavis for the conversation, and I said good-bye to Harvey, but not before I gave him another brief lecture about standing up for himself, prodding him to put up his little furry dukes and give Mavis the ol' "one, two."

I don't pretend to know how animals can foretell future events. Not all animals make prophecies. Most are content to talk about chicken sandwiches and rides in the car. I can only listen to the fortune-tellers when I find them; then, over the years I watch their predictions come true. I surmise that the part of the animal that talks to me, the spirit, or what I call the Speaker, has a much larger perspective on human life than we do when we're caught up in it. Besides, cats see farther than the rest of us do.

But it was not Mavis who took away my breath in this reading. It was Harvey. A few days later, I got an excited call from the fathers to tell me they witnessed Harvey take action for the first time in his life: Mavis was screaming at him the way she always did, but this time, instead of running away to hide under the couch, Harvey turned around and punched her in the nose. One paw to the face worked like magic. The old broad hasn't bothered him since.

PURRING PROPHETS

JUST TO BE FAIR, let's address this question of fortune-telling animals from a more scientific viewpoint. Dr. Edgar Mitchell might say that the animal is not telling the future at all, but is merely giving us an indication of what direction some energy is traveling. As Ed says, "If you see someone walking toward the kitchen, chances are, he's going to end up in the kitchen." I see his point, but I don't entirely agree, because I've also heard predictions of sudden moves, deaths, or other changes that the person couldn't possibly foresee.

Still, Dr. Mitchell's argument is thought provoking: When humans and animals get caught up in the karma and energy of each other's fields, they form what is called a "quantum entanglement." A term of similar meaning in psychology is a "family constellation." I like this image: you have your own personal solar system, meaning that you, your human loved ones, and your animals revolve around each other and affect each other with thoughts and actions. There's a certain sense of gravity and magnetism that holds your behavioral patterns in place. When one person or animal in the system heals or changes his behavior, it alters the dynamics of the entire constellation. That's why the idea of healing yourself is so important. If your spiritual and emotional growth can impact everyone on your pathway, eventually we can heal the world, one by one, by initiating a cascading catalyst, like divine dominos tumbling all over the world. "Love, love, love, love, love…" Wouldn't that be nice?

Some psychiatrists in Germany are now exploring the possibility of including animals in family constellations, and I am helping to pave this new road. But this is virgin territory — highly controversial and mysterious. My new hypothesis would suggest that a major shift needs to occur in the separatist science of recent centuries, whereby we get to know something by dissecting it to its smallest parts. In this new, more compassionate form of investigation, we stand back to get a broader point of view instead of narrowing our field of vision; this wide range of focus includes all the animals who are energetically tied to a person through relationships.

In my opinion, we can use an animal as a "coordinate" in a family constellation using contact with the animal to ricochet off or through his energy field to access the humans around him. Think of a family constellation as a psychic subway system, where we are all connected on a web of light. Every person or animal is at an intersection on the web, and we can use that fork in the road to split off into various directions in order to mentally contact anyone in their lives. It works the other way, too. If I have a client on the phone, I may access his body to connect with the animal in his life. I'm not using my client's conscious mind — that would trap me in his thoughts and fears — but I use his "field" as a vortex to move to the next stop on the psychic subway.

If we acknowledge that even inanimate objects are composed of Q-forms and vibrate with a distinct signature frequency, then we may interpret Dr. Mitchell's model to suggest that using an animal as a coordinate is no different from psychometry, whereby one can use, say, a person's watch or car keys to access his energy field. I've performed this type of psychokinesis as well, and while I agree that inanimate objects are laden with Q-forms and history and can provide sort of a "map" into their owner's family constellation and future, the energy does not feel as vibrant to me as that of a living, organic being, or even that of a spirit on the "Other Side." This is all up for speculation, of course, and I don't claim to know things I don't understand. But I am honored to be able to open a dialog about this so that we can talk about these mysteries all over the world.

On the subject of fortune-telling, I'll never forget a reading I had with a horse in a posh barn in Palos Verdes Estates, in horse country just south of Los Angeles. I initially went there to work with one horse, but as I passed another's stall he said, "Please talk to my Mommy!" When I asked what his mommy looked like, he said, "She's the pretty blonde girl with the broken hand." Sure enough, my client confirmed that this horse's guardian, Suzie, had a cast on one hand. The horse then went into elaborate detail about where he had taken a fall and how horrible he felt about hurting his beloved rider. What's more, every single horse in the barn was aware of the fall, and they were so concerned about this woman's injury that they were all wary about going on the particular part of the trail where the accident occurred. As I passed each horse, they all asked, "How is Suzie? Is she okay? Is she out of the hospital?"

But that's not the clincher; as you can tell already, that sort of miracle has become fairly business-as-usual in my life. Later, while I was speaking with Suzie and her horse, the horse next to hers began to tell me about *his* mom. He showed me her abdomen, and there I saw a vision of blood accompanied by crippling pain. When I looked closer, I saw the problem was her uterus, and on even closer inspection, I saw that the issue was endometriosis. With this, I heard the words, "She needs to have emergency surgery right away." To make matters even scarier, the horse told me that the operation would be risky and that the woman would almost die on the operating table. When I asked him why, he said she was very unhappy, and that given the opportunity to slip away, she just might take it.

I scheduled an appointment with the horse's mother. We talked about the chronic bleeding and pain that had been plaguing her for years, and she confirmed she was starting to suspect it was endometriosis. Despite the intimate nature of our conversation, I made no mention of her horse's deadly prediction because I didn't want to scare my client or project any negativity to her about her medical condition. Within the month, the woman had to have an emergency hysterectomy, and sure enough, she flatlined on the table. The doctors barely resuscitated her in time to bring her back.

How could an animal know so much about his owner? This woman's horse not only described a medical condition she wasn't even aware of, but he predicted her future. How could this be possible? The only explanation is that animals' capacity for logging and storing information and for tapping into a quantum field is far greater than what we once imagined, and our models are outdated. But fortunately, now we have a new way of looking at all this.

ANGELS ON THE HEAD OF A PIN

HAVE YOU EVER WONDERED exactly how much information could be packed into your cat's little tangerine-sized brain? According to Michael Talbot's book *The Holographic Universe*, holograms might be the answer. (Here I must give you, dear reader, a word of encouragement: If you don't understand all the technology of holograms, not to worry! Neither do I. You don't have to know *how* it works *for* it to work!) He tells us that a hologram is produced when a single laser light is split into two separate beams. The first beam is bounced off the object to be photographed. The second beam is allowed to collide with the reflected light of the first. When this happens they create what is called an "interference pattern," which is then recorded on a piece of film. To the naked eye the image on the film looks nothing like the object photographed but resembles the concentric rings that form when a handful of pebbles is tossed into a pond. But as soon as another laser beam is shined through the film, shazam! A three dimensional image appears that is eerily convincing. You can actually walk around a hologram and view it from different angles, but if you reach out to try to touch it, oops. Your hand will go right through it. More importantly, unlike normal photographs, every small fragment of a piece of holographic film contains all the information recorded in the whole. Michael Talbot writes that if you cut the film into two or even smaller pieces, each piece will contain all of the information intact. Cool, huh? What does this have to do with animals and brains? Lots, according to Michael Talbot.

He tells us that Dr. Karl Pribram, a neurophysiologist at Stanford University and author of the textbook *Languages of the Brain* established a landmark work with the holographic brain theory, even though, unfortunately, Dr. Pribram was not an animal champion. Dr. Pribram believed that the model of a hologram finally provided a way of understanding how memories could be distributed rather than localized in the brain. Before Pribram's research, one of the biggest mysteries that scientists battled was how to locate where memory is stored in the brain. No one could find it. But Dr. Pribram felt that if a portion of a piece of holographic film could contain all the information necessary to create a whole image, then it seemed possible for every part of the brain to contain all of the information necessary to recall a whole memory.

Are you with me? What I propose is that all living beings are logging their experience of life on earth into the Divine Computer called the Zero Point Energy field in the same fashion that images are logged onto a piece of holographic film. Your consciousness functions as the laser beams that can "light up" the holograms in the animal's experience and make their memories visible to you. How many holograms can be stored in one brain? Michael Talbot gives us some eye-opening figures:

"The brilliant Hungarian-born physicist and mathematician John von Neumann once calculated that over the course of the average human lifetime, the brain stores something on the order of 2.8 x 10 to the twentieth power (280,000,000,000,000,000,000) bits of information. . . . Interestingly, holograms also possess a fantastic capability for information storage."

Now, when we're speaking of holographic wave interference patterns, what we're dealing with is little squiggly energy waves packed on top of each other. In this mode, the entire U. S. Library of Congress, which contains every book ever published in English (minus maybe a few), would fit onto a large sugar cube. The holographic model would also explain our ability to recall memories instantly, often in three-dimensional images.

This also brings up the question of brain size in relationship to intelligence. People ask me about this often. If the size of our brains were a measure of our intelligence, surely whales and elephants would be making *Homo sapiens* look like a bunch of pinheads. There's also the question of brain size in proportion to body mass — if a larger relative brain size indicated more intelligence, ants would make humanity look like a big top of Bozos (and if you look at how efficiently ants run their society and communicate with each other, there may be some truth in that). Einstein said that the existence of genius is determined by the way the two hemispheres of the human brain communicate with each other, and I agree that intelligence may not be determined by the size of the brain or even by the size of the brain in proportion to the body, but by the capacity for interaction between the brain's parts. A big surface area increases this capacity, so the surface area of the brain is important. Animals that have highly convoluted brains (a big surface area all wrinkled up to fit into a skull) tend to be the most intelligent. That includes dolphins, whales, apes, and humans. In this instance, size really *doesn't* matter. And, recalling the frequency packed sugar cube, even your parrot or iguana's pea-sized brain may have the space to store the entire Library of Congress between its owner's furry or scaly ears.

When we Resogenate (sorry, kids, it's time to conjugate) with an animal, we expand our consciousness so that we can access this library of information. Now, to make matters even more fun, your brain will not function in this luminous realm in the manner to which you are accustomed. Welcome to wonderland! You will no longer be restricted to thinking thoughts in a point-to-point manner, whereby your thoughts follow a linear path through time. You will be subject to great masses of information getting downloaded and dumped in your lap at warp speed. There is no A-to-Z delineation in the reading of these "records." You will be shown A to Z all at the same time, like watching a movie beginning, middle, and end all at once and probably not in any logical order. You may receive all manner of pictures from an animal's mind: her physical ailments, her medical history, her hopes and dreams, her emotions, and a lot of other seemingly disjointed information all at once.

Dr. Pribram tells us, "The brain primarily talks to itself and to the rest of the world not with words or images, or even bits or chemical impulses, but in the language of wave interference: the language of phase, amplitude, and frequency — the 'spectral domain.' We perceive an object by 'resonating' with it, getting 'in synch' with it. To know the world is literally to be on its wavelength."

When you are completely "in synch" and on the same wavelength as an animal, you may indeed hear his thoughts. But in order to "download" the Animalogos, the first step is to envision a new world, one where animals can talk. With this, we must envision a new "us," a remodeled human race who can hear them.

One of my favorite metaphors comes from one of my favorite movies,

The Matrix. When the dashing hero stumbles in to a room of telekinetic children, he happens on a child who is making a spoon wiggle and dance like a caterpillar in a hurricane. When the hero asks the child how he "bends the spoon," the whiz kid replies, "There is no spoon. There is only me. I bend my mind."

CONSCIOUSNESS IS NOT THE SLAVE TO DESIGN

"THINK OF YOUR BRAIN AS A PIANO," Lynne McTaggart tells us in her book *The Field.* "When we observe something in the world, certain portions of the brain resonate at certain specific frequencies. At any point of attention, our brain presses only certain notes, which trigger strings of a certain length and frequency. This information is then picked by the ordinary electrochemical circuits of the brain, just as the vibrations of the strings eventually resonate through the entire piano."

I love the piano analogy because it seems to help me answer the questions I'm asked so very often. "Can you talk to turtles?" "Are elephants different to talk to than lions?" "Rats aren't as smart as chimps, are they?" and best of all, "Can you talk to insects?" With the analogy of musical notes, we can wrap our minds around the answers to all these questions simultaneously. Different species of animals, and different animals within species, are simply resonating to different frequencies, or notes, and yes, insects can talk, but you need to expend a lot of energy to "hear" them. Trees can talk, too, but they're farther up the frequency scale and are even more difficult to hear. Remember, though, that it is not the insects and the trees that are doing the "talking" — your mind takes the frequency packets (Q-forms) you find in that animal's quantum field and turns them into what sounds like language inside your own mind. It is a harmonic resonance that you can translate.

Humans are accustomed to communicating only with other humans. Using our piano metaphor, that limitation means that if you resonate to, say, the note of middle C, you can identify only other notes identical to yours, and if someone else is not sending out the vibe of middle C, you don't hear them at all. Or perhaps you will learn to talk to cats and dogs but not insects. That would mean you can reach a few additional notes to form a few chords, but other notes are out of your reach.

Another analogy is that of a radio, picking up different stations. Some stations come in strongly, while some are full of static, far-away, and fade in and out. You'll be surprised to find that a mouse might come in crystal clear for you, while your own horse sounds like she's phoning in from Japan. You will have different levels of connection with different animals, and I find that the intensity of the communication has nothing to do with species. Even I, practiced as I am, may have trouble tuning into a particular dog, even though I've successfully tuned into thousands of dogs.

Now, you may be asking if all animals are equally intelligent. In this new model, all living beings are experiencing life on earth and logging their experiences holographically. As you learn to tune into these other species, you can discover the answer to that question directly. Once you've listened to enough rats who are grieving the loss of their mates, ferrets who are concerned about their human owner's medical condition, horses who still miss another horse they were separated from years ago, snakes who are in agony because they're isolated in glass tanks, lonely turtles who desperately want to have children, and cheetahs who can name the other cheetahs and human volunteers in the sanctuary *by name*, you'll find that the playing field is far more level than we once thought. *Homo sapiens* aren't the most intelligent animal on earth; we are simply one of the four types of primates who, along with the cetaceans, are thought to be the whiz kids of earth (and as far as I'm concerned, there is only one low primate on the intelligence totem pole, and it's the one who created Reality TV).

Here's a story about a really smart primate, a little male orangutan who was able to tell my American protégé exactly what disease he had come down with. Listen to how my student, Darren, baffled the vets with his diagnosis of this orangutan.

No More Monkeying Around with Vets!

One of my many animal-related positions is a veterinary internship. We were working with Julian, an orangutan that had been sick.

Although a couple of people had their theories as to what his problem was, no one was sure what was making him ill.

One day I was in the building just outside his enclosure with one of the doctors as she was observing the orangutan. Julian looked at me and said, "Tell her I have pneumonia." How did he know I was the one to talk to? I try to talk to many of the animals there, of course, but I don't remember talking to any of the orangutans. Later, while the doctor and I were washing our hands, I asked her if he could have pneumonia, since he had been coughing recently. She said probably not because he didn't have any of the other typical symptoms. I was stumped. I couldn't figure out why he thought he had pneumonia, or how he even knew what pneumonia was. Later that day, I found out that one of the other doctors thought he had pneumonia, but no one else agreed with her. So I figured that she had told someone in front of Julian. He didn't get better, so several days later they immobilized him and did a complete exam, and sure enough . . . he had pneumonia.

It seemed that all along, he knew *exactly* what was wrong with him, and there he was, asking me to tell the doctor so that she could treat him. I am amazed at the fact that he knew the word "pneumonia," and he knew it so surely that he told me about it and asked me to tell the doctor!

This taught me to listen to what the animals say, rather than try to figure out how they came to that conclusion, even if they don't have the typical symptoms.

I asked Darren if animals' voices sound different from his own thinking process or if the words sound simply the same as his own thoughts. Darren said, "I usually have trouble telling the difference but I will periodically hear a specific voice, especially if an animal has gone out of his or her way to talk to me. Not only do I hear a voice from them, but it is almost as if a miniature alarm is going off in my head telling me to listen (similar to the instant reaction you have when someone calls your name and you turn your head). In this particular incident with Julian the orangutan, I heard the voice of a very mature man. It was deep."

I asked him if he felt the pain in Julian's chest. Whenever I am diagnosing pneumonia, and I've done it several times myself (on humans!) the red flag for me is always the crushing pain in my chest. Darren, though, has a blessed gift in that he is a clairaudient medical intuitive who does not always have to suffer the pain of the animals right along with them.

"I didn't get any sensations with this," Darren explained. "I think Julian took it for granted that people couldn't understand him, but what confuses me is how he knew to tell *me*. It wasn't like he was saying to just everyone, "I have pneumonia!" and hoping someone would listen. He just looked at me and calmly said, "Tell her I have pneumonia," as if he *knew* I was the only person in the place who could hear his message and he was simply tired of the vets getting it wrong. I suppose maybe some animals just know who can do this and who can't. Maybe you can help me figure that out."

Maybe I can't, but I'll try. For some incredible reason that defies all description, animals can identify animal communicators. I recently visited two cheetah sanctuaries in South Africa to assist their vets and staff, and as I approached each cat, I said, "I'm different from other humans. I can hear you." Most of them said, "Good grief! I *know* who you are, Amelia! We've known you were coming for *months!*" Some were even miffed that I didn't have enough time to talk to each of them, because they had known I was there that day and were waiting eagerly at the front of their enclosures.

I had a similar experience when I went to Pilanesberg National Park to visit with some elephants. As Sandy, my workshop coordinator, drove me up into the park, she said, "Don't get your hopes up. This reserve is huge! You can drive for hours without seeing anything!" We were short on time because we'd gotten lost. I kept "sending" the thoughts to the elephants, "We're late, but I'm coming! I'm coming! Please come down to the road and see us!" (We were getting there just as the park closed after a hot, frustrating afternoon of driving.) When we frantically raced into the park, a huge young elephant was waiting yards from the front gate. He yelled at me, "So you finally made it!" He paraded around while I fawned over him, snapping photos, and he said, "I've told the others. They're coming down to see you."

Well, sure enough, within the hour, three gigantic females paraded out of the bush and brought their four babies to see me. I gaped and howled with glee as they surrounded our car.

Now, from a normal human's perspective, it might seem like I am making up the transmissions I receive. But remember, the proof is in the pudding. When the elephants are *waiting at the gate* of the national park to see you, you know you've succeeded in making contact.

But back to our orangutan: I asked Darren how he felt about his triumphant connection. "Well, the part that impressed me the most," he said, "was that he was right about his own medical condition, even knew the exact medical term for it. It wasn't like he simply said, 'I have lung problems,' or 'There is bad stuff in my chest.' The actual use of the term 'pneumonia' is what hits me the hardest. Even knowledgeable humans who know a lot about medicine don't always know what type of condition they have, much less the actual term for it. But again, I guess somehow he just knew. Perhaps there is no real explanation for it."

Well, there really is an explanation for it, but we're going to have to stretch our minds a little bit in order to understand it. The model for this type of phenomenon is quantum holography, which suggests not that animals are actually "talking" to you at all but rather that you are accessing information in a remarkably effective data retrieval system.

Here are a few examples: When I worked with the ailing rider in Palos Verdes, her horse actually seemed to "tell" me that his mommy had endometriosis. One of the cheetahs in South Africa "told" me he had had two cases of cystitis (bladder infection) and a birth defect in his hips that caused hip dysplasia. On another occasion, a very famous gorilla explained to me a problem she was having with the eustachian tube in one of her ears and claimed it was related to an allergy she has to oatmeal, of all things. All that data was verified by the animal's keepers. I actually received the words "endometriosis," "cystitis," "dysplasia," and "eustachian tube."

There's no pat explanation to explain why an animal could tell me medical terms and know more about their own afflictions than we humans

know about our own bodies, but there is a delig
entertain. When I train doctors and veterinarian
communicators who are also walking encyclopedi
tion, and all their cerebral data can be accessed thr
of signature frequencies. Because they are medically
apt to be able to identify specific conditions. Darr.., neard" the word
"pneumonia" because he knows what pneumonia is. I should stress that
you can't diagnose anything that's outside your frame of reference. I know
what endometriosis is, so when a horse shows me that affliction, something in my consciousness can mirror it back. If I don't know what I'm
describing, I won't have words for it. Vets have words for a litany of medical conditions that a layperson wouldn't know. The doctor is the one who
knows the words for the condition; the language does not come from the
animal. The words resonate with the part of you that recognizes them.
Here's a way to make this clearer.

THE LIBRARY OF LOVE

I USED TO THINK that when you "asked" an animal a question, she would
volley the answer back to you, as if you two were engaged in a game of
telepathic ping-pong. But then my workshop students started asking this
clever question: When a group of one hundred people asks a dog the color
of his food bowl, does that mean he has to say, "It's blue with white trim!
It's blue with white trim! It's blue with white trim! . . ." one hundred times?

Ah. What a magnificent question. When I put it to Dr. Mitchell, he
suggested that the animal *might* send the information to each person who
asks, but it's more likely that the Q-forms in an animal resembles a library.
All the memories of the animal are stored within every cell of her body,
and with practice and discipline, you can learn to go in and read the
records. Remember Dr. Schempp, who discovered that it is possible to
extract three-dimensional images from sound waves? In a nutshell, that's
what we're doing when we Resogenate. We concentrate our focus and
beam our consciousness onto the animal and the records inside the animal's cells are "lit up" so that we can see them.

re are a couple of stories from two of my brightest students, whose ccesses can show you how this process works. The first story comes from one of my students at the Omega Institute in upstate New York. Patty Gibbons had one of those struck-by-lightning epiphanies in my class and discovered that she was a lot more powerful than she thought. The topic she's covering here is one well worth addressing — what to do when a woman gets pregnant and her animals feel rejected. But, I'll let Patty tell you for herself:

I Was Here First!

My sister asked if I would speak with Sylvester, one of her dogs. My sister and her husband had just had their first child six and a half months earlier, and most everyone seemed to believe that Sylvester hated the baby. He certainly was not his usual happy self.

Well, during my discussions with Sylvester, he did not say that he "hated" the baby, but he was fearful of being "displaced" by him. Sylvester wanted to know why the baby had a special bed (crib) and room, and he said that he would also like to have "stars and blue" — the very decorations and colors that were in the baby's room! He showed me my brother-in-law going straight to the baby when arriving home from work, walking passed the dogs without saying "hello" to them. He said he was jealous of the attention to the baby, as well as the baby's things (toys, and so on). Sylvester also complained about no longer being picked up. Prior to the baby's arrival, my brother-in-law would often carry Sylvester around in his arms like a baby.

The thing that truly surprised me was Sylvester's request when I asked him if there was anything he would really like. He said he would like a bright blue turquoise bandana! When I asked, "What if they can't get a bright blue turquoise one?" he responded, "A purple one would do."

I called my sister to report what Sylvester had to say. She said that Sylvester had been taking the baby's toys, and yes, her husband had been walking right passed the dogs to say "hi" to the baby after work. And now for the real kicker — *over ten years ago*, while they were living in Manhattan, they would take the dogs to a rather pricey groomer. I guess to make you feel you got your money's worth, the dogs were each dressed in a bandana when they were done being groomed. I'm sure you can guess the rest by now . . . Sylvester had been given a bright blue turquoise bandana, and his "brother" Sam had been given a purple one!

After our discussion, my brother-in-law made a point of saying "Hi" to the dogs when returning from work and immediately went out and bought the turquoise bandana as well as a purple one. And Sylvester has been a much happier dog. My sister reported that he's even grown affectionate again like he used to be and once again rides around in her husband's arms.

Patty is now practicing professionally here in the States and her contact info is in the back of this book. And on this same theme, here is a revealing story about another forlorn dog. This report comes from one of my most beloved students and friends, Wynter Worsthorne, a South African who is now practicing professionally as an animal communicator in London. Here's what she has to tell us about her conversation with a pooch in a similar fix.

The Tail of Daisy, the Dachshund

The very first time I helped an animal and her human with my newly found skill, I had just returned to South Africa after attending Amelia's workshop on the Isle of Man. A very good friend of mine, Amy, had just had a baby, but her other child (Amy's eight-year-old four-legged child) was having problems; Daisy the dachshund was feeling neglected, displaced, ignored, and completely worthless, not part of the family at all. She was now "just a dog" — whereas before she had been an integral part of the family unit.

Daisy had started chewing her tail, literally eating it! She had chewed about an inch off the end. She was forced to wear a bucket collar over her head and she had been given cortisone injections, but nothing helped! The next step was Prozac and removal of her tail!

97

Amy was so stressed; she was at her wits end and did not know where to turn or what to do.

I offered to try to connect with Daisy and see what the problem was. I had no photograph of her but had known her since she was a pup, so I didn't think there would be a problem with making contact. I am an artist, so I drew a quick pencil sketch of Daisy and wrote her name below it — then I started focusing. (I have since found that this works as well as having a photograph to work with. Even if I have never met the animal in the physical, a name and a description will help me "connect" quite easily over any distance.)

I started by holding an image of Daisy in my mind and sent a huge feeling of love toward her. I visualized sitting together with Daisy in a bubble of light — with no one else around us, nothing disturbing us — just the two of us. I felt this deep sense of connection. In that moment, there was no one else in the world except this beautiful little dachshund sitting in front of me.

Before I'd even started to ask Daisy any questions, I immediately got this overwhelming sense of despair — I felt emotionally dead, had no will to live, I did not understand what was happening. Suddenly I realized I was inside Daisy's reality, feeling her feelings, not mine. As the dog, I got shouted at whenever I barked a warning that someone was coming, whereas before, my barking was always appreciated. I was not allowed to sleep in the bedroom with my mom anymore or be near this new baby that had suddenly come to live with us. I was left at home alone so often, whereas before I would go everywhere with mom. It was literally eating me up, and I wanted to chew my tail in frustration. The physical pain, at least, was something I could understand.

All this information came rushing at me at the moment I *was* Daisy. Her pain was so overwhelming and I was so deeply affected by it that I wanted to burst into tears. Then I remembered Amelia telling me that when you are communicating in this way, you need to go in, get the information, and then get out as quickly as you can. Amelia said we have to act like firemen, whose job is to go in, locate the fire, put it out, and get out without getting hurt. I now understood this completely. If I stayed with Daisy's pain for much longer, I would be in too much pain myself to do anything about it.

I stepped back into myself and disconnected from Daisy's pain by becoming aware of my own body, and my own physical self. I was still in the bubble of light with Daisy, but I was not "inside" her body anymore; we were two separate beings.

I started talking to Daisy — sending her huge amounts of love, explaining to her all about the new baby. I told her that her job now was even more important! She had a baby sister to look after. I explained how stressful it had been for her mom, who did not realize the pain she was causing. I told her I would speak to Amy and set her right.

While I was speaking I visualized or "imagined" Daisy in her new role, part of the family again — seeing her together with her mom and the baby. I immediately felt a sense of calm — and I knew Daisy would be all right. In the bubble of light, I saw Daisy curl up in her basket and fall into a peaceful sleep. I thanked her for talking to me and reassured her that I would speak to her mom and that everything would be all right.

I then saw Daisy in her own bubble of light and myself in a separate bubble — this separated us, so that neither of us would carry any lingering physical or emotional feelings that were not our own. I have found that it is really important to do this because not only do we pick up the animal's emotions, but the animal we are working with is also exposed to all our problems. We need to make absolutely sure that we are separated once we have finished our work.

Throughout the day I "tuned in" to Daisy, visualizing her at peace and sending her huge amounts of love and reassurance. That evening I called my friend. Her first words to me were: "What on earth did you do? Daisy hasn't chewed herself for hours. She's been sleeping peacefully, curled up in her basket." I spoke to her at length about what Daisy had been going through. I discovered Amy had been feeling guilty all along about the way she'd been treating her dear friend. As a new mom, she had been taking advice from "those who know better," and of course in our separate human world, there is no place for dogs in babies' nurseries.

Daisy recovered fully, and Amy made a supreme effort in making her part of the family again. Daisy and the baby now love each other to pieces, and never again has Daisy felt unwanted.

Let's take a brief look at all the things Wynter is doing right: When she "went into" Daisy's body to feel the dog's emotional pain, Wynter established Unimorphosis. This trance state is deeper than Resogenesis, where you stay in your own body to establish the psychic connection with the animal. Remember, in Unimorphosis, you actually merge your mind with the animal's, enter his body and look out his eyes. Wynter was smart to do it that way. She was even smarter to pull out when she did. She moved back into Resogenesis so that she could function as a counselor for the dog.

Furthermore, she demonstrated what I meant when I said, "Tell the animal you are an attorney for the defense, not the prosecution." Wynter did not go into this situation trying to fix Daisy or make Daisy change. That's why it worked. She did not say, "You'll have to suck it up because your mom has another baby now and that's that!" Wynter did just the opposite. She said, "I'll set your mother straight!" And boy, did she! And boy, did it work!

The third technique she employed that worked so beautifully was her sending Daisy the Q-forms (the imagery) of what she *did* want — for Daisy to feel loved once again in the family unit — not what she did *not* want — for Daisy to continue to be miserable and chew her tail. When Wynter sent the telepathic command of what she did want the dog to do, Daisy saw the "film clip" of holographic instructions and did exactly what Wynter asked. We will explore how to send telepathic commands in depth in the next chapter.

But first, one last story. This comes from one of my honky-tonk, cowgirl students in Texas, Janet Ballard, who stunned me with her accurate readings in my workshop at The Crossings in Austin. Janet is the only contributor offering a story to this book who does not want to be a professional animal communicator. She's a mule expert. That's right. She's more than content to simply be the country's mule-goddess, but here she offers a happy story about motherly instincts that cinched her pack saddle.

Feed the Turkeys, Turkey!

I had read and reread *Straight from the Horse's Mouth* so many times I pretty well had it memorized. I'd practiced some of the exercises but didn't have much luck with my horses. I found on Amelia's website that she was giving a workshop four hours away in a couple of weeks. I was determined to "do" something before going to the workshop or else not waste the money or make a fool of myself in front of a person who I thought so much of.

So after the farm chores were done, I sat down in the porch swing to watch the sun set. I opened my book and went step by step one more time. But this time my sidekick, Jaycee, the black and tan coonhound who follows my every step, was plopped in the swing with me. So I asked her, "Jaycee, tell me anything, anything at all! I'm desperate here!" Instantly, a picture of her white plastic food bowl appeared to me, empty! My thought was, "Oh, come on! I filled it before we sat down here!" I was so mad, I started to get up, and in a flash, there was a picture of our baby turkeys. You see, Jaycee is a natural-born mother — she has mothered baby deer, fox, chickens, and even kittens. She will mother any babies. She was right. I had not fed the baby turkeys! This was the only day in three weeks since they were born that I'd forgotten them. But she had not! Needless to say, I got up and fed the turkeys, and just in case, I looked at her bowl. Sure enough, it was full of dog food!

Janet's story provides us with the beautiful scenario of animals helping other animals. You will encounter this daily as you master this work. If you succeed in learning to listen to one of your animals, that token one may be the spokesperson for the other animals in your family or even in your professional practice with whom your communication is not yet strong. If one of your dogs is missing, ask the other dogs where he is. If one of your cats is sick, ask your other cats what is wrong with her. You'll find that enlisting their help also helps clear your emotional blocks. When there is fear blinding you from seeing a situation clearly, turning your focus to one of your other animals may provide the wellspring of love and support you need in order to grasp the answers you seek.

In the next chapter, I explore the mysteries of medical gestalt, which might help you understand the aches and pains of your beloved four-legged friends. It is, without contest, the most important thing I could ever teach you.

CHAPTER FIVE

Unimorphosis

The Magic of Merging Consciousness

There is no unnatural or supernatural experience.
There is just experience.

— DR. EDGAR MITCHELL

HARRY AND THE TENNIS BALL

I FIRST MET HARRY when I made a house call to inquire why this German shepherd was destroying the carpets in his parents' palatial house. His human mother, Rachel, was a vivacious beauty who, like many rich housewives in L.A., schedules appointments with psychics between manicures, private Pilates lessons, and weekend trips to Las Vegas. Rachel warned me over the phone that Harry had been trained as an attack dog in Germany; he barked at absolutely everyone, so I should not be put off by his ferocity.

On my drive to their house, I contacted Harry in advance mentally, to see if I could avert a hostile greeting. It worked. I was incredibly relieved when I arrived at the house and the ferocious attack dog not only greeted me with a big grin instead of a bark but promptly curled up at my feet like a puppy. Rolling onto his back, he proudly showed me his golden belly.

Rachel and her husband, Vince, were flabbergasted. They had never seen Harry act this way before with anyone. They told me he sometimes even barked at them. I was thankful to find Harry so receptive to my advance contact; it helped Vince and me get off to a good start. Vince was a big, handsome bear of a man — not the teddy variety, but more grizzly — and he made it clear that he was only humoring his flamboyant wife with my presence. He had built his fortune through his business of international exports, so he had acquired the shepherds as watchdogs. To him, the dogs were valuable investments, but property just the same. Not about to be bamboozled by a little curly-headed doggy psychic, he rationalized that I just had a "way" with dogs.

Harry and I made some progress with his problem that day, and we established a strong rapport. Fortunately, Harry was a great "sender," so when a frantic call came some months later from Rachel and Vince, I had no problem tapping directly into Harry over the phone.

Rachel told me that x-rays showed a free-floating, apple-sized object next to Harry's intestines. Then Vince told me in his booming baritone, "When I take him to work, he pees on the carpet in my office. The vet can't tell if the thing is putting pressure on his bladder or if it's an inflamed bladder. Harry has been eating rocks and throwing them up, but the vet says the thing is not a rock." Their utterly baffled vets wanted to perform exploratory surgery immediately in case the big round object was malignant. Instantly, I took a look inside, using a gestalt method I will explain in the next section. Inside Harry, I saw a hard object encased with fluid. I checked the signature frequency to determine if it was cancer and got a resounding "no!"

Later that night, I mentally checked in with Harry again. When I made contact he was boarded in a cage at the vet's office and was too panicked to "talk," so I spent some time trying to calm him down. He kept sending terrified pictures of what he expected would take place in surgery, and in return, I sent reassuring images of a long nap, followed by a happy homecoming; then a reunion with his beloved Patsy, the couple's other dog. The next morning, I contacted Harry while he was still sleepy.

"What is the object in you?" I asked.

"It feels like I swallowed a rock," Harry said.

"Did you?" I asked.

"I swallowed a lot of rocks."

"To try to make the object pass?"

"Yes."

"Is it a rock?" I asked.

"Well, I feel like I swallowed a tennis ball."

Again, I looked inside his body and spied something that looked like a herniated intestine: a huge round ball was protruding from a wall of soft tissue.

"Does it hurt?" I asked.

"Pressure," Harry said.

"Is it putting pressure on your bladder?"

"Yes."

"Is it malignant?"

"No," he answered.

Harry was so convincing, I knew this thing couldn't be cancerous, but I kept asking nervously over and over like a worried mother. Fortunately, he seemed too chipper to be battling a life-threatening illness, and this helped me trust that my intuition was right. I surmised that it was only a cyst and that for some reason, it *felt* to him like he had swallowed a tennis ball.

"Are you planning to be well after the surgery?" I asked. This is a telltale question with potentially terminal illnesses. Animals seem to know whether or not their surgeries will be effective. This precognitive wisdom is one of the many astonishing powers animals have that few humans possess. His reply made me breathe a sigh of relief.

"Yes. Tell Daddy not to worry about me, and tell Mother I want her to come pick me up from the vet. I want her to be there, too."

"Is there something you're upset about that caused this problem?" I asked him.

Harry sent me a film clip of Q-forms showing how he spent his days in his father's office, enduring high levels of stress. His father's international business was a volatile one, and Harry took his job as a guard dog very seriously. Harry sent the feelings of anger and tension in Vince's stomach, and thus in his own stomach, with a soundtrack of men violently arguing.

"Sam. Daddy's had problems with a man named Sam. I'm worried about his safety with the two dark-skinned men." (With this, he showed me a shadowy perception of land on the other side of an ocean. I got the distinct feeling these two men were coming from the Middle East.) "Daddy is involved with these men in a new venture. Sam! And Sampanaro! Very bad!" Harry transmitted the feeling of dread.

"Is the stress of Vince's job making you sick?" I asked.

"I have to protect Daddy from Sam . . . Sampanaro!"

"Would you like to stay home from Daddy's office?"

"I have to protect Daddy from the bad men." With this, I got a sinking feeling in my stomach. I felt that Vince was in over his head.

"Tell Daddy I like the funny music in the car," Harry requested.

"Okay," I agreed. "What if you stay home from the office to rest for a while? How are things at home?"

"Iris doesn't love me anymore." I got hit with an aching wave of sadness, even though I did not yet know who Iris was. I continued to probe, and Harry continued: "Carrie. Mother works with a woman named Carrie. Tell Mother not to worry. Something will go wrong with Carrie. Tell Mother not to get involved."

I assured him, "I will talk to your parents for you. Your surgery will go smoothly and you'll be home soon — "

"Patsy! Home with Patsy!"

"Yes. You'll be resting at home with Patsy soon. I'll tell your mother that you want her to come pick you up. So, say it again — this is just a cyst, isn't it? It's not a cancer."

"Not cancer. I feel like I swallowed a tennis ball."

"Is the cyst a tennis ball?" I asked.

"It's a cyst. But I feel like I swallowed a tennis ball."

Thanking him, I called his parents, who put me on a three-way call. I assured them that Harry was confident the object was a nonmalignant cyst, not cancer. I warned them that Harry had been very agitated in Vince's office lately and gave them the names Sam and Sampanaro. I told them Harry thought these men were a threat to his father. I heard a muffled gasp on the other end of the line. I think Vince dropped the phone. For a few seconds, I heard nothing but dead air. Finally, Vince found his voice.

"Sampanaro's in the office every day," he whispered. "How did you do that?"

I tried to explain how mental telepathy works, how simple it is, and how observant his dog was. Vince quietly confirmed that Sam was his ex-business partner, with whom Harry had witnessed an ugly breakup. Also, Harry had overheard many yelling matches between Vince and a business partner named Sampanaro lately. I was glad I had not edited my information; I would have guessed there was *either* a Sam or a Sampanaro, but not *both*, because the names were so similar. Fortunately, I was learning to blurt out *all* my information without analyzing it.

"Sampanaro! Sampanaro! Oh my God!" Rachel cried, breaking into incredulous laughter. This was one of those moments I live for — when I witness the end of a personal battle that's been fought for years. Vince had not been a believer. His wife had hornswoggled him into all this psychic business; I knew the moment Rachel hung up the phone she was going to wag a triumphant finger at her husband and say, "I told you so!"

I advised Vince to proceed with caution and cut off his partnership with Sampanaro. Rachel agreed she had never trusted Sampanaro and had always opposed the partnership. I also sensed this Sampanaro was an unmarried lady's man (or so he'd like to think). Vince confirmed Sampanaro was single and unsuccessfully playing the field. Vince agreed to terminate the partnership as soon as he could but grumbled about being involved in something he couldn't get out from under yet.

Vince confirmed he had some prospects with two Middle Eastern men. The "funny music in the car" turned out to be Creedence Clearwater Revival on the oldies station, with Daddy singing along, so we all understood why Harry thought it was pretty funny.

Vince and Rachel confirmed that Iris is their daughter, who had recently left for college and thus had stopped taking Harry for long walks in the park. No one in the family had realized how much those walks had meant to Harry.

I suggested that Rachel be the one to take Harry home because he requested his Mom come to the doctor, too. She was touched — she had always thought of Harry as Vince's dog. Rachel joyously confirmed that she worked with a woman named Carrie who had been rather problematic lately.

"But how could Harry have known about Carrie?" Rachel asked. "He's never even met her."

"He's heard you talk to her over the phone," I said.

"But that's incredible . . . it's so incredible!" Rachel laughed giddily. True, but Harry had something even more incredible hidden up his paw.

I recounted Harry's words about the tennis ball, to air my confusion: Harry had said, "I feel like I swallowed a tennis ball," but went on to say that the cyst was not a tennis ball. It would have been quite a feat for a German shepherd to swallow a tennis ball whole, and because he called it a cyst, it didn't seem very likely. Still, I kept wondering if a tennis ball was involved. We were all anxious to get the mystery solved, and we didn't have long to wait. Harry's surgery was scheduled for that afternoon.

The next night, Rachel called to update me on Harry's progress: the vets had discovered a nonmalignant cyst on Harry's prostate. (Harry had not been neutered.) The vets neutered him and opened the cyst so that it would drain, but they had to hold him for a few more days to keep an eye on him. Excited, Rachel described her visit with Harry: rather than running straight to Vince the way he always had, he ran to her instead. She had never known how much he loved her.

But the best was yet to come. The next night, I got a phone call from Rachel, absolutely elated. The vet had called to tell her Harry had been vomiting, and guess what he was throwing up! Chewed up tennis balls! Apparently he had eaten tennis balls back home and was now throwing them up after the surgery.

A few weeks later I got a triumphant update: Harry had made a full recovery, and Vince had chosen to part ways with his charming pal, Mikie Sampanaro.

Now you may be wondering how I can see inside animals' bodies. What the Sam Hill am I doing? It's called Medical Gestalt.

I AM YOU AND YOU ARE ME
AND WE ARE ALL TOGETHER

WEBSTER'S DICTIONARY DEFINES GESTALT psychology as: "the study of perception and behavior from the standpoint of an organism's response to configurational wholes with stress on the identity of psychological and physiological events and rejections of atomistic or elemental analysis of stimulus, precept, and response." Good grief! In plain English, that means that through gestalt you can share the experiences of other living beings from their own point of view.

When I perform a body scan, I establish Resogenesis so that I can hear the animal's thoughts; then I take it a step further and move into Unimorphosis, where I can align my consciousness in the animal's body, briefly, and with her permission cohabit the same physical form. It's easier than it sounds. In Unimorphosis, you see the world through the animal's eyes, which will be essential later when we explore the possibilities of tracking lost animals. Unimorphosis is the best way to give effective commands (from the inside out) and to search for painful problems in an animal's body.

Medical gestalt is nothing more than a concentrated form of creative visualization — a game really — that we all engaged in as children when we pretended we were something else. If you pretend you are the animal, you can identify a myriad of physical complaints. It is so simple, but we've forgotten how to do it, and many of us who remember how have forgotten how to *trust* it.

MULTITASKING

I'LL BET YOU'VE BEEN TOLD all your life that you can't see inside other people's bodies, haven't you? If that's true, I'll bet you've learned that you can't feel other people's physical pain inside your own body. Well, now I'm going to ask you to put aside your ideas for a while — the things you know or think you know. I'm going to ask you to jot down your questions as they arise because you might experience opposition as you read my words. Save those questions for later. For now, let these new ideas and thoughts cohabitate with your old belief systems. After you've entertained these new ideas, sift through your ideas and ask yourself this: Who taught me this? Where did I learn this? Why did I come to accept this as absolute truth? Was this belief something I formulated on my own, or was it taught to me as someone else's vintage belief? If I used my own reasoning, what event made me deduce that this idea was an absolute truth? Remember, you are not here to reiterate outdated beliefs. It's time to burst forward and recalibrate your energy. There's a whole new world out there that few people are talking about . . . yet.

As we learn to scan animals' bodies, we discover that records are not stored in the brain alone. Most of our scientists are now willing to admit that no one has ever been able to locate where memory is stored in the brain. Although there may be some truth to the idea that certain parts of the brain control certain attributes, the philosophy of the new millennium describes the mind differently, with the holographic brain theory. In this more sensible paradigm, we are not "reading minds" but actually reading "energy fields."

Michael Talbot, author of *The Holographic Universe*, agrees that the sum total of our experience may be present holographically in every cell of our bodies, but he goes on to point out that this model is no less mysterious than many of the tenets in physics that our scientists have adopted but never fully understood. Michael points out the paradox when he tells us, "It is worth noting that we don't really know what any field is. Dr. [David] Bohm has said, 'What is an electric field? We don't know. When we discover a new kind of field, it seems mysterious. Then we name it, get used to dealing with it and describing its properties, and it no longer seems mysterious. But we still don't know what an electrical or gravitational field really is. We don't even know what electrons are. We can only describe how they behave.'" Similarly, we can also observe how gestalt therapy and telepathic communication behave, even though we don't know exactly what they are.

The most miraculous explanation of holographic brain theory I can provide for you is the odd and shocking behavior that sometimes accompanies organ transplants. We've all heard the stories: someone receives a kidney from a concert pianist, then suddenly the recipient not only has the desire but the ability to play the violin! The most comprehensive collection of these studies is compiled by Dr. Paul Pearsall in a book called *The Heart's Code*. Pearsall points out that Albert Einstein proved that matter and energy are interchangeable; therefore, energy and information are also synonymous. What he means is that memories appear to be stored in the actual organs of our bodies; and even more revolutionary is his theory that the heart itself, like the brain, generates and receives information from the world around it. Here's one of his most profound examples, which Dr. Pearsall tells from his point of view.

I recently spoke to an international group of psychologists, psychiatrists, and social workers meeting in Houston, Texas. I spoke to them about my ideas about the central role of the heart in our psychological and spiritual life, and following my presentation, a psychiatrist came to the microphone to ask me about one of her patients whose experience seemed to substantiate my ideas about cellular memories and a thinking heart. The case disturbed her so much that she struggled to speak through her tears.

Sobbing to the point that the audience and I had difficulty understanding her, she said, "I have a patient, an eight-year-old little girl who received the heart of a murdered ten-year-old girl. Her mother brought her to me when she started screaming at night about her dreams of the man who had murdered her donor. She said her daughter knew who it was. After several sessions, I just could not deny the reality of what this child was telling me. Her mother and I finally decided to call the police and, using the descriptions from the little girl, they found the murderer. He was easily convicted with evidence my patient provided. The time, the weapon, the place, the clothes he wore, what the little girl he killed had said to him . . . everything the little heart transplant recipient reported was completely accurate."

According to Dr. Pearsall's findings, the history of the body is stored in the body, and according to my own research, the ability to read the records is through a quantum process fundamental to nature. Evidently, when I scanned Harry's body, I simply used my mind differently than the way you currently use yours, but if I can learn how to do this, so can you, because organically you and I have the same equipment. Let's revisit what Dr. Mitchell has to say about all this.

Earlier, our favorite astronaut tells us, "The Quantum Hologram is the name we give to coherent emissions from objects, which means that all the information about you is contained in each molecule in your body. To have a complete description of an object, you need both its space/time and quantum information — the nonlocal connection. The inner subjective experience (the emotion) seems to be rooted in the nonlocal attributes discovered in quantum mechanics." The properties of nonlocal connection are those we receive in Resogenesis.

Going further, the terrain we want to illuminate in Unimorphosis is inside the animal's body, and this may require that you stretch your paradigm considerably. As an animal communicator, my perspective on physical bodies may be very different from yours. When I enter Unimorphosis with Harry, for instance, I'm functioning on a nonlocal level, which means I'm focused on the content and meaning of the electrical field to the exclusion of all else, and I'm fueling my inquiry with unconditional love. In this sacred realm, there are no judgments, no thoughts of my own, no projections. There is only listening. In that silence, my concentration is so absolute that I cease to exist. Within this commitment to selflessness, I elect to view Harry's body differently. I don't accept that Harry's body stops at his flesh and keeps his medical conditions and thoughts separate from me. I don't view him within the Explicate Order at all. I can move into his quantum field and into Implicate Order because I love him so much, I'm not afraid of anything he could show me or any of the pain he could make me feel.

WHAT IS YOUR PAIN THRESHOLD?

YOUR SUCCESS IN MEDICAL GESTALT will revolve around your pain threshold. You need to be able to withstand pain and still function. Courage and compassion are attributes of self-esteem. If you can honestly look at any animal and silently say, "Let me feel your pain. I can handle it. I don't care how much it hurts me. If it helps you, I am willing to shoulder the burden," then you've launched yourself into that magical realm of loving kindness where you've declared that you are so powerful and strong, no pain can affect you. This is where we want to go. Here, you're not separate anymore. You are not two bodies in two divorced energy fields. You and the animal have merged into one unit by virtue of your love.

In *Creating Affluence*, Deepak Chopra writes: "Life is the coexistence of all opposite values. Joy and sorrow, pleasure and pain, up and down, hot and cold, here and there, light and darkness, birth and death. All experience is by contrast, and one would be meaningless without the other . . . . When there is a quiet reconciliation, an acceptance in our awareness of this lively coexistence of all opposite values, then automatically we become more and more nonjudgmental. The victor and the vanquished are seen as two poles of the same being. Nonjudgment leads to quieting of the internal dialogue, and this opens the doorway to creativity."

In this unnamable space beyond opposites, communication between all living things is possible. Just look at what Dr. Chopra is asking us to do: "quiet the internal dialogue." Sit in silence and realize that you and your animal are *already* one. Joseph Campbell had something really beautiful to say about this: "The ultimate word in our English language for that which is transcendent is God . . . Now, in religions where the god or creator is the mother, the whole world is in her body. There is nowhere else."

Here's how this relates to us. When Harry was in pain, I went into his energy field to alleviate his suffering. There was nowhere else for me. The world melted away, time stopped, I lost myself, and my entire identity morphed into that of a terrified dog, locked in a cage at the vet's office all night. But then I needed to step back into my identity in order to offer him strength, so I established *two* voices inside his head: his *and* mine. I could feel his fear and pain but still keep my wits about me enough to perpetually soothe him, bathing him in peaceful energy, enough to repeat loving words of comfort every few hours. When I'm working in this healing space, I gradually take over, coaxing the other being to vibrate on my frequency, and as my loving presence gains dominion over their fear, I establish what's called "coherence." This is the tuning fork phenomenon, where all the tones around the instrument are encouraged to align to the highest frequency.

For another simple way to look at this, let's go back to Campbell's description of the Divine Mother — Mother Nature — as having the entire world inside her body. Similarly, during Unimorphosis, you are present to the entire world inside you. Remember the quote from *The Matrix*, where the little whiz kid bending the spoon says, "There is no spoon. There is only *me*. I bend my mind." This is also true. All of the animals on this planet, indeed, every living thing is inside your mind. As a drop of water in the divine ocean, you have the macrocosm inside you. When you acknowledge your connection to the cosmos, your perception changes, because in that instant, you are no longer choosing to operate as a particle but you operate as a wave, or indeed, an entire field of energy.

So, when you're learning how to perform a body scan, you're not actually looking for answers inside the animal. You're looking for answers inside *you*. When an animal or person is in pain, I locate their vibratory rate, match it, then change it, and in essence absorb their negative feelings. When they touch me, they become me, and I usher them into my energy field like a mother hen scooping her chicks under her protective feathers. In this way, gestalt is a method of not only retrieving information but giving healing.

Medical gestalt requires you to acknowledge your relationship to another living being, and the clarity of your vision will revolve around your relationship to yourself. You already have a quantum relationship with every animal in your world that allows you the ability to feel what they're feeling. I'm just asking you to pay closer attention to it. Because your own body is the instrument through which you measure what other animals are feeling, we must first ask how aware you are of what *you're* really feeling. In gestalt, your body and emotional well-being are your only instruments. How clean are your tools? Are they sharp, or dull and muddy?

Gestalt therapy always reminds me of the old TV show I watched as a child, *Kung Fu*. The opening sequence always shows the lead character, Grasshopper, being tutored by his master. The master has Grasshopper fixate upon a candle while the master chants, "You *are* the flame. *Become* the flame." This echoes the wonderful phrase many people hear when learning meditation, "You are your attention." This concept is frighteningly simple and yet ultimately empowering because it puts us back in the driver's seat; it makes us absolutely responsible, not for the events in our lives, but for our interpretation of the events.

THE BODY SCAN: AN EXERCISE

Now we're going to revisit some ideas I explored in my most recent book, *Straight from the Horse's Mouth*, with a new slant. If you haven't read it, you might find it useful. But for now, just remember, the laws of gestalt don't change, and practice always makes perfect.

The challenge is this: You must have an acute awareness of what is happening in your own body so that you will be able to differentiate between your physical sensations and those of your animal friends. Your first challenge may simply be to learn how to get in your own body. The emotional challenge is the same. When you know and accept your own emotions, you can sort out what you are generating, as opposed to what emotions and sensations are emanating from your animal. Therefore, we will concentrate first on cleaning our slates and getting in touch with our own bodies.

For the sake of consistency, I am going to write this exercise as it would pertain to a dog or cat, but feel free to substitute "hoof," "wing," or "hand" whenever "paw" is not appropriate.

Before you look inside your animal, let's take a quick inventory of your own aches and pains. Where are you tight and stiff? Let your focus glide down your body, down each arm, into your neck, back, pelvis, legs, and feet. Breathe into the tight spots and let the tension go. Make a mental note of what hurts inside your own body so you won't confuse your own issues with those of your friend. Gently bringing your focus back into your heart, retreat into the sanctuary of the light, and prepare to pray along with me. This meditation is designed to put you in a gentle rollicking trance, and if you say it out loud, it will actually increase the amplitude and decrease the frequency of your brain waves to foster a more receptive state in mind.

I Stay Centered in Love

I believe there is only One Power in the universe and this Power is God, the source of all peace, love, and creative expression. This Power is present in every atom of my being, in every person, every flower, every tree, every star, every body of water on this beautiful planet, and in every single cell of my beloved animal. I reach deep within, into the quietest space within my soul, and here I find it easy to unite with this Power. I am now in perfect alignment with this Divine Intelligence. My consciousness expands as I acknowledge this love, and the loving kindness that pours from me is an umbrella that shelters other living beings from harm. I know that the love in me is so strong that it can calm, soothe, cheer, and enlighten any person or animal I greet into my life today. This wellspring of confidence and healing energy shines from me in everything I think, say, and do. Each moment I live is a joyous celebration that showers me in the knowledge that I am God's perfect love in action, forever expanding and unfolding to bless the world around me. I enjoy staying balanced and perpetually coming home to the God Consciousness within me. This truth I know for myself, I know for every person, and I know for every animal everywhere. I am grateful for the joy this sacred knowing brings. I release this blessing out into the world, knowing that Divine Intelligence will shine wisdom into my own mind to help me understand this animal today.

Practicing Unimorphosis

Next, ask your animal for permission to mentally "see" inside his body. You would be entering his physical form with your own spirit, and your animal might not be comfortable with that level of intimacy.

If he gets up and leaves the room after you ask permission, go practice your tap dancing, then try this technique again later.

Most animals enjoy this communion and welcome the attention. The feeling of merging consciousness is usually very pleasurable. If your friend seems to relax at your suggestion, go ahead and make contact. Picture yourself as a very small being: an elf, a fairy, or a tiny point of light. Hop out the top of your head and fly over to your friend. Slip into the top of the animal's head, through his crown chakra and slide down into his left forepaw. You are now inside the animal.

Feel the shoulder. Feel the knee. Feel the paw, the bottom of the pad. Is it tired? Is it sore? How is the circulation? Is there any obstruction in the leg? How is the alignment? Does the leg function properly?

Now climb back up the left front leg, cross over to the other leg, and glide down to the other forepaw. Again, you are looking for stiffness, problems with bones, skin, muscles, and circulation. Envision applying pressure to the paw. Envision yourself walking. Envision the flexibility of the ankle. Is there pain present, or does the joint move smoothly?

If you feel sensations in your *own* arms and hands, this is *exactly* what you are looking for. Sensations are as valid as the language you receive in Resogenesis. Remember that you are now in two places at once, projecting your attention inside the animal in your very small astral form while simultaneously recording sensation in your own body. If you are investigating known problems, ask for the answers you seek. For instance: "Did this bone not mend correctly?" When your friend offers up information of his own volition, you might get flashes of pain in your own body or see pictures in your mind. Your animal may send a message like, "The hot concrete burns my feet," showing you a glimpse of the sidewalk with the sensation of stinging in your hands. As you've learned, these messages may or may not be accompanied by language. If you don't get clear images, just keep going. This work takes practice.

If your patient is a cat, see how it would feel to extend your claws. Fabulous, isn't it?

Now rise up into the animal's throat. Check his larynx. How does it feel to meow or bark? How does it feel emotionally to speak and not be understood? If your friend is a dog, how does it feel to be silenced? Do you ache to speak? If your friend is a cat, how does it feel to purr?

Descend into his heart. Look around. Is it strong? Is it clear? Does it function properly? Does it feel good? How does it feel emotionally? Are you lonely? Do you, as your animal, need more love? Are you left alone too long? Would you like the company of another animal? If you get hit with a wave of sadness or joy in your own body, you know you have successfully made contact.

Slide over into the left lung. How does it look? Is it pink? Is it clear? How does it feel to take a breath? Is the breath loose or constricted? Move to the right lung. Is it healthy? Is it strong? Do you feel any irritation, burning, or constriction in *your own* chest as you explore your animal's lungs?

Next focus your attention on the animal's stomach. Is it upset, or at peace? Is he hungry? Ask questions like, "What kind of foods are difficult to digest?" Picture the food going into the animal's mouth and wait for a response in your own stomach. You may see a color, feel a texture, smell an aroma, hear a word, or taste something.

If you suspect allergies, envision the animal ingesting or in contact with the potential culprit, then wait to see if the irritant has any effect on your own body. Use your own feelings while you're in here. The thought of a "bad" food or drug may make you cramped, queasy, panicky, or even tearful. The presence of disease may be perceived as a darkness, heaviness, pain, or sadness.

Ask the animal to pull your attention into any organ that is in pain or is not working properly. Feel free to ask general questions like the following:

"Do you think acupuncture or a chiropractic adjustment would help?" With this, envision the procedures performed by a qualified holistic vet.

"Do these treatments help make you feel better, or do you want to get better on your own?" Check your body to see what it feels like "before" and "after" the therapy or adjustment.

You may not hear "yes" or "no" answers, but a feeling of discomfort or a rush of relief is enough information to let you know you're on the right track. If you feel anything at all, consider it encouraging feedback.

Now rise up into the spinal column and slide along it, vertebra by vertebra. How is the alignment? The cartilage? Is it supple and flexible? Is there any pain? If there is sign of injury and you have a good connection with the animal's inner voice, you may ask: "How did this happen?" Be aware of any emotions such as fear or rushes of adrenaline and any accompanying imagery.

Put your focus on the animal's right hip. Is there any pain or stiffness, or does it function like a well-oiled machine? Envision it in motion. Is it creaky? Glide down the animal's right hind leg. Put your focus in the ankle, the foot, the pads under the foot. How does it feel? Envision it supporting the body's weight. Now how does it feel?

Glide over to the left leg and feel the muscles, the strength of the bones, and the structure. If the animal is in good health, you will feel a burst of vitality in your own left leg. It feels especially thrilling to be in the body of a strong, sinewy horse or a happy, muscular dog. Psychically exploring a healthy animal may feel better than being in your own body.

Concentrate on the animal's tail (I love this part). Feel how it connects to the body through the coccyx. Travel down to the tip and see how it feels to have a tail. Check every link. Imagine that you could wag your tail. Does every inch feel good?

Check the skin. Does it feel comfortable, or dry and itchy? The skin is a particularly good gauge of your connection. If your animal suffers from skin allergies, you will find yourself itching and wanting to scratch the spot.

Next, let your attention float up into the animal's head. Go into the sinuses. Ask if he gets headaches. Go into his eyes and check his vision.

Investigate his ears. How is his hearing? Is he prone to mites or infections? Go into his mouth and check his teeth. Are they fairly clean? Look for pain and inflammation. Check the alignment of his neck and jaw. If you salivate slightly and want to smile, all is well; but if you feel pressure or pain or see red or black flashes, you have hit a hot spot.

Go wherever you need to go in the body. Ask. Look. Listen.

When you've finished your psychic spelunking, hop out of the top of the animal's head. Return to your own head and thank your friend for letting you explore his body. Awesome, wasn't it? Now is the time to build a wall of protection. Visualize a cocoon of light around your animal friend and a separate wall of white light encasing you, safely dividing your physical and emotional issues from those of the animal. You need to make a clean departure for the health and happiness of the animal. In order to avoid leaving any of your unconscious negative patterns or residue in your friend's energy field, see him safely protected in a bubble of light. If you pick up his aches and pains in the meanwhile, aspirin won't help you. If you feel any unusual sensations or emotions, construct the cocoon of light around yourself and go about your business. With time, the sensations will fade away.

In the course of this exercise, you may have received nothing more than a wordless command. You may simply have had a gut feeling. Watch your urges closely for the next few days. If need be, call your vet and have your friend checked out. Better safe than sorry.

You may also find that the drugs or diet your friend is on is not working. I highly recommend seeking out a veterinarian with knowledge of holistic, alternative, and Eastern medicine. Keep an emergency surgeon nearby but find a holistic vet, even if you have to visit the next state.

When you feel comfortable with the body scan technique, feel free to practice on human beings. Make it a game you play with your spouse and children. Teach your children how to perform the body scan on you and record their findings, as most children have not yet forgotten how to use their X-Ray Vision. The beauty of working on humans is they can actually answer you in English.

READING AN ANIMAL'S SIGNATURE FREQUENCIES

THE WAY YOU'RE GOING TO IDENTIFY a physical problem is through the animal's signature frequencies. Spiritual author and aerospace wizard Gregg Braden tells us that living beings are electrical in nature. He says, "Each cell within each component of our body generates a charge of approximately 1.17 volts at a specific frequency for that organ. This unique vibration is termed a Signature Frequency. Each cell is in constant motion, the rhythmic oscillation of a subtle beat, generating its Signature Frequency."

Okay, let me translate this into Amelia-speak. Each organ has a design. When that design is out of whack, you will pick up the distress signal like a sinking ship's SOS. According to Braden's interpretation, we could say the geometry of that organ is messed up, even if the problem is not structural but viral or bacterial. If nothing's wrong with a particular organ, you may not feel anything when you tune into it, except maybe waves of peace. However, if there's pain in the body, your attention will be drawn to it like a noisy smoke alarm. This is how the tigers in Florida showed me Raja's tooth as I explained in chapter 4. My awareness was drawn to his upper left molars like a full-blown fire alarm. The signature frequency is not only the blueprint of the internal organ but the "song" that body part sings. It might help to imagine that every cell in your body is singing. The "singing" of each cell is what makes each design hold its shape. Vibrationally, you'll sense when a signature frequency is off-kilter, because it will be "singing" out of harmony. It will be oscillating at the wrong rate, which means the rhythm of the organ will be off. Put back into the context of my reading with Harry, I could "see" that the design of his intestines was out of whack — I could envision the huge tumor clearly — and on closer examination, I could go inside the tumor and see that it was filled with clear fluid. This is how I determined the tumor was not cancerous. In addition, the signature frequency was offbeat, but I new it wasn't life-threatening because it wasn't that syncopated against the rest of the body. To me, cancer feels like symbols crashing over a harp solo. It's that harsh.

Okay, let's answer some of your questions through the example of one of my students. Laurie Filsinger emailed me this provocative question with a success story. Check it out.

Explain the Spleen, Please!

I did my second ever body scan right before I came to your class in Nashville. My first one was done on a healthy cat, so nothing came up. Well, my friend was low on cash and wanted to see if her cat needed to go to the vet or not as she was dropping weight. (To me it was obvious that she did, but I humored her.) I did your body scan exercise on her. I told my friend that I felt that there was a problem with a tooth in the upper left back part of the mouth and that there felt like some sort of soft blockage in the abdominal area. Well, the day of the class, she took her cat to the vet. When I returned home from Tennessee that night, I had an email waiting from her. She said that the vet found two abscessed teeth and that one was in the upper left back of the mouth. I was flabbergasted!!!

But when he palpated her abdomen, nothing was found. I thought I was shooting at 50 percent, but I was still pretty happy about that. Well, two weeks later, she takes her kitty back to the vet to have the teeth worked on. Her kitty had difficulty waking up from the anesthesia, so they kept her overnight. I thought this was very odd. Anyway, when my friend picked up her cat, the vet told her that her spleen was quite enlarged. Now, this troubled me as he had said that everything was hunky-dory in the abdominal area two weeks prior. Is it possible to actually be able to detect upcoming organ issues, or did this vet just miss this the first go around?

I actually don't have a spleen anymore, or a gall bladder, or an appendix, for that matter. Apparently this has little effect, as I still felt "something" in my abdominal area when I scanned the cat. It felt more like a blockage, though — not exactly a tumor but like something wasn't able to pass. I'm assuming since the spleen was enlarged, it was holding onto blood cells, which would account for the blocked feeling I got. I was wondering if you thought I would have been better able to identify that it was the spleen that was the problem if I actually had one? Also the sensations I felt with the tooth and the spleen were dull, but I would imagine abscessed teeth would be quite painful. My friend said that part of the tooth actually broke off in the vet's hand upon examination. Do you know why my sensations were so diminished?

Oh, and I also wanted to ask you something else. Have you ever had a dog ask you why you don't potty out in the yard like they do? I've never had much luck hearing my own dogs, but since your class, I think I've been catching snippets of their thoughts! Last night, my littlest dog followed me into the bathroom like she always does, and I swear I heard her ask me "Why don't you potty in the yard like I do?" Again, flabbergasted!! After *all this time*, I can actually *hear* her and that was her pressing question! I thought it was humorous and just wanted to see if you have ever gotten that one before!

TROUBLESHOOTING X-RAY VISION

IN ANSWER TO LAURIE'S QUESTIONS: yes, you can feel pain in the spleen area even if you don't have one. Likewise, if you're checking an animal's tail and you don't have one but that invisible tail is broken, boy, will you feel it! Ditto with elephant's noses and bat's wings and the pedestal tail of a kangaroo. You feel the signature frequencies of those appendages, maybe not in your invisible tail, but in your energy field. Would you be able to better feel body parts that you also share? Not necessarily. If you tune into a bird with a broken wing, it will hurt like hell.

Can animals predict future health problems? Apparently so, because they seem to know which body parts are deteriorating and diminishing in energy better than humans can understand their own health problems. Again, these predictions probably originate not in the "mind" of the animal but in the quantum field of the organs themselves. But in this case, I would assume that the cat already had the blockage before the vet discovered it.

Why were Laurie's feelings of pain so minimal? Because God has a heart. She should simply thank God she could locate the pain in the teeth without feeling its full force. My opinion here is that, like Darren and his orangutan in chapter 4, Laurie stayed more in her own body than in the cat's. She established Resogenesis more firmly than Unimorphosis as she moved into the animal's field. If she had put her entire focus inside the cat, the pain in those teeth would have knocked her over. It's a gift beyond measure to be able to locate pain without feeling its full force.

And finally, *have dogs asked me why I don't poop in the yard?* Indeed they have, and much worse. This question was a wonderful indication that Laurie actually was hearing the animal's thoughts clairaudiently; the more outlandish the question from our human perspective, the more likely it is that it is actually coming from the animal's perspective. When you get kooky questions like that, it's one of the best ways to assure that you're truly "tuned in."

Dr. Mitchell's view is that in Unimorphosis we are accessing holographic records, as if we were nothing more than MRI machines scanning energy on a quantum level. In this model, the animal's cellular memories are an unguarded library of holographic records, and you simply walk through the cosmic door and "read" whatever you want. But this is where I differ from him. Although I do agree that on the deepest level that is exactly how we perform a body scan, I ascertain that there is also a level of mental awareness where the animal is "answering" your questions as you ask them, and this part of the animal feels closer to the ego or personality than the soul. Perhaps it is just another layer of mysterious quantum process. In any case, that was the level where I could actually telepath with Harry the German shepherd as I psychically strolled through his body.

Another thing that leads me to think I'm communicating with the animal as a conscious personality is that once in a while an animal refuses contact. Here's a rare and poignant case when an animal said, "no!"

DINO'S PRIVATE HELL

WHILE TEACHING IN NEW YORK, I had the distinct pleasure of working with some of the animals from the Catskill Animal Sanctuary. Julie Barone, whom you read about in chapter 2 (the girl who "had whiskers!"), brought to my workshop many splendid animals as our guest teachers, including a perpetually pooping ram; a big, bossy duck who completely ousted me out of the teacher role and took over the class; and a lovely cow who spoke to us all about the dilemma cattle face in the hands of cruel American factory farmers.

But the animal I fell in love with was a little pony named Dino with a soft, pumpkin-colored coat, a shaggy blonde mane, and warm, honey-colored eyes that would melt your heart. He complied with all the questions from the group and patiently let everyone telepath with him, but when Julie asked us all to "go into" his past, I immediately moved my consciousness inside his body to scour his cellular memories. Suddenly, I heard a voice yell, "No! No! Amelia! Don't come in here!!!" As Julie tried to brace us and tell us something terrible had happened to Dino, I silently argued with him, "It's okay, Dino. Whatever it is, I can handle it." Instantly, I moved into his past and "rolled back" in time so that I could see his past. But he argued adamantly, "NO, AMELIA! GET OUT OF HERE! Get OUT! You don't understand! You CAN'T handle this! I WON'T show you!"

But even as the voice yelled out its warning, it was too late. Suddenly, I was in a blind panic — perhaps the worst panic I've ever felt in my life. I was in utter blackness, desperately trying to get out of my stall, but I was choking on smoke. The crashing of the fire was deafening, and I felt my face stinging, and my lungs burning, but through it all, Dino's thoughts drowned out the outer noise. I could hear him screaming inside my head: *"I've got to save my friends! I've got to free them! Let me out! Let me out!"*

I pulled back into my body as fast as I could, but I was already heaving with tears in front of my entire class, and I was so shaken I could barely stand. A crashing wave of pain and regret hit me so hard I almost threw up. I said something like, "Holy shit, Julie. What happened to this pony?" When she told us about his past, tears streamed down all our faces, the horror of it was so inconceivable.

Dino was the only survivor in an arson fire that killed twenty-three horses in Brooklyn. One of his beautiful eyelids literally melted from the flames, but throughout it all, the only thing this heroic little pony could think about was rescuing his friends. His heart was utterly broken as he heard all the other horses trapped in their stalls, dying in terror all around him. Is it any wonder he didn't want to share that agony with me?

Dino is now living a long, happy, healthy life at the wonderful Catskill Animal Sanctuary, and it's only a further testament to his loving nature that he didn't want to burden even the "horse-therapist" with his tragic past. Animals can say "no" to a body scan, and when they do, it's best to honor their requests.

MUTINY IN THE MEDICAL PROFESSION

NOW LET'S HAVE SOME LAUGHTER. At the end of this chapter I'm going to share with you one of my very favorite stories in the world. First I want to explain how I met the human star of this hilarious and naughty story. I was on stage in Cologne, Germany, and had just asked the crowd if animals ever spoke to them in their dreams. A few shy hands went up. I asked if the animals literally "spoke German" and if their mouths moved liked humans. This time only a couple of hands went up, one from a radiant woman with long blonde tresses.

"That's how it started for me," I said. "My cat started coming to me in my dreams and talking to me in English."

When I took my break and walked out into he crowd, this beautiful blonde woman approached me tentatively.

"I have a message for you," she said. "Last night, before I left England, my cat came to me in a dream. She spoke English to me as if she were human. Her mouth moved. She's never done that before."

"What did she say?" I asked, mesmerized.

"She said to tell you she said 'hello,' " the woman said breathlessly.

"What?" I asked, astonished.

The woman was clearly shaken, and her eyes filled with tears.

"She said, 'Tell Amelia I said hello.' "

The woman pulled out a photo of a wild-eyed little gray and white striped cat. My knees gave a little. When I looked back up, I saw tears trickling down the woman's cheeks. My eyes welled up with the shock of recognition.

"Oh my God! Dr. Bertram! Is it you?"

She nodded and gave me a nervous hug. Julia Bertram and I been emailing each other for a while, and I had asked her to step forward out of the crowd in my seminar and identify herself. This woman was not the kind of spiritual seeker you might imagine attending my workshops. She wasn't someone who talks to fairies, obsesses on past lives as Cleopatra, or chases gurus around India. She was a veterinary surgeon, and she was married to another vet who was also a surgeon. The couple were both highly respected traditional vets.

Suddenly, I had in my arms a woman who had gone to vet school and was now conversing with her cat in her dreams. Mutiny in the medical profession! The look in her eyes I'd seen many times before in the eyes of my students who are doctors and psychiatrists. She was so rattled that she was on the verge of a nervous breakdown. Her very own cat had catapulted into one of her very own dreams and spoke to her in perfect English like a Cambridge professor of literature. This woman's psychic abilities had stormed the fortress of her analytical mind and they were wreaking havoc on the mental antiquities she'd collected in vet school. One look at her flushed cheeks and the crazed look in her eyes and you could see the whole story. Yesterday, her brain processes were all law and order, and today, there were monkeys in the temple.

Over the course of the next two days, Julia's psychic skill blossomed and she quickly became one of the best students I've ever had. She revealed details about the guest animals that she never could have known, describing the inside of the human guardians' homes, the guardians' occupations, physical descriptions of their spouses, and details about animals who were not in our presence — including the breed, size, shape, color, and names of the ones who had been left at home. She could tell me the color of the dogs' beds, what they saw on their walks, and what other species they encountered, and she provided detailed accounts of the guardians' activities behind closed doors. She explained each animal's emotional state and relationships, both with humans and with other animals.

At one point, a parakeet was brought out onto the stage, and Julia said to the German girl who was his guardian, "He says his favorite thing is to watch you dance." I, too, saw the guardian playing CDs and dancing wildly around her flat. When the German girl confirmed that she does this often and that her parakeet dances along with her, Julia and I let out squeals of laughter, and I gave her a joyous high-five. Nothing in the world is more fun for me than to telepath simultaneously with one of my students.

Later in the workshop, a dog was brought out onto the stage, and we asked, "What are the other animals at home?" Julia described a brown and white guinea pig who had died and was in spirit, a sandy-colored rabbit who was also in heaven, and a goldfish the family was about to buy. When the dog's guardian confirmed that those were indeed exactly the animals she lived with and wanted, even I almost fell off my chair. I'd never before seen such accuracy.

The real test would be if she could go home and practice her new-found techniques on the job. We humans heap a huge amount of stress on our precious vets, while we look on, always frightened, often frantic, and sometimes even hysterical or belligerent, as our dear, wise vets try to hold their balance to make a clear diagnosis. I'm going to share two of Julia's shining success stories with you, one breathtaking and one naughty, to demonstrate what big risks she takes and how beautifully they pay off.

Divine Intervention — With a Scalpel

Two weeks ago at work the receptionist came in and said there was a cat waiting to be seen with breathing problems. It should have been one of the other vet's cases, but they were all busy so I took it.

The thirteen-year-old cat was dying — gasping for breath, limp, with blue gums. The owners were both in tears. I listened to her heart. Without thinking, I gestalted her body and saw a hole in her diaphragm. I told the owners I was convinced she had a diaphragmatic hernia. I said I would take her in, put her on oxygen, take an x-ray, and phone them with the results in order to make a plan what to do. The owners wanted me to do everything to save the cat but were absolutely convinced she would die.

I took her to our kennel area and put her in an oxygen tent. She was deteriorating. She went from bad to worse, so all the other vets said: "What are you doing, Julia? Just put her to sleep! She is already half-dead anyway!"

But I thought, "No, I can save her." When there is a hole in the diaphragm, tissue from inside the abdominal cavity can slip through the hole and press on the lungs. I thought, "If I lift the cat up at the front end and shake her gently, maybe whatever has slipped through will slip back."

So I did — before the horrified stares of my nurses. And it worked! The cat immediately settled down, her breathing eased, and the color of her gums went back to pink. I took an x-ray and could see nothing. I was still convinced I was right, although all the other vets thought I was a little crazy. I phoned the owners and told them I would stabilize the cat and operate later. So I kept her for three days and she improved greatly.

Then came the operation, a very tricky one, because as soon as you open the abdomen, air gets sucked through the hole in the diaphragm and the lungs collapse. You have to breathe for the cat with a machine. When I opened her up, her breathing got worse and, yes, I found the hole, about two centimeters in diameter. I was right! The operation went fine. Yesterday, I took out the stitches and got an enormous bunch of flowers from the delighted owners.

All the other vets in my office would have put the cat to sleep. None of them even thought about a diaphragmatic hernia, so was it a coincidence that this particular cat was my patient and I managed to save her? Or was it divine intervention? The main thing is that the cat is alive and well. The owners changed surgeons so I can see this cat from now on.

Incidentally, Dr. Bertram recently told me she hums as she performs her surgeries. She said that while the other vets sometimes panic and say things like, "This cat is never going to make it," she only envisions the outcome that she does want and mentally talks the animal through the surgeries. I observed that not only does she send calm, assertive energy to the animal under anesthesia, but she does so in feline body language, by humming, the best way to calm a nervous cat. When we hum, we mirror their mother's purrs. Julia confided that even her most challenging surgeries go remarkably well when she hums and enjoys her work. She says she loves to perform surgeries, and it shows.

And now, here's Dr. Bertram's most infamous success story. There's no PG rating on this book, so I can only suggest that if you're under the age of eighteen, please skip this story and go on to the next chapter.

Good Vibrations

A lady brought her dog in to see me because he had been vomiting for the past few days while nothing was coming out the other end.

I thought he probably had a "foreign body" obstructing his bowels. I told the woman to book him in for x-rays, and if we found an obstruction we would have to operate.

When the dog was under anesthesia, he was relaxed enough for me to feel something in his abdomen, so we did not need to take any x-rays. We prepared him for the operation. I asked him what he had swallowed and he "showed me" something that looked like a banana. I thought, "A banana couldn't cause this much trouble," and was very curious about what I would find. I cut him open and found the obstruction. When I opened up the intestines I found the top part of a vibrating sex toy! I took it out and showed it to my colleagues and yelled: "Hey guys, is this what I think it is or is it just my imagination?" There were little rubber rings on it that looked like a face. The British vets looked on stoically and pretended they had never seen one of these objects in their lives, but one of our Irish vets said: "It's got a smiley face on it! That is a #@$* dildo, that is!"

So I wondered what to tell the owners. Asking, "Have you been feeling a little dissatisfied lately?" seemed out of the question, so I just phoned and told them I had found something. When they asked me what it was, I said: "Err . . . some sort of rubber toy. I'll show it to you; maybe you'll recognize it!" The other vets and I had great laughs and joked about it a lot. A few days later, when one of my colleagues asked me how the dog was, I said: "A little shaken until the batteries went flat!"

When I showed it to the owners, they asked, with completely blank faces: "What is that? Where could he have got that from?" (Maybe their neighbors are having orgies in the garden!)

In the next chapter, I explore techniques for finding lost animals who have run away. But keep in mind that this chapter does not apply to you if you are one of Dr. Bertram's clients and your dog simply collapses when his batteries run flat.

CHAPTER SIX

Tracking

Follow the Trail of Stars

Indecision is actually a decision. It's a decision to fail.

— DR. RAYMOND CHARLES BARKER

CHLOE'S COURAGE

SEVERAL YEARS AGO on an Easter Sunday I got an SOS call from an old friend. Liz had devoted most of her life to animal rescue work, but I had never heard her this upset before. This case was a real doozy.

Liz had just brought home a dog who had been in a terrible accident. Liz didn't have a cell phone with her and she didn't know where the nearest emergency clinic was, so she raced the dog home so that she could look in the phone book. When she got a phone machine instead of a person at the emergency clinic, she panicked. When she found all the vets closed, she called me.

"Thank God you were home," she cried, "I think the emergency clinic is closed now for a lunch break."

She wanted to know if I could work sight unseen over the phone. While I prefer to work with photographs, in this crisis I was able to establish communication merely by listening to Liz's description.

After Liz described a gorgeous Labrador/shepherd mix, I mentally located the dog and immediately felt the immobility in her hind legs. Meanwhile, Liz told me her story between deep, wrenching sobs. She was driving down a country road a few blocks from her house, in the northern suburbs of Los Angeles. She could not see whether it was the blue Chrysler in front of her or the red pickup in front of that that had hit the dog. "It happened so fast I couldn't tell," she sobbed. Liz was crying so hard I could barely make out her words.

She saw the dog's body fly up into the air and land in a field off to her right. Neither the car nor the truck in front of her had bothered to stop. Liz pulled over and bolted out into the field where the dog had landed. The dog was wide awake and did not appear to be in any pain, but she seemed to be paralyzed from the waist down. Liz carefully picked up the half-limp dog, hoping she would not injure her further. She knew she was this dog's only hope of survival.

I asked the dog's name: "Chloe," I heard. When I asked Chloe where her back hurt, I heard: "It is broken in only one place." She sent me a picture of her spine, in the region of her third vertebrae above her tailbone. I moved my awareness into her through gestalt, checking for pain. I found sharp pain in her back only when she tried to move.

She showed me her attempts to sit up by pushing her weight onto her front paws, attempting to drag her body forward. Liz confirmed her position as being sort of a "half-sit." I sent the thought to Chloe to be still. I was relieved to find much more fear and shock than actual physical pain. Chloe was utterly bewildered. I ask Chloe whether it was the hit or the landing that caused her injury; she said that to the best of her knowledge, it was the impact of a truck hitting her.

"So it was not a blue Chrysler?" I asked.

"No, it was a red truck."

"Thank God they were going so slow," I said.

"Why did he hit me?" she asked.

"He didn't know you were there."

"Didn't he see me?"

"No, he didn't."

"When he hurt me, why didn't he stop?" she asked. I had no answer for her. My eyes stung with tears. The cruelty of the human race is something I can never explain to animals — maybe because I don't understand it myself.

At that moment Liz's call-waiting beeped in. The emergency clinic was responding to the hysterical message she had left. I told her I would be at her house by the time she got home from the vet's. I turned back to Chloe, knowing I could not hesitate before asking the most painful question I am ever forced to ask an animal:

"Chloe, do you want to live?"

"Yes . . . oh, yes. I'm not ready to fly away. I'm going to get well," she replied.

"Liz," I pleaded, "Under no circumstances should you let them put this dog down. Do you hear me? She wants to live! Promise me you *won't* let them kill this dog, no matter what!"

She gave me her word and asked how she might lift Chloe up to put her in a carrier without hurting her. Liz kept the phone pressed against her ear while I guided her hands under the dog, according to Chloe's instructions. Because her hips had been shoved to the right on impact, she didn't want any pressure twisting against the injured vertebrae. Liz carefully eased her into the carrier. Just before she hung up the phone, I heard Chloe's sad bark, her quiet call for help.

I got to Liz's house right after she and Chloe returned from the emergency clinic. Liz ushered me into the living room. Shaken and bedraggled, she tried to pull herself together. She said the vet warned her that Chloe may never walk again and there was absolutely nothing he could do. Liz had to fight like hell to keep Chloe from being put down because the vet was convinced there was little hope of recovery. He also told her the odds of finding Chloe's family were one in a million and that she had better be able to accommodate a crippled dog for whatever its life span may be. Liz was devastated.

"You are our only hope," she murmured. The words rocked me to my very soul. I started praying desperately for guidance.

"Now, just wait, just wait," I assured her, trying to keep a veneer of calm. "Let's let Chloe speak for herself."

Liz pointed me to a cage in the corner where Chloe was lying. I saw two delicate paws protruding through the open cage door. I bent down to look into the face of one of the most precious dogs I had ever seen. Sitting in front of Chloe, I encouraged Liz to quiet her mind so I wouldn't pick up on her fears and get cross talk.

First I asked, "When will you be able to walk?"

"Three days," Chloe responded.

"Pain?" I asked.

"Just resting," she said.

When I body-scanned her, I felt hot and cold tingles pulsing up and down her legs. Liz confirmed that the x-rays showed a ruptured disk in the third vertebrae. "Broken only in one place," had been Chloe's transmissions to me, and to a dog, "broken" must be a fair description of "ruptured." We thanked our lucky stars the spinal cord itself hadn't been damaged.

"Three days," I told Liz. "She says she would be well enough to walk in three days."

"Slowly," Chloe added. Liz repeated the horror story of the vet's grim prediction. He didn't think we could ever find this dog's owner. I asked Chloe to retrace her steps to show me exactly where she lived, backtracking from the street where she was hit. She gave me a rough blueprint of how many blocks east and north she had traveled. When I encouraged her to show me a street sign, I had Liz scribble down the word "Centennial." As I mentally searched for landmarks, I saw a big yellow sign just before the last turn. The sign pictured stick figures of humans.

"Child crossing?" I asked Chloe. "Miniature people?"

"Yes! There is a school on the corner." I whispered the good news to Liz, and she jumped to her feet.

"Oh, I know exactly where that is!" she cried.

"Show me your house," I asked Chloe casually, so that the images would flow smoothly and not be stilted by my urgency. She showed me a pink stucco house with a big tree and a tall stone object in the front yard.

"What is it, Chloe?"

"It's a monument."

"A monument?"

"Yes."

She sent me the image of some sort of concrete statue or structure, but I couldn't put a name on it. I tried not to translate it but to take the words at face value. The world looks very different through the eyes of a dog.

"Tree?" I sent the picture of a tree.

"Smells good," she replied.

"Anything on the ground?" I formulated images of pecans, acorns, and crab apples.

"The yellow fuzzy balls smell good."

"Thank you, Chloe. Thank you so much!" I said.

"Liz," I said, "There's a sycamore tree in the front yard!"

"Birds," Chloe added.

I sent the mental pictures of sparrows, then pigeons. She shot down my transmission.

"No, no," she said. "Pretty colored birds."

I couldn't see her birds clearly, but I took note without question.

"Tell me about your backyard. Is there a pool?"

"Yes."

"Is there a fence or a wall?"

"A fence."

"Do you live in the yard with the pool?"

"No."

"I thought you said there was a pool."

"Yes."

"Do you live in the backyard of the house with a pool?"

"No."

I was stumped. These kinds of logistics often get twisted when talking with animals. I filed it away and tried another tactic.

"Mom?"

She sent me a picture of short, fiftyish lady with red, shoulder-length hair and very Irish features.

"Names?"

"Robert."

"Robert," I yelled to Liz, who was frantically scribbling notes at the dining room table.

"Daddy?"

"Baby comes. Baby human." With this she sent a picture of a blonde toddler in a very disturbing walker.

"The walker annoys me," I heard.

I asked Chloe to tell me about the day before the accident.

"I had liver for breakfast. I love liver." Her Animalogos was high, with an elegant lilt, or at least that's how I interpreted it.

"The baby was coming so I went next door to get Boots."

"Boots?" I interjected. She showed me a large golden mutt with imposing white feet.

"He couldn't come out." She displayed the yellow dog longingly looking though a bay window with lace curtains.

"His parents were still sleeping." Instantly, I saw a dark-skinned young couple. "Finally, the sleepyheads got up and let him out. We walked to the scary road. He told me not to cross, but I didn't think the car would hit me."

"Where did he go?"

"He ran back home to get help."

Liz didn't remember seeing another dog fleeing the scene, but she was so upset she said she wouldn't have noticed.

"What else can you tell me about your house?"

"Noisy machines in the backyard. Awful machines."

"Thank you, Chloe." I got up to confer with Liz.

Chloe added at the last minute, "Mother has a beautiful voice. I love the singing."

"You will be up in three days?" I reaffirmed.

"Yes. I'll walk in three days and go home. Mother will come get me." She was very confident.

"Chloe, is there anything you'd like to tell me?"

"Yes," she added. "Tell Liz thank-you."

I shared the message and we both bit back our tears. I gave Liz the general location of the area Chloe had described. Liz whipped out a *Thomas Guide* to search for a Centennial Street in her neighborhood. She found a Centinella.

Liz grabbed her purse and hurried out to the printers to make flyers, and I drove home to rest and pray. She called me that night to say she had posted flyers up and down Centinella Street, which *was* by a school. Sure enough, she had found a pink house in the middle of the street! The "monument" appeared to be a flagpole, and the "colored birds" were wooden lawn decorations! The yard was adorned with tole painted birds! Eagerly, Liz had knocked on the door, but no one was home. She wondered if the owners were out looking for their dog, so she posted several flyers in front of the pink house.

The next morning, a short, ruddy-faced Irish woman named Patricia Roberts knocked on Liz's door, looking for her dog, Lowie.

"It was my mother's name," she explained. Patti confirmed that her granddaughter had come to stay with them for Easter. The "noisy machines" in the backyard were men working on the pipes. And Socks — the golden pooch next door who Chloe called Boots — was Chloe's neighborhood pal. His parents were a young East Indian couple.

"So, do you have a pool?" Liz asked Patti. Liz chuckled when she told me Patti's reply, "Well, yes I do."

"I saw it though the fence," Liz lied. "Do you usually keep her in the yard?"

"Oh, it's impossible to keep Lowie in anywhere. She's a regular Houdini! She can get out of anything to roam the neighborhood. She's a roamer." That explained why Chloe *was not* kept in the yard with the pool.

Liz told Patti the bleak diagnosis from the emergency clinic. Patti gratefully compensated Liz for the expensive doctor's bills, assuring her that she didn't care if Lowie never walked again. As long as Lowie wasn't in any pain, Patti would take care of her for the rest of her life. Lowie was her everything. She would love her unconditionally no matter what. Thank God for animal lovers — they are the angels of the human race.

Three days later, I got an update that was even more exhilarating than the last. Patti called Liz to share the wonderful news: that very morning

Lowie had stood up on all four feet and taken her first few steps. True to the dog's own words, *she was walking!*

On the phone with Patti, Liz was struck with a mischievous impulse: "Maybe it was your beautiful singing that revived Lowie." Liz never told Patti about me, so she never knew her dog had spilled the beans.

THE INVENTION OF LIGHT

MY READING WITH CHLOE was not a typical occurrence. Most attempts at tracking are not that successful, but when they are, I almost feel like the animal has been "lit up" so that I can see him.

One of my all-time favorite art teachers once taught me an unforgettable lesson that may help me explain how it works. On the first day of two-dimensional design class, Dave "The Fox" Starrett began a lecture about inventions.

Dave is a seventy-five-year-old sly character who seems to have been created by Charles Dickens. "Can one person change the world?" he boomed at the class of wide-eyed freshmen. "Oh no!" he roared. "One person could *never* change the world! You could never change the world! *I* could never change the world! *One person* could *never* make a difference!"

He stalked over to the panel of light switches and with a dramatic flourish, snapped them all off. The enormous art studio went pitch black. A hush fell over the room full of terrified students.

"*Before* Thomas Edison," Dave challenged the inky darkness. Then, he flipped the lights back on and illumined the room.

"*After* Thomas Edison," he snarled with a sly smile. He did it again to milk the moment. "And what did Thomas Edison do that no one else was doing?" he boomed. "He dared to *think differently*."

Animal communicators share something in common with Thomas Edison. We are "inventing light," too, but this is a different type of light. When we learn to track lost animals, we illumine the Q-forms inside the animal's memory and shine light on the "maps" they left when they strayed away from home. Psychically, it's as if they've left traces of electromagnetic energy in their wake, leaving a trail like the hazy tail of a comet as it soars across the sky. We can learn to "read" the hazy traces as we uncover and log any hint of what the animal saw and felt on his road to trouble.

In many respects, the process is identical to the other techniques we've already covered, Resogenesis and Unimorphosis. The only real difference is your level of concentration. If in Unimorphosis you are using a mental pen lamp to light the inside of an animal, you'll need a psychic floodlight to locate a lost animal. The stakes are high, nerves are raw, the clock is ticking, and chances are that the client you're dealing with is a hysterical wreck. Not a fun combination, if you ask me. Tracking is about as pleasurable as a root canal, so my advice is, learn it *now!* Drop everything and learn it this instant! Please "fix the roof while the sun still shines" because when it's your dog or your cat that's missing out there, you're going to wish you had invested the time to learn this discipline.

TRACKING: THIS IS HOW WE DO IT

IN ESSENCE, TRACKING IS SUPER-ADVANCED GESTALT. You have to locate the animal's energy field, then look out their eyes. In order to see what they see, you must focus on that animal to the exclusion of all else. Recall for a minute the Zero Point Energy field I described in chapter 1. This theory assures us that every living being is part of a seamless matrix, connected on one gigantic web of energy. Coupling this with the idea that "you are your attention," it makes sense that we can move our focus effortlessly into other living beings and look out their eyes. You might call this "mobility of consciousness," meaning you can move your spirit and cognitive awareness outside your own flesh and into the world around you. We just have to wrap our self-absorbed brains around the idea that our minds are not separate, that we are all part of one infinite Divine Mind that has many billions of bodies.

In practical terms, this means that when an animal's guardian calls you and is freaking out because her dog is missing, you first reach deep within yourself to that sacred, peaceful place inside of you where Universal

Intelligence lives. You anchor that energy, which means you commit to staying in this calm, loving place at all costs, and you let this love and serenity shine from your heart like a lighthouse. You are not here to get caught up in other people's chaos. You are here to be the eye of the storm. Chances are, if you master this technique, you'll never do anything in your life that is this difficult . . . or this rewarding.

A friend once told me that he functioned best under incredible stress. If there was nothing traumatic going on in his life, he'd simply bumble around creating chaos all day, but when something terrible happened, he'd go into red-alert mode like an emergency-room doctor. Marianne Williamson has written some insightful words about this phenomenon, saying that if someone calls her in a state of panic, she moves into a realm of perfect peace and calm. Time stops until the person is comforted and the emergency passes. That's what we have to do when we track. We can't react emotionally, in any way, and we absolutely can't get caught up in the fear and anguish of the humans who have lost their animals.

After anchoring yourself in peaceful energy, next you build the bridge of Lumensilta, extending from your own heart to wherever the animal is in space. Ask that you can see out the animal's eyes, and, fueled by prayer, *command* that it is so. You must *pretend* you are the animal until it mentally "becomes a reality"; you'll know you've succeeded when the feelings in your body start to change ever so slightly. You may see fleeting images or feel temperatures on your face or textures under your "paws" or "hooves."

Once you've established contact, your first directive is always to see if you can locate a light source and determine the amount of oxygen available — that way you'll know instantly if a missing animal is trapped somewhere, like in a car trunk, a garage, or a dumpster. Next, you do a body scan and check for injuries or hunger. Feeling pain or hunger is a clear signal that the animal is still alive. Animals in heaven are never hungry or in pain.

If you're tracking a missing cat or dog and your question is, "Are you still alive?" check for two things: headlights and impact. If the animal was locked out at night and you see blinding headlights, then everything goes white, you know she got hit by a car. If you feel impact on your body, you know she was in an accident, and if you feel a sharp pain on the back of your neck, you know she got bitten by a coyote.

Another way to tell whether the animal has gone to heaven is by the imagery he sends. If a missing dog shows you a picture of himself sitting peacefully in Grandma's lap, and you know that this Grandma is no longer alive, it's a pretty clear indication that the dog has moved on. If you pick up any names of the person's deceased parents or grandparents, there's a huge chance this animal is gone.

Determining whether an animal is dead or alive can be very tricky. There is one animal that will blatantly lie. Wanna guess which one? Cats. If I ask a missing cat if he's still alive, she'll say, "Of course!" If I know for a fact that she got killed by a car, I have to say, "Remember that cold, stiff dead body you left in the road?" The cat will say, "Oh . . . that?" And chances are, a cat will say next, "I meant to do that."

I think that felines are Mother Nature's most magical creation, and being that they are asleep and out-of-body for 80 percent of their lives, it can be very difficult to determine whether they are alive or not. Even when they're alive, they are not exactly "alive" the way other animals experience life on earth. Felines are dreamwalkers; they straddle the worlds — this 3D world and the other dimensions — where they dance freely and come and go in mystical ways. We'll talk about this more in a future chapter on death and dying, but for now, I'd like to share a story about tracking a missing cat. Then I'll provide you with exercises so that you can try it yourself.

BOO BOO IN THE MOONLIGHT

THE REMARKABLE DR. BERNIE SIEGEL wrote the foreword to my most recent book, describing how I found his missing cat, Boo Boo, in Connecticut even though I had never met her and I lived in Los Angeles. Bernie got to tell his side of the story, but I've never told you mine. This was one of the most successful cases of tracking I've ever performed in my life.

I met Dr. Bernie Siegel in July of 2000, after he gave an extraordinary keynote address at the Kinship for Life conference in San Francisco.

Shining in front of us all like a floodlight, Bernie told tales of having over one hundred animals fostered in his home at different times for different reasons, speaking of them as lovingly as if they were human children. Like a cross between the Pied Piper and Dr. Dolittle, Bernie lectured on the healing properties of animals, their importance as teachers and friends, and how dramatically they have transformed human lives. Evidently, animals gravitate to Bernie for the same reasons humans do — they are drawn to the same open heart, gentle humor, and unconventional wisdom that has cured the incurable and healed the hopeless. Bernie spoke of Dickens and Gabriel, his Maine coons, and Smudge, his rabbit, with the same glee as a five-year-old boy unwrapping his gifts on Christmas morning. His contagious excitement spilled over onto every person in the room.

When I bumped into him in the elevator and told him I was an animal communicator, he was wary, but he kept an open mind: "Well, if she says she can talk to animals.... I wonder if she *really* can..."

Three days later, he called me to find out. When my home phone rang back in L.A. and I picked it up to find Bernie Siegel on the other line, I almost dropped dead on the kitchen floor. (I hadn't published a thing yet. This was very early on in my career.) He was near tears when he described his emergency: A beloved cat had been missing in coyote territory for a week and a half.

Bernie had been house-sitting for his son, Jeffrey, whose declawed house cat, Boo Boo, was Bernie's workout partner. Every morning, Bernie would work out with his beloved feline friend while she played on the exercise equipment. Boo Boo had disappeared while Bernie was in San Francisco, while a friend was moving some furniture out an open door. Bernie didn't find out she was missing until he returned to Connecticut. Was she still alive? Could I find her?

Holy-jumped-up-catfish! If there's one thing I don't like to do, it's to psychically track lost animals. If there was one time in my life I didn't want to be wrong, it was with Dr. Bernie Siegel!

I gave Bernie my common-sense, how-to-find-a-cat lecture. A house cat will often get lost in areas where other cats have already sanctioned their territories. I liken it to the movie *The Warriors*, in which a New York gang attempts to make its way home through an entire city of rival gangs, who thwart its every move. I felt that Boo Boo was trapped "down under" a house where another cat was standing guard, refusing to let her out. I didn't give myself any credit for "tuning in" to Boo Boo because this situation is almost always the case with lost cats. I suggested that Bernie go out with a can of tuna after dark and look under houses, calling down low.

Then I overnighted to Bernie the entire chapter from my upcoming book that explains how to track lost animals. If Bernie was so intuitive, maybe he could learn to do it himself? Close, but no cigar.

I then tried to palm off the job to my friend, Marty Meyer, an excellent animal communicator here in Los Angeles to whom I refer my tracking cases. I called to find her out of town. A couple of days passed, and when I got another plaintive email from Bernie, I succumbed, agreeing to give this tracking case a shot if he could mail me a picture of Boo Boo. But Bernie was so overcome with grief, he couldn't bear to search for a photo of Boo Boo in his son's house. He couldn't even send me a picture of the cat! "What are the odds that she's alive anyway?" I argued with myself. I hadn't told Bernie the truth: I usually throw in the towel when an indoor cat has been missing for more than three days, much less a missing *declawed* cat. Between the coyotes, the cars, and the hostile neighborhood cats and dogs, what chance did Boo Boo have? And Bernie couldn't even send me a picture. Good grief.

The only clue I had that Boo Boo was still alive was a name I "picked up" while on the phone with Bernie.

"Who's Michael?" I asked. There was a feeling of longing attached to the name.

"Michael is Boo Boo's vet," Bernie answered. That gave me an indication that Boo Boo was alive and that I had made contact.

"She wants to see Michael," I said. A dead cat would not be asking for her vet. Still, my demons of self-doubt had me by the throat. I didn't want to take this risk. However, later that day, I picked up a notebook, flopped down on the couch and started praying out loud.

"Boo Boo, if you're alive, tell me what you see!" I begged. Then I decided to go directly to the Source.

"God, *command my hands*. Please show me where this cat is." My hand started to write.

I jotted down a page of notes that looked like this:

I see her as very lithe with a triangular head. I feel like when she left Jeffrey's house, she went to the left. Which means, if you were standing inside his house looking out the front door and you were to exit the house, you would go to the left. I don't feel like she's been very far away. Uphill. She says her favorite food is tuna. I hear the names Michael, Bobbi, Margaret, Simpson, Terry/Teresa, Steven, David, Rebecca/Reba/Rodney.

She's seen two dogs in someone's backyard — fenced in. A big one and a little one. She saw red brick and ivy and a black metal grate. She's been hiding down low, in a garage or under a house. She's seen large white stones around concrete steps or a patio.

Marjorie, Jeff, David. Close to home. Wants to come home. Tammy, Tamera. Thirsty, found some food one night. Hungry. Wants to come home to Jeff. Cold at night.

Big black cat has her trapped. White paws. Lots of wild dogs in the neighborhood at night. (Coyotes?) She's seen a "fountain" in stones in someone's yard. Fear in chest. Wants to see Michael. Pine trees, pine cones on the ground. Ate by dumpster/garbage cans once. Ran from "sprinklers" in a yard.

I psychically body-scanned her for major injuries and didn't find any, only fear and hunger and a feeling of being banged up. When the transmission stopped, I looked down at the page of notes. They were very specific. If I was off, I was off by a country mile. I'd written the name "Steven." My eyes settled on the name. "No, I could be wrong," I chided myself. "I can't take this risk." In an attack of cowardice, I put the notes aside and tried to dismiss it all from my mind.

I had never read any of Bernie's books, so a couple of days later, I went to the bookstore and bought *Love, Medicine and Miracles*. That night, I opened the book and read the dedication, "I'd like to thank my children...*Stephen*." My knees buckled. "Steven!" Bernie had given me no other names but that of one son, Jeffrey. And he thanked his wife, "Bobbi."

"Good Lord," I thought, kicking myself. "What an idiot I am! This poor cat really is alive, and she's suffered two more cold, hungry nights under the house because I was too chicken to send Bernie the notes!"

In a moment of desperation, I ran out into my backyard. This was the night of July 16, 2000, and the moon was very full, like a gigantic golden pumpkin heavy on the horizon. Gazing up into the summer sky, I mentally reached out for the little cat and called out to her:

"Look up, Boo Boo! Look up! Can you see the moon?"

I heard her voice ringing like a bell over the thousands of miles between us.

"Yes," she said. "I see it!"

My eyes welled with hot tears.

"That's it! She's alive!" I convinced myself. "If she were on the Other Side she wouldn't be on the ground looking up at the moon."

"Are you all right?" I asked her.

"Yes, but *he* won't let me out." Once again, I saw the dark cat with the white paws holding her hostage under the house. I felt her fear and hunger. "Okay," I told my demons, "if this cat were dead, she wouldn't be trapped under a house, cold and hungry." I gave myself another kick in the head for making her suffer needlessly before I ran to my computer and emailed Bernie the page of notes. Even as I typed the words, I feared he would never find her.

The next day, I saw a message in my inbox from Bernie entitled, "SUCCESS!" When Bernie read my email, he recognized many of the names, so he printed out the letter and followed my directions like a map. He went out the front door, to the left, up a hill, and under Jeff's very own house, which had sprinklers in the yard and cat food by the dumpster, surrounded with pinecones. Two dogs had been kept in the backyard, fenced in. One was still there, and one was a memory. In the front yard was a "fountain," an aerated pond where Bernie's dark cat with white paws, appropriately named "Meanie," was holding Boo Boo hostage under the house. Bernie called down low and heard little Boo Boo answer with a frightened meow. Absolutely elated, Bernie scooped her up and took her inside. It was the happiest homecoming of his life! Boo Boo had been outside, fending for herself for almost two weeks! Although she was thin and scraped up, thus "wanting to see Michael," Boo Boo was in perfect health. Bernie verified almost every detail of my reading; Boo Boo was exactly where she told me she was.

In the meantime, I'd been sending Bernie exercises describing how to telepathically communicate with animals, determined that I wasn't going to stop until he could do it, too. Every day, I'd receive three or four excited emails from Bernie testifying that he was suddenly able to talk to his cats and talk to his bunny, and "hear them answer" inside his head. What might have taken most people years or maybe even a lifetime of diligent practice took Bernie about a week. Bernie turned from skeptic to star student overnight, but is it really any surprise? Dr. Bernard Siegel is one of the sharpest tools in the shed.

FINDING THE COURAGE TO SOAR

COURAGE IS THE KEY to tracking. Just as your success with telepathy hinges on your level of self-esteem and your success with gestalt hinges on your pain threshold, your success with tracking hinges on your level of courage. My favorite definition of courage is "Finding something to hang onto when there is nothing to hang onto." You've got to commit to taking huge risks. You might be wrong, you might make a fool of yourself, or you might save a life. If you're wrong nine times and right once, it was worth it.

One aspect of the courage required to track is a willingness to make mistakes. I was terrified when I first tried to perform for Dr. Siegel, but I never would have been able to help Boo Boo if I couldn't withstand my own level of fear. At first you might not understand the images you receive. Remember when I was in Unimorphosis with Chloe and she said that there was a "monument" and "colorful birds" in the yard? Those references sent me into a mental game of charades to try to determine what she meant from her point of view. Please take into consideration that a "lake" could be a puddle if you're talking to a frog, and a "mountain" could be a molehill if you're talking to a hamster. (This reminds me of one of my favorite jokes: Two snails were standing on the sidelines, watching the tortoise races. Two of the tortoises collided into each other. Bang! And one of the snails asked the other, "Did you see what happened?" And the other snail said, "No! It all went by so *fast!*")

Most things in life can be explained by looking at them from a new perspective. Why does your pet run away? It depends on your perspective. Animals do not run away from home for no reason. Maybe you did something to bug your animal friend so much that he was willing to take off. Why did you do that? Again, this depends on your perspective. I don't track anymore because it exhausts me; 99 percent of the time the missing animal is already dead, and most of the few that are still alive ran away because the humans were driving them crazy. Remember, human beings do not own cats. Cats have the right to live wherever they want. But if you master these techniques, your chances of having a contented, satisfied cat will improve dramatically. The more we practice Unimorphosis, the more accustomed we become to viewing our world from animals' very different perspective.

Let's do a tracking exercise. We won't be tracking, just practicing the perspective techniques you'll need to track. I've crafted these questions for animals that are present and not missing, and in this exercise we'll revisit some of the techniques from my previous book. Rather than focusing on your pet's location, I've designed them to help you practice looking out of her eyes and understanding her thought processes.

IF YOUR FRIEND IS A CAT

- What do you see (through your cat's eyes)?
- How does your food taste?
- What food do you like best? What texture? What temperature?
- What does it feel like to purr? To stalk? To hunt? To play? What is your favorite toy? Why?

- How do you feel about the birds outside your window or in your yard?
- How does your litter box feel? Smell? Is it clean enough?
- If your cat goes outside the box: Why do you do this?
- How does it feel to sharpen your claws on your scratching post? On the carpet? On the couch? On a tree? On my panty hose (or some other human belonging)?
- Do you know I don't want you to claw the couch?
- Do you understand what I say to you?
- Are you deliberately careful with my fragile, "hairless" skin?
- What do you see in the backyard?
- How do rodents make you feel?
- How does catnip make you feel?
- What does it feel like to climb a tree?
- How do you feel about humans?
- How would you feel if you met a dachshund?
- How would you feel if you met a Great Dane?
- How do you feel about television noise?
- Are you afraid of cars?
- What do you think cars are?
- Do you have a special place in the house?
- Do I leave things in your special place that I shouldn't?
- Do you have possessions that you're attached to?
- Are there possessions that I could provide to make you happier?
- Do you know what books are?
- Do you understand why humans have a written language?
- How does sunshine make you feel?

- What's it like to see in the dark?

- How does nightfall make you feel? Moonlight? Stars?

- Can you see inside your own body?

- Do you understand your own medical conditions?

- Do your vaccinations work?

- How does a house full of human children make you feel?

- What do you feel like when your parents are angry? Late? Anxious? Sick? Too loud?

- What does God look like to you?

- What do you think is the meaning of life?

- Where do you go when you leave your body?

- What do you dream about?

- Where do you go to get help healing your body?

- What does it feel like to be outside in tall grass?

- What do roses smell like? Pine trees? Sycamore trees? Rosemary?

- How does it feel when I pet you?

- Where do you like to be petted the most? Your head? Your back? Your ears? How hard? Am I too rough? What touches do you not like?

- What would you like changed about your household?

- Am I too loud? Is my voice too high when I talk to you?

- Do I scare you? Do I move too quickly?

- How do you feel about another animal in your household? Do you love him? Are you jealous? Does he scare you? How does he look from your perspective? Is he beautiful? Is he bigger or smaller than you are? Do you feel threatened? Maternal? Protective? Do you enjoy spending time together? What do you talk about? Do you have friends who are not cats? What do you talk about with other species?

- Do humans look strange to you because we have only two legs?
- How do you feel about me? Do I leave you alone too long?
- How does it feel to sleep with me?
- What's your favorite thing I do?
- What's your least favorite thing I do?
- What kind of music do you like?

Other Questions to Ask If Your Friend Is an Indoor-Outdoor Cat

- What animal fascinates you the most?
- How does it feel to make a kill?
- What does a sparrow taste like? A mouse? A cricket? A lizard?
- Whom do you not like? Why?
- What do you think about while you sit?
- What do you dream about when you sleep?
- Do you have friends I don't know about?
- Where do you go outside?
- Do you visit other humans? Do they feed you?
- Do you know other cats in the neighborhood?
- Have you befriended any "night animals"? Skunks? Opossums?
- Do you see raccoons?
- How big is your territory?
- Do you understand how dangerous cars are? Coyotes?
- Do you have a curfew?
- Do you have a mate? Are you in love?
- Can you see animal spirits on the Other Side? People?

- Do other spirits live in your house?
- When cats die, where do they go?
- Have you lived before in another body? What was your life like then?

IF YOUR FRIEND IS A HORSE

- Do you like to be ridden?
- How does a rider feel on your back?
- Do you like to wear a saddle?
- How does the bit feel in your mouth?
- How does it feel to be shoed?
- How does it feel to be in a turnout with other horses?
- How does the hot walker make you feel?
- Do you like to gallop? How often do you need to run?
- How much time do you like to spend in your stall?
- How does it feel to be locked in your stall all by yourself?
- Would you rather sleep where you can see other horses?
- Would you like to have a pipe stall?
- Do you like to be groomed?
- How do cross ties make you feel?
- Do you like to jump?
- What is your favorite food?
- Do you get enough to eat, or do you feel hungry?
- How do you feel about humans?

- Am I gentle enough with you?
- Do you understand your commands, or do I confuse you?
- Who's your best horse friend?
- Have you ever been in love?
- Do you have a mate?
- Are you lonely?
- Do you have friends who are not horses?
- What is your favorite activity?
- How do you feel about your horse trailer?
- Do you like to go to shows?
- Do you enjoy competing with other horses?
- Are you in any pain?
- Would a chiropractor make you feel better?
- Do you prefer flat surfaces or trails?

In the thousands of readings I've done over the last few years, there is one question that is the most popular. In fact, I don't recall ever doing a reading in my life where the guardian didn't ask this single question. So end your reading with: Do you know how much I love you?

DO YOU SEE WHAT I SEE?

WHEN YOU FEEL you've made a connection with an animal who is present, it's time to practice with one who is not. One of the best exercises is to simply tune into one of your friend's animals and try to locate where they are. You can make a game out of it: ask a friend to take her dog for a walk to a new place, or engage in an unusual activity, and let you practice tracking. Make a list of all your impressions, and ask your friend to give you questions about the animal and her surroundings.

Answer them quickly, bravely, without thinking, then let your friend confirm your answers.

Aside from actually finding a lost animal, never does tracking come more in handy than when you are on vacation. Tracking skills allow you to check in on your animal friends while you're away and to let them know when you'll be back. Animals *do* have a sense of time, by the way; never underestimate how much your animals know about time and place. (The best method to explain to them how long you'll be away is to send them the image of five days and five dark nights, or whatever applies.) I've had dogs tell me, "Mother went to New York last June and she's about to go to Italy in August and I don't want her to go without me." I've had cats tell me, "I'm going to the vet on Wednesday," and I've heard horses say, "I'll see you in the morning at 10:30." Holographically, they pick up and record *everything*. We are the ones that are so preoccupied and tuned-out that we can't comprehend what's going on in their lives. They even know our plans for the future, our fears, our hopes and dreams, and our medical conditions.

When I'm touring, which is about a third of the year, I stay in daily telepathic contact with my cat Aunt Flo. Once this last year, while I was teaching on the Isle of Man, I had what appeared to be a nervous breakdown. I kept hearing in my mind, "Mommy, I'm locked out! I'm *locked out!*" I had a panic attack and burst into hysterical tears over lunch. Two of my best students — both professional healers — had to take my hands and literally hold me down to keep me from running to catch the next plane out of there. So I raced to the phone and left a message for my cat sitter. (Time zones are a real pain in the butt.) A few hours later, I got a reassuring call from my cat sitter: Flo was inside and everything was back to normal, but she had gotten locked out and had a good scare.

Another even more dramatic incident occurred a few years back when I was teaching in Maui with bestselling author and spiritual teacher Alan Cohen. My cat Hopkins needed have a checkup for her teeth. The poor darling had hideous gingivitis and was in terrible pain. I hadn't been able to get her in to see my wonderful vet, Karen Martin, before I left town, so I let my cat sitter schedule the appointment after I left. I'd given the okay to pull teeth if necessary and spare no expense to help little Hopkins finally have a healthy mouth.

I didn't know the day or time of the appointment. Suddenly, while on blissful Maui, I got a splitting migraine and my entire jaw went numb. I could barely talk for two days and I certainly couldn't sleep. When I called home, I found that beautiful little Hopkins had had ten teeth pulled. Over the course of the next few days, I tried to pull out of the pain and send her strength, commanding her to sleep and let God heal her. Eventually, the pain in both of our jaws drifted away.

Now here's a funny story. One of my students in San Diego flew to Hawaii and left her Dalmatian at home with a house sitter. When the woman made telepathic contact with her dog to see if she was all right, she heard the words, "She burned the cookies!" With this, the woman got the smell of smoke and a sense of urgency. (Smoke is a big deal to dogs. Remember how much more sensitive their noses are than ours.) Apparently the dog was concerned that the sitter was going to burn the house down! When my student got home, she found a big plastic bag in her fridge filled with chocolate chip cookies. None of them was burned. She checked the cookie pans for traces of charcoal. Nothing. When she asked the dog sitter, "Did you by any chance burn any of these cookies?" the woman was mortified. "How on earth did you know?" she asked. She had thrown out two entire pans of charred cookies and carefully scrubbed the cookie sheets!

FLYING LESSONS

This next exercise works best with a photograph of the animal you'd like to locate. Look into the eyes of the animal you'd like to find and let your mind slip into motion. You will feel that you are traveling through space as you search for the soul. You're reaching. Jumping off a cliff. Letting the roller coaster dive. Simply letting go. Surrender your ego as you seek. Think of the animal and yourself as two polarities of a magnet. Let yourself be drawn to wherever she is. Let your imagination take flight.

You may experience subtle sensations of dizziness or lurching. This is the motion that defies description. In this instant, we work our alchemy. We reach outside ourselves with our own minds. Think of it as psychic skydiving — a moment of mental free-falling. But the gravity does not pull us down to earth; the gravity pulls us toward the being we seek.

To find Divine Intelligence, we look within ourselves — at our own icing and filling, flavor and texture. Finding the God within animals is even easier. They can't hide it — each one is a spiritual masterpiece. Acknowledge that your animal's soul is a beacon, like a bright star twinkling in the darkness, and fly toward it in your mind. Record your impressions in a notebook and see how much information the human guardian can validate.

Take a Walk on the Wild Side

Now I'm going to rave like a proud mother about one of my students again. I've had the distinct pleasure of training my European protégé, Esther Yesudas, for the last four years. Esther logged the reading she describes here when she was fifteen. She is now sixteen and my youngest professional animal communicator. She is also the best remote viewer I've ever seen in my life. She speaks both English and German fluently, and she lives and practices in Germany.

I thought I'd write you about the cat Blacky. She's totally black with green eyes — a short-haired breed. And she's got a cheeky-looking face and there's something mystifying about her. When I first looked at the pictures the owner sent me, it was like she was calling at me. "Come on, take me, speak to me." So here's what I asked her:

"What rooms do you know?" She showed me much more than other animals usually show me. She showed me a staircase that came down from the attic and led into a corridor with four doors. Two of the doors were opened a little, so I was able to walk into the rooms, looking at them from her point of view. The first room had a computer and a dark carpet. The other room was a sort of bedroom with white walls that seemed to have a dark floor. The owner said it was true! It was a bedroom and the walls were white, but the floor was the same color as in the room with the computer.

I had gotten curious, so I asked Blacky about the garden. She showed me a light-colored wall curved in a semicircle. Right in front were flowerbeds, and in the middle there was a statue. On the way out of the house into the garden there were some chairs and a table. On the left hand side of the wall was a little roof bordering the neighbor's winter garden, and opposite that was a door to get out of the garden. Leaving the garden you stepped right onto light brown tiles. I've never, ever had a cat describe her home to me so exactly — and the owner confirmed it all — *all of it!*

I wanted to know where she liked to sleep. I saw a blue-green blanket that the owner told me was a couch. To the left of that I saw a long cupboard, and in the middle I saw a plant. I couldn't actually see the living room, but I knew I could look into the living room from the place where Blacky liked to sleep. I also saw a TV. The owner told me everything was right. So I asked about the color of the food bowl and what she liked to eat. I pictured a dark blue food bowl. And then I saw a silver-blue one. I questioned the owner and she told me that the food bowl was silver-blue with a dark blue cat on it. Isn't that *fantastic!*?

Blacky told me she loved taking risks and said she would also jump along dangerous paths. She also admitted, pretty proudly, that she provoked her owner a little. I was also supposed to ask her if she had been trapped the two days she didn't come home. She said she hadn't, she had just looked around something (I thought it was a wooden house that was under construction), and when I asked her why she hadn't gone home she answered, as if I were simply crazy: "Why should I go home that *far* out of my way when I'm coming back to this place again tomorrow? Apart from that, sleeping outside is far more interesting. It would be a waste of energy to go all the way home and then come back!"

The Psychic Bounty Hunter

Few of my students get names when they track, but getting a name can mean the difference between success and failure. The next story comes from one of the most gifted students I've ever had the honor of teaching. This miracle worker, Marcel Stoller, lives and practices in Switzerland. In this case, Marcel was actually working as a detective for lost kitties and answered a plea he found in a newspaper!

Every day before I go to work, I go into the same restaurant and take the same chair (which is always free when I come in!) and I drink a cup of coffee. A couple of weeks after my first workshop with Amelia, I was simply sitting in this chair — I had stopped looking at the television and reading the newspaper, as Amelia had suggested — when suddenly I heard a soft voice.

I looked around and saw a dog sitting on a woman's legs. "Hi. My name is Nora and I have to go to the vet this afternoon at three o'clock. Please talk with my woman and tell her: 'Don't give me painkillers. I can't take tablets. Don't forget they make me sick!'"

I paid for the coffee and stood up to go over to this woman. We said hello and I said, "Wow, what a beautiful dog." Then I began to caress the dog and I asked, "What's her name?" The woman said: "Nora. She's a lovely dog, but we must go to the vet this afternoon." I told her I thought the dog shouldn't have painkillers. The woman looked at me, surprised. "Thank God you reminded me!" she said. "I'll have to tell the vet. A couple of years ago, she nearly died from taking painkillers. She can't tolerate any sort of tablets in her stomach." I changed the subject, said good-bye, and slipped out the door before she could ask me anything else.

A couple of weeks later I saw Nora again, but this time she was walking on three of her four legs. I asked her guardian what had happened. She told me that the vet had to do an operation on Nora's meniscus, and she wouldn't be able to use that leg for a while. I silently "said" to Nora that the operation worked perfectly and that she could now use this leg without a problem. I sent Nora a mental picture of her running on all four legs. Meanwhile, I talked with the woman about the weather and then said good-bye. As I left, I looked back and saw the woman riding her bicycle and Nora following behind her on four legs. Nora was careful, but she was walking on all four legs! I yelled, "Success! Yes! *Yes!*" The people around me looked at me like I was crazy.

It was in this chair in this coffee shop that I knew for the first time what it felt like to contact an animal. This experience gave me confidence because everything I said to this woman turned out to be true. I'm telling you this story first so that you'll understand why the next week I was absolutely certain that I could find Dusty.

On the following Wednesday, I was sitting in this same restaurant, drinking my coffee. Suddenly, I felt the same sensation I had when I made contact with Nora. But I couldn't see an animal. I thought it was weird. Then, I had the sudden urge to pick up the newspaper, but I didn't know why. Then I saw a short ad with no photo. It said: "Missing tomcat: 'DUSTY,' 5 months old, in Küssnacht, Switzerland." And there was a phone number to call.

In this moment, that strange feeling came rushing back to me. The transmission starting pouring in so fast, I couldn't think of anything else. I grabbed my mobile phone and called the number. The woman who answered the phone was named Beatrice Stauffer, and she was in tears over the loss of her six-month-old kitten. I told her I work as an animal communicator and that maybe I could help find Dusty. She agreed to send me a photo. Once I got the pictures, I looked into the bright eyes of this tiny grey and white tiger cat and started to work.

"What is your favorite food?" I asked Dusty. "Fish," I heard, very clearly.

"What is your favorite place to sleep?" He said, "In my basket with many soft toy animals."

"Can you show me where you live?" I asked. He said "Yes" and sent me a mental picture of his house.

"What happened that made you leave home?" He showed me and image of him walking toward a playground.

"Can you get back home?"

"No," he said.

"Why?" I asked.

"Because I'm trapped in a house. I can't get out."

"Can you show me the house?" I asked. He said, "Sure, but only the inside."

"Are you well?" He said, "Yes, I'm in good health. I'm okay."

"When you can, you will come back home?" He said, "Yes, of course. I'll be happy to get home and tease the dog. I like to make him angry."

After this first reading, I called Mrs. Stauffer and told her what Dusty said. "He is alive and not far away from you. Please make flyers and post them all around the children's playground."

"We don't have a playground," Mrs. Stauffer said. Dusty had shown me the directions to this playground, so I told Mrs. Stauffer where to look. She agreed and called back two days later.

"It's amazing!" she said. "I found the playground! And it was right where you said it would be!" I had been continuing to track Dusty in the meantime, and he had given me a lot more information, so I shared this with her. He had sent me these thoughts:

"When I was by the playground, I saw a funny, interesting child, so I followed him. Then a very old woman picked me up and took me to her home. We drove about ten or fifteen minutes. We went through a glass door and up two or three stairs. And now I am arrested. I'm stuck here. The woman loves yellow clothes. She cannot get going. She has a problem with her leg. She is very slow."

And then he showed me many things in this apartment. I asked him, "Are you okay?" He said: "Yes, but a little bit sad." I told him that we were going to make every effort to find him.

Mrs. Stauffer called me regularly for forty-eight hours straight to hear the results from every reading. She did everything I told her to do to try to find Dusty. I sent her to many houses in her neighborhood and insisted she knock on dozens of doors.

Two days later, she called back again: no results. No one had phoned about the flyers she posted, and she had visited all the houses in the neighborhood and nobody knew anything about Dusty.

"My nerves are shot! We must stop all this," she said, choking back sobs.

I told her I was certain we'd find Dusty. I knew he was alive because he had showed me so much detail in the readings. I begged her to call all the nearby veterinarians again. I assured her that I'd contact the poor lost kitten for more details.

That evening, I talked with Dusty again. It was the last reading where he sounded "normal." I begged him to show me something new so I could find him. He showed me everything he could, but I had seen it all before. I told him that this was not enough. Then he said to me, "Please help me! I have had enough of this woman. I want to go home. It is not fun here. It's a boring and sad place. Please get me out of here!"

So I said to him, "Dusty, make the woman mad so she'll put you out and then you contact me. We'll find you more easily outside. Act like you're crazy! When she picks you up, bite the woman. Climb the curtains. When she opens the door, run out very fast!"

He only said, "Okay, I'll try this." I called Mrs. Stauffer and told her that she must go outside and look for Dusty every day because Dusty might be out free soon.

A few days later, Mrs. Stauffer called me again, sad and discouraged. She said, "I definitely give up! I thank you very much for your work, and I hope we can meet sometime. Have a nice day and goodbye!"

I was frantic. I wasn't about to give up on this cat. That evening after work I spoke to Dusty again. I asked him, "Are you inside again or are you outside now?"

"I don't know."

"Where are you?"

"I don't know."

"Hmm, what's happened?"

"I don't know."

I asked him everything I could think of about where he was, what he was eating, and about the woman. No matter what I asked, all he said was, "I don't know." I was mystified and terribly frustrated. Eventually, I stopped trying to contact him. In hindsight, I realize that the one thing I forgot to ask him about was his health!

After that terrible night, I committed to mailing the photos back to Mrs. Stauffer. But for maybe four or five days, I forgot to send the photos back and I couldn't stop thinking about Dusty. Finally, one evening I decided to try one last time. Suddenly, I got a new idea! I thought I'd ask him what he heard when the telephone rang. He said, "Hi. I'm sleepy, but many times a day I hear the name 'Meyer' when the telephone bells ring."

I called Mrs. Stauffer as fast as I could to tell her that she must call all the "Meyers" on the street where she lives and the next five streets over. A few days later, she called me, really heartbroken. She said, "I've called more than twenty Meyers in the last two days but I haven't found the right Meyers."

She wanted to give up again, but I pleaded with her to call all the local vets one last time. I felt that Dusty was near, and I simply couldn't give up on him. The next morning, she called me and began to cry.

"I found Dusty!" she cried. "He's in a nearby vet's office, and he has a broken leg. I told the vet about the last few horrible weeks and a little bit about you — but not too much, because the vets don't believe in you or your work. No one would believe my story, but then a medical secretary came into the room and overheard me talking. She said really loudly: 'My name is *Meyer!*'" Mrs. Stauffer said the veterinarian was about to give Dusty to an animal shelter. If she had waited even one more day, it could have been too late.

After the happy ending, I did one last reading with Dusty to say thanks for the help and to ask him why he didn't tell me more about the situation so that I could find him faster. He said, "At first I was drugged for the operation on my leg, so I was very tired. And secondly, you didn't ask me the right questions. In the future, when you speak to a cat, you must keep your questions short. Humans talk and talk and talk, and at the end of your talking you have said nothing really important. Next time, when you talk with animals you must have a short chat and you'll know all you need to know. I wish you much fortune in the future to help many animals on the earth." Wow! This cat was no more than six months old! And with such sagacity! I was very impressed!

I realized then that when I contacted Dusty and all he could say was, "I don't know," he had just been put under anesthesia for the operation on his broken leg. I never felt the pain of his broken leg, but then, I never did a body scan on him. This was a big error. After this experience with Dusty, I made a big note and taped it on the wall in my room: "EVERY TIME YOU READ AN ANIMAL, DO A BODY SCAN FIRST! ALWAYS!"

FIX THE ROOF WHILE THE SUN STILL SHINES

MARCEL ISN'T ALONE IN THIS EXPERIENCE of having an animal who didn't report an injury; I've had this happen to me as well. But from what I can make of their conversation, I suspect that Dusty actually did tell Marcel that it was the woman in the yellow dress who had hurt his leg but that Marcel might have scrambled that information. Perhaps he heard "hurt leg" and assumed those words went with the image of the woman. Perhaps Dusty was disoriented. Perhaps the leg was numb. But more likely, Dusty was a little cantankerous tomcat who didn't want to admit he had been injured. For me this conjures up memories of my cat Mr. Jones coming home all beat up and bloody but only willing to say to me, "Ah, hell, honey, that's nothing. Don't worry your pretty little head." Cats are the animals that are least likely to complain about their problems, so if you want to get medical information about a cat, sometimes you have to hang on like a bulldog.

Persistence is everything. Making these techniques work takes discipline and confidence, and Marcel showed us that tenacity is worth a million pipe dreams. I'm in awe of Marcel's gift but equally in awe of his courage. He also showed us the importance of learning to ask the right questions.

Now, about the weekend holiday that Blacky described to Esther: let's try to see the vacation from her point of view. First of all, cats roam. Especially boy cats. If you own a boy cat who stays out through the weekend, he's undoubtedly explained his plans already. He might say something like this: "You know what, Mom? There's this really cool construction site down the street, and I need to go check it out. I'll probably pull an all-nighter because there's this hottie calico cat who lives right next to it, and I want to go hit on her. There's also a mean yellow cat down there who's been teasing me through the window, so I need to go kick his ass. No worries. I'll be home by Monday. Don't wait up." And chances are, if you're a modern woman, you may be so busy and distracted that you won't hear him. So when he takes off, you panic.

The best way to alleviate this needless suffering is to practice tracking *now!* Every single time you walk into your house, try to mentally locate your cat. Or even before you enter the house, reach out with love to your feline and try to visualize exactly where he is. Test your skills daily. If you're inside and your cat is outside, just try to determine if he's in the front yard or the back, then go get your suspicion validated. At one time the love of my life was a glorious green-eyed Maine coon cat named Mr. Jones — I mentioned him before. During the eight years we shared together, I was in constant telepathic communion with him every single day. I would mentally say, "Where are you?!" and I'd get the image of him on the porch. When I went out onto the porch, there he'd be, basking in the sun. Or if he said he was out back, I found him out back. I never gave him a reason to step out on me, and he never did. There were a few terrible scares when he needed to SOS me about problems while I wasn't home, but because our communication was so seamless, I was always able to thwart disaster by heeding the warnings of my little informant. I poured my undying love and devotion into him and was careful to never do anything to get on his nerves, so for eight solid years he never let me out of his sight. He usually couldn't even stand to be in another room. We were in love.

If you don't irritate your cat (by being noisy, neurotic, or obnoxious), he's not very likely to stray far from his food bowl. However, dogs run away for different reasons. Usually, when your pooch is digging his way out of the yard and taking off for dear life, he's simply not getting enough exercise in captivity. When your dog shoots off in a blind sprint of runaway joy, she, like Chloe, is simply not getting enough exercise trapped in the backyard. Walking on a lead is no fun. Dogs need to run (in places approved for dog running!). If you can't run with your dog, perhaps you could find a neighborhood kid to run your dog while roller-skating. (The kid, that is. Not the dog.)

Another major factor comes into play with runaway dogs is loneliness! Dogs are incredibly social animals who like living in groups. They take off to find other dogs. If your dog is bored, and especially if he can hear the bark of another dog in the neighborhood, it's a pretty sure bet he's going to try to dig his way out of the yard to go find her. Imagine you were in a prison cell and could yell to the inmate in the cell next door but you were never allowed to meet face to face. Or let's say you're fairly happy but you have a friend you can only speak to over the phone and you're not allowed to meet in person. Wouldn't you want to change that? If we are sensitive to these problems before they happen, we may be able to avoid a lot of agony down the road.

In the next chapter I troubleshoot many practical problems. I also take time out to address some common questions — not just about nonlocal communication but about animal behavior in general — which might help you make more thorough assessments.

CHAPTER SEVEN

Troubleshooting with Grace

The worst sin toward our fellow creatures is not to hate them,
but to be indifferent to them. That is the essence of inhumanity.

— GEORGE BERNARD SHAW

I WAS TEACHING A WORKSHOP in the idyllic countryside near Hanover,
Germany, when I learned a very big lesson from a very small teacher.
Although I was grateful to be surrounded by so many curious, bright-eyed
German students, I was recovering from a monstrous bout of bronchitis
and I was absolutely bushed. After I retired to my room every night, all I
wanted to do was fling myself into bed, have a good cough, and enjoy
being absolutely alone. My relationship with solitude was like most
women's relationship with chocolate; I couldn't get enough.

But on the first night, I returned to my room to discover I had unwit-
tingly left my screenless window open. Much to my chagrin, I found that
although I had booked a single room at the inn, I suddenly had a roommate — a really noisy roommate. I tried to shoo her out the window, but
she dodged me like a top gun in a dogfight. The more irritated I grew, the
more ridiculous my antics became as I chased her around the room in a
wild monkey dance. Finally, she landed on the curtain rod to catch her
breath. I couldn't see her little face, but I'm sure she was laughing.

I don't know anything about the vocal capacity of houseflies, not even what makes their infernal buzzer buzz. Perhaps some flies' buzz is like the purr of a cat or the chug of a tiger, but this was the Beverly Sills of houseflies — that is, Beverly Sills vocalizing on the back of a Harley and riding with the Hell's Angels. I'd never heard anything like it in my life. Utterly irritated, I jammed some earplugs in my ears and tried to get some sleep. "Buzz, buzz, buzz!" She landed on my arm. I shooed her off. "Buzz, buzz!" Louder now, she landed on my ear. "Ugh!" I swatted. "I said, 'Buzz, lady, buzz!'" She landed on my cheek and gave me a good bite. "Argh!" I screamed and flailed at the air. Somehow, I fell into a fitful sleep.

I woke to find her standing on my forehead, bending over my eyelids like a vulture. "Hello! Guten tag! Buzz, buzz!" she said. "Go away!" I yelled and swatted. I ran to the window, flung it open, and begged her to leave, but she stood her ground on my pillow instead. I guess now that she'd kept me restless all night, she was ready to get some shut-eye. I smacked the pillow around, but she outsmarted me, landing over and over on the blanket like a little kid joyously jumping on the bed. She liked me. I was great fun.

I had flown to Germany to teach animal communication. The techniques of nonverbal commands that apply to large animals also apply to insects. So it was particularly humiliating that I couldn't get this little beast to cooperate. Bleary-eyed, I stumbled out of my room to begin the day's teaching. I returned that night to find her still in the room and still energized. Apparently, she had had a really good day's rest. By now, I was furious and hating her. I chased her around, threatening to kill her, but she just laughed and laughed. Once I finally piled into bed, she performed a blissful ballet dance all over me before she gave my finger a good bite and fell asleep on my hand.

The next morning, there she was, or should I say, there we were. Housekeepers had been in my room twice by now, but apparently they had not been able to evict my roommate. The mystery of the passage of time was working its magic on me; something had profoundly changed. That day when I returned from a long day of teaching and opened the door to my room, my first thought was, "Where's my fly?" I searched the room for her and when I found her on the shower stall, I breathed a sigh of relief.

"Thank God, you're okay," I whispered. Then it dawned on me that I had not seen her eat anything in the forty-eight hours we'd been together. I had food in the room, but it was all locked up tight in plastic bags.

"You must be hungry," I said, ripping back the peel on a too-ripe banana and setting it on my bedside table. Manna from heaven! She flew right over to the banana and lit on it, eating voraciously. She was famished. "What a knucklehead I've been," I sighed to myself. The poor kid's natural life span was probably less than thirty days. She just spent a tenth of her life starving, and here I call myself an animal lover! If a lost puppy showed up on your doorstep, you would feed it, right? But a housefly? Never! Why not? I watched my fly munch away with delirious bliss. I put a glass of water and a handful of trail mix next to her and fell asleep with her by my head.

I woke at three o'clock in the morning like a shot. Jet lag is the most committed lover I've ever had; he follows me everywhere I go. When I reached out to switch on the lamp, my first thought was, "Where's my housefly?"

She was on the lampshade, digesting peacefully. This is when the second epiphany occurred. The idea suddenly dawned on me that she was locked up alone in my room, three days of her precious life already spent, and maybe even far more, considering I didn't know how old she was. How many days did she have left? What if she was lonely? What if she wanted a boyfriend?

I went to the window and ducked my head out to peer up through the mist at the blanket of stars. The countryside in the German forest is cool and ethereal, the air is thick with magic, and the fairytales of our childhood linger in these woods, drifting like ghosts in a timeless fog. I breathed in the dreamy air and peered out into the darkness. I held the thought of attracting my friend's soul mate, but there was no movement in the silence. It was a bugless night. I stood for perhaps ten minutes before I reached out to shut the gingerbread window. But just before the frame clicked shut, something flew in front of my face. He zoomed directly to the lampshade and landed next to my roommate. I crossed the room to get a closer look.

He was much bigger than she and a strange shade of green. There was something sort of awkward and clumsy about him. He wasn't a housefly. I have no idea what sort of critter he was, but when I can't identify an insect, I call it a "bearbeezbooze." The bearbeezbooze stood near her, but not too near. He shifted his weight from foot to foot, not knowing what to say to my fly. It was clear he wanted to stand on her banana, but he was trying to drum up the courage to ask. Even though he was polite, he obviously wasn't her type. Now my little friend had to have dinner with a guy who wasn't even her species. My brain got preoccupied with other things and I started to doze off, even as the odd couple on my bedside table were still nervously trying to end their first date. All of a sudden, I felt compelled to jump up. I ran to the window and threw it open. I stood there for a moment, not knowing what I was doing or why I was there. Eventually, one single housefly came sailing in. He flew directly to my roommate and stood very, very close to her. I put on my glasses for a focused view.

He was slightly smaller than her, darker, taller, more angular, and with much longer legs. He was not only the closest thing to tall, dark, and handsome I'd ever seen in a housefly, he looked to be younger than she. "Rock on, sister!" I squealed. I wanted to high-five one of her little bristly feet. She had manifested her knight in shining stubble, and he was a gorgeous younger man! He stood faithfully by her side on the lampshade and didn't go anywhere near her banana. Clearly, he was not after her dowry.

We all slept silently through the night, and nobody bugged me (excuse the pun). The next morning I noticed the two little pie-eyed intruders were still entranced with each other's company, while the bearbeezbooze looked on like a proud uncle. Now I didn't have one roommate, I had three.

Of course you know I'm making some assumptions just to tell you a good story. I don't know for a fact that she was a she or that he was a he. Maybe the newlyweds were two gay guys. Maybe they were lesbians. All I know is that they were happy together and I was very proud to have had a part in instigating that. I had become a matchmaker for the multilegged. They were "my" flies now, so I fed them and took care of them until I checked out of the room. The day I left, they all flew out the window together.

I've thought extensively about the ideas of ownership. The "mine" and "not mine" concept seems to be central to the restoration or destruction of our natural world. "Mine" means the claimed object is worthy of love. "Not mine" means it is someone else's responsibility. One of my favorite quotes is from the Bhagavad Gita: "Until you learn to love every child in the world as if it were your own child, there will always be war in the world." We've been taught to carve off pieces of the world around us and shelter "our own" under the umbrella of our love. We've learned to rationalize that the rest of the world is not worthy of our protection. It can take a long time to unlearn this. Maybe my little housefly had a love at first sight experience with me; I was "her" person from the very first moment. But she was not yet "my" fly. She spent a long time and a lot of effort to teach me to be loving.

You may think my story about my tiny insect friends is ridiculous or insignificant, but it's not. Emmet Fox, a master teacher in the Church of Religious Science, tells us, "The aim of the metaphysical movement is to teach the practice of the presence of God." How do we practice the presence of God? We bear silent witness. We sit, and we watch. I think the Divine speaks the loudest in life's most simple moments, when we quietly watch God's voiceless creatures. The Divine Creator was in that housefly, in that room, in that misty night, and when I asked Divine Intelligence to bring my friend a companion, the Universe answered without hesitation. Fox goes on to say, "We practice the presence of God by seeing God everywhere, in all things and in all peoples, despite appearances to the contrary. So when we see the appearance of evil, we look through it to the truth that lies beyond it." My hatred of the little insect was not only ruining my life, it was ruining her life, too. When I viewed her as a nuisance and cursed her, I was seeing her as evil. Divine Intelligence couldn't work through me when I was busy being a jerk. So the first step in this process was seeing the God in my nemesis, thereby becoming concerned about her welfare.

BURNING QUESTIONS

WHY DID I OPEN THIS CHAPTER with a story about a housefly? Because everywhere I go there are two subjects that people ask about more often than any other: death and bugs. In later chapters we'll focus on the miracle of ascension and an even more miraculous phenomenon, reincarnation. But first, I want to talk to you about insects because I want to try to answer some of the questions about creatures and consciousness that might be rolling around in your head.

Insects and spiders are without a doubt our most mysterious neighbors on this planet, and in many respects they resemble teeny-tiny aliens more than they resemble animals. Yes, they are responsive to quantum fields and telepathic thought, even from big, clumsy humans, and the success stories that have poured in from all over the world of people who have made mental contact with spiders, praying mantises, moths, and butterflies, to name a few groups, are numerous and beautiful. I've had many personal successes with spiders and many failures with ants (whom one of my German friends calls "the Police Force of the Ground"). Whereas winged creatures almost always cooperate with telepathic commands in order to save their own lives, ants are more likely to say, "Wiggle your antennae somewhere else! I've got my orders, lady!"

It's also possible that because we are so large, we may be completely outside the insect paradigm and they may not really understand we're here. Size is a funny thing. If you consider how often we overlook insects, it's easier to understand how they could overlook us. Of course, insects can think and feel just like every other creature, and it's not their fault that we're terrified of them because they have wings and too many legs. And it certainly isn't fair that we question their intelligence when the social structures of ants, bees, and termites make human society look like a bunch of Keystone Cops. Apparently, ants communicate with each other better than humans communicate with other humans. Can they talk? I dunno. It sure looks that way. I'm told that chemicals called pheromones are important in insect communication, but could there be something else?

Does one ant have to walk out of my apartment and go all the way back to the mound in order to get his friends? And what if he does? Does he then tap his brother on the shoulder and whisper, "Party at Amelia's house! Tell the whole family." Or can he simply stand on my balcony and beam out to his entire neighborhood, "Amelia's vacuum cleaner is broken! Come on in! She's a trailer park chick and there are enough Cheeto crumbs under her couch to keep us all happy for weeks!"

I'll tell you one ant story, and it's not very funny. My friend Linda Sivertsen loves God's creatures as if each and every one were her own child. One day she found ants in her kitchen, and although she would normally let them peacefully cohabitate with her, on this particular day, she was having company over. She didn't want to use any poison, so she started sweeping ants into a handheld dustpan. She looked down to find one ant standing on his back legs, waving his two front legs over his head. He was looking up at her as she was murdering his family and friends, wildly signaling her as if to say, "Oh, the humanity! Stop the killing!" Linda's heart is so huge that she broke down and wept, calling her son, Tosh, into the room. Tosh, who was at this time about nine years old, looked on with astonished eyes as she gently picked up this one heroic ant, who had climbed onto her finger. He continued to stand on his back legs, waving two legs over his head, all the way out into the front yard, where she gently set him down in the grass.

She called me screaming with this outrageous news. She said he waved at her for at least ten solid minutes. Then, to add insult to injury, less than two weeks later the exact same performance happened to me. One hot California summer night, I found myself killing ants. In my very own kitchen, on my very own sink, one ant sprung up and stood strong on two legs, like a little man. He waved up at me, frantically, like a man on the runway trying to flag down a jet. "Stop the massacre!" he yelled. I, too, picked him up and burst into tears, and apologized for being such an idiot. I then asked one of my European students to telepath with my ants, and she emailed to say, "Amelia, they're just looking for *water!*" Duh.

So, this summer, we have a truce. I created a swimming pool for them out of a shallow plastic plant holder and placed it just outside my front door. There's even a slide for the kiddies made out of a popsicle stick. I leave dollops of honey or tidbits of food near the slide every day, so that they can have a poolside snack. Have they come into my apartment since I created their luxury resort and waterslide? Of course not! If only I had figured this out years ago, I could have spared so many teeny-tiny lives.

So, in summary, yes, insects can probably telepath, and yes, they're probably always trying to talk to us, and yes, they probably think human beings are a bunch of numbskulls. We can't even get along with each other, much less them.

In this chapter, I want to teach you how to send telepathic commands that will apply even to insects, but let's address some other practical concerns first. We've covered everything from tracking lost animals to seeing inside bodies. Let's back up now and investigate some more fundamental concepts in case I lost you somewhere along the way. I'd like to address a few of the questions most commonly asked by people who contact me.

Do Animals Understand Human Language?

Without a doubt! The more socialized the animal, the higher the probability that you can learn to hear words clairaudiently. You are more likely to pick up words from small dogs who go everywhere with their humans, cats who are very people-oriented, and parrots who have human companions than you are from exotic animals, farm animals, and fish. Poodles who accompany their mothers to the grocery store and the nail salon are more apt to tell you the names of their mother's friends, who she talked to on the telephone yesterday, and what kind of music she listens to on the radio.

Music is always mentioned by my animal clients. More often than not, animals like classical or jazz, but remember how Harry the German shepherd loved the classic rock his daddy played in the truck? I never met an animal who didn't love music, but they all have their own personal tastes. That said, this does not include canned human voices. Most animals *hate* the mindless human chatter that they are subjected to when people lock them in with talk radio so that they "won't get lonely." Not many complaints about this come from dogs, but television or radio chatter is *torture* for cats. Cats have inner resources, even in the silence of sleep, that we can barely imagine. Human voices disturb their dreams.

When communicating with exotic or farm animals you must rely more on your clairvoyance than your clairaudience. Horses are usually more responsive to pictures than to words because that seems to be how they communicate with each other in the herd, but many horses are very familiar with human languages as well. I once had a horse client who wanted me to compliment his owner on a song she sang to him often: I heard that it was about "white angels" and "birds in the sky." He showed me these pictures after he sent a few beautiful notes into my ears, followed by a warm, glowing feeling in my throat. I heard his rider through his own ears, singing on his back. Sure enough, the human turned out to be a songwriter, and she had written a love song for her horse about a couple of her friends who had passed away, thus the "angels" were "flying in the sky." She sang this special song to him often. The horse claimed to be her inspiration, and she confirmed that she did her best music writing on his back. Little wonder.

If My Animal Can Hear My Thoughts, Why Does He Disobey Me?

Many behavioral problems are a cry for help, so health problems need to be ruled out before all else. After health disorders are ruled out, the most common problems are inadequate space, poor relationships between the human owners, poor quality food, and simple loneliness. In fact, whenever a client comes to me with behavioral problems, the second question I ask is always, "How long do you leave him alone at home?" Many people leave a dog locked up alone all day and then expect him to be perfectly behaved when they get home. I strongly believe that animals who naturally live in groups should be kept in twos (at least!). Better to have an old bickering couple than no couple at all. I liken it to the movie *Planet of the Apes*. How would you like to live out your life being the only human in a world full of apes? (As it is, many of us probably feel that way right now!) Mixing species is also better than having no social outlet available to your animal friends. I have known some dogs who had profound friendships with cats, birds, and even tortoises!

Usually when a human gets punished by his pet — wetting the bed, chewing the furniture — the human did something to deserve it. The animal is trying to send a signal the only way he knows how. I have *never* met an animal that misbehaved who did not have a very intelligent justification for his behavior. Sometimes animals will disobey us when they don't trust us because they feel our behavior is inconsistent. Animals are creatures of habit, and they look to us for consistency. Animals will often punish parents who do not feed them at regular intervals. The lesson here: Establish a reliable routine. They also resent being sent mixed messages. Always speak and "send" in affirmatives. (For more on this, see the section entitled "Always Use Positive Statements" later in this chapter.)

Never use your animal's name to mean "No!" Your animal's name is not a reprimand for bad behavior. For instance, don't yell "Barney!" when you mean, "Be quiet!" Many of us have terrible childhood memories of our parents yelling our names when what they really meant was, "Stop that or I'm going to smack your bottom!" In fact, my childhood nickname was used so often to mean "Stop what you're doing!" that I actually had to change my nickname because the mere thought of it would make me cringe. Don't do this to your animal! "No!" means no. "Stop" means stop. "Be quiet" means be quiet. But let "Barney" or "Spike" or "Lucky" mean, "I adore you. Come and get your love."

Also remember that you cannot "fix" a mirror. The vast majority of my clients have animals whose issues simply mirror their own. If the animal's problem is your problem, the only way to "fix" the animal is to take the steps needed to work on yourself. Sometimes even health challenges can be mysteriously contagious. This phenomenon, called "reflective illness," is so controversial that it has never even been addressed in the United States by traditional medicine, and I don't pretend to understand how it works. Our new understanding of electromagnetic fields and quantum entanglement may provide the first model we've ever had to help us guess what's really going on here.

Apparently, germs are not the only way to spread illness. And I don't speak here from any of the research I've done, just fifteen years of personal experience. Dogs with blood-sugar or liver problems often have an alcoholic in the household. Animals with cancer often have a history of cancer in the human family. I once worked with a golden retriever who was obsessively scratching her jaw; we finally determined she was having a sympathetic reaction to the pain of her human owner, who'd had his wisdom teeth removed. Sometimes pets won't eat when their mother or father is dieting. Now, if even these medical issues are shared between pets and owner, certainly our emotional negativity takes its toll on our animals.

Human drama *always* affects our pets. Animals often complain to me of fights and arguments that go on around them, and like children, they sometimes blame themselves. Unfortunately, their only recourse for resolving their pain and aggression is "acting out." If we understand it when a man who spends the day working for an angry boss wants to punch the wall when he gets home, isn't it also easy to understand that a dog who is subjected to an angry owner may want to chew on the table legs? Our animal friends need a place to dump their pain, too. Furthermore, pets are a great barometer for our emotional state. When your pet is deliberately defying you, you must be humble enough to ask, "How can I help you? What behavior of *mine* can be corrected?"

I never met a "bad" dog. There are wild dogs, abused dogs, and misunderstood dogs; there are dogs who are expected to act like miniature humans, but no bad dogs. There is no cure for instinct, nor should there be. All these creatures evolved from wild animals, and we should treat them as if it's a privilege to have them in our presence.

Sure, our animals' instincts may inconvenience us. But then we should learn to make compromises on their terms. Always offer an alternative; give them their own possessions. For example, when you take back your sock, offer your dog his own chew toy. Give him something he can chew, a place where he can sleep, a ride that he can go on. And if he complains, honor his wishes.

Do Animals Have an Awareness of Time?

Absolutely. Contrary to popular belief, animals can tell time. Don't ask me how... the position of the sun or an internal clock, I guess. All I know is that they have an acute sense of time, much better that ours. Remember my story about Mr. Jones showing up out of nowhere and pressing his little nose up against the sliding glass door at 4:57? And believe me, I would get "the business" if I stayed out later than my regular schedule. He hounded me like a possessive dad: "Where were you? It's past my dinnertime! Why didn't you *tell me* you were going to be out late?"

(Telepathy has its drawbacks. Wait until the first time you accidentally step on someone's tail and hear a voice yell "Klutz!")

In coyote country it is essential to set curfews. Don't hesitate to send to your cat pictures of what will happen to her if a coyote catches her, or if she gets caught by an owl or hit by a speeding car. These images are nowhere as grueling as the real thing, and difficult as it may be for you to conjure them up, you must. These warnings are *essential*. This is the only instance where I recommend sending pictures of what you *don't* want. I actually double up the commands, positive with negative: First I send a picture of the cat safely crouching in the yard, watching the cars go by. Then I send a picture, with feelings, of my cat getting hit by a car. This is called a "psychic sandwich," and I'll explain it in detail in the next section.

When planning to leave your animals, tell them how long you will be gone. Count nights or moons. I say, "I'll be away for three dark nights." Believe me, they understand you and will usually let you know by disappearing the night before you leave, ignoring you, or taking a leak in your suitcase. (This is Rodney's trademark. Once after I had returned from working as a model at a convention in Palm Springs, I unpacked all my laundry in a heap. Then Rodney dug out the uniform I wore for the convention and peed *only* on that! "No wife of mine is going to work!" And of course, I was forbidden to leave town. From that day on, I took him with me.)

As soon as you know you are leaving town, explain it to your animals immediately so that they do not think you're going behind their backs. Only send mental pictures of a happy homecoming, not the separation itself. Always return bearing gifts, because they think the only excuse for you to leave them and go "out there" is to hunt. Always have something to show for your hunt and lavish them with time and attention when you return. Every time I leave the house I tell Aunt Flo where I'm going and approximately how long I think I'll be out. This prevents her from waking in a panic when she finds herself alone.

Another word on travel: Many of the people whose pets run away are in the process of a move. For some reason, the animals are usually convinced that the humans are moving without them. All of my animal friends are alarmed if they have even caught wind of a *possible* move! Remember, they see the pictures in your mind, even the pictures of your future plans. If at all possible, take them to the new location before the move and show them their new territory. Let them *in* on your plans as if they were active participants, not pieces of baggage. Ask their *permission* to relocate them and hash it out. Then allow plenty of time for them to say their good-byes to their old friends and neighborhood. Be respectful of their process. When moving day comes, never expose them to the hubbub of big objects getting moved about. Moving-day chaos is terribly upsetting. Always move the animals first. Tuck them away in a quiet room or keep them at a friend's house until the dust settles and their new territory is intact.

Do Animals Know What Gender They Are?

Of course, but they don't usually care. Two male horses are as likely to bond as a male horse with another female. The same is true of almost all species of animals. So, don't despair if you can't determine the sex of the animal just by looking at a photograph. It is not always easy, especially if they're neutered. I am often wrong about this myself, especially with dogs, tigers, bears, and elephants. This just makes me smile, and I quietly hum to myself my favorite Aerosmith song, "Dude Looks Like a Lady."

And if I had a dime for every time I've been asked if animals can be homosexual, I'd be a very rich lady right now. Yes, animals can be "gay," and animals can fall in love with another animal of the same sex because for them, love knows no boundaries. Note: Animals *do* fall in love, and they *do* feel married, so always allow adequate grieving periods for your non-human friends if they have lost a loved one. Some never fully recuperate. (Just like us.)

Can Animals See in Color?

Contrary to popular belief, yes. Some species may not "see" color but they can somehow comprehend color, even if they do not perceive it in the manner currently recognized by science. Scientists tell us the rods and cones in the retina respond to light: rods interpret black and white and cones interpret color, therefore most scientists may disagree with me, but animals do describe to me the full spectrum of color. I don't have an explanation for this. Now, whether animals are perceiving different wave lengths of visible light as humans do or using some other form of ESP, I can't tell you. I worked with a little pug dog on *The Mo Show* years ago who described her daddy's green and purple flowered bedspread. Another dog described to me a gray, sky blue, and mauve oriental rug with "little animals" on it. The owner confirmed that the dirty oriental blue and mauve rug was woven with pictures of little deer. Many a new dress has been described to me in great detail, as well as dog toys and beds in every color under the sun. So far, I've heard about pink, red, orange, green, violet, yellow... everything! One of my favorite fashion consultant animals was the cat of actress Leeza Gibbons. When I met the big, butch tuxedo cat, I was about to shoot a segment of the television show *Extra* in Leeza's front yard. Her cat told me he loved her new lime-green minidress with the matching handbag. Leeza confirmed she had come home in a new lime-green dress the week before and spent more time than usual petting him that night. (Apparently, he didn't just like the dress, but what she did in the dress!)

Do Animals Reincarnate?

I think so. Do they change species? I think so. Can animals be humans and humans be animals? I believe we can. Am I willing to be one of the only psychics in the world who will attest to this? Yes.

We'll cover this topic extensively in chapter 10. For now, let's just say animals do indeed change species when they reincarnate, with one exception: cats. Once you've been a cat, you may never want to be anything else. Why bother?

If Animals Do Reincarnate, Do Our Own Animals Come Back to Us?

Animals go where the love is. A lifetime for most pets is short compared to ours, and they often return to the people they love again and again. I've heard many dogs and cats tell me about prior lives with the same owners. One of my clients has a schnauzer who told us he had been a little golden long-haired dog "before." He described many things from their life together before he was a schnauzer: my client's older brothers, the house where my client grew up, and even how old she was when he got hit by a car. My client tearfully confirmed that when she was a child, she had had a little gold Yorkie who got hit and died in front of her house. What's more astonishing, the schnauzer told us he had deliberately "waited" on the Other Side until my client grew up and got married so that he could be with this particular *daddy* "again." His connection to her husband was from a prior life they had shared together! And here is an amazing example: I recently had a dog tell me that he liked his "old vet" better. He described the man in detail and even gave me the vet's last name. His owners told me that *this* dog had never seen *that* vet, but that their *last* dog, who had passed away, used to see *that* vet.

Reincarnated animals often tip off their human parents about their identity through some behavior that was unique to the animal who had passed on. They sometimes set up codes so that their parents will recognize them. For example, once I spoke to a kitty who had just joined the angels. Her human mother, who was a vet, was utterly inconsolable until her cat gave me this message: "Tell Mommy I'll be the little black and white kitten who licks eyebrows. And I'll have extra toes." The vet confirmed that her departed little kitty had always licked her eyelashes and brows, and that she had always wanted a polydactyl cat (a cat with extra toes). Her cat knew what she wanted, and she knew how to get her human mom to recognize her when she returned as another kitten. We can also negotiate when they will come back and what kind of form they will take. I'll teach you how to do this in chapter 10.

Can You Communicate with Animals Once They Have Passed Away?

Of course. I see and hear departed animals as clearly as I see and hear animals who are alive. Often I don't even know the difference. One of my clients once sent me five animal photographs. The spokesperson for the group who came forth was a big, white cat who slept in the window. She described to me all the comings and goings in this house, to the minutest detail. It wasn't until I got on the phone with the owner that I discovered the cat had passed away two years prior.

Here are some more related questions:

- *Where are animals on the Other Side?* Our deceased relatives usually keep our animals until they rejoin us or we join them.
- *Do they remember us and their lives?* Yes. They spend time in both worlds. The deceased animals frequently check in on their former owners and spend many happy nights cuddling in bed with their beloved humans. Your angel-animals are sleeping in your arms or at your feet, almost every night as you doze off to sleep. This is the best time to commune with them and in your drowsy state, you are more likely to catch a glimpse of them or feel a warm comforting presence somewhere near your body.
- *Can we call them back?* It is their option. If they had difficult lives or long illnesses, they will want more time in their spirit bodies. Sometimes they need time to detox after traumatic deaths. Remember, they are in a place where they are never in danger, they never get sick, and they feel no pain. It is a big sacrifice to come back to this world, no matter how well-loved they are here.

If I'm Communicating with an Animal from Another Country, What Language Will She Speak?

Now this may sound like a kooky question to most Americans who only speak English, but this in a very common dilemma around the world. I once got an email from a girl who had moved with her dog from Spain to Japan. She wanted to know if she should speak to her dog in Spanish, or Japanese. Can animals be bilingual? And if you're telepathing with an animal from another country, will the Animalogos be in her language or yours?

My German protégé, Esther, is bilingual and she hears extensive conversations from animals in both English and German. I even experienced it myself the first time I telepathed with a German cat. I found that the words inside my head were spoken in English, but of course the names of the humans and streets were in German. So if you're tracking a lost dog in Norway and you don't speak Norwegian, the human's names and street names will be tricky, but the transmissions themselves will be absorbed by your brain and patterned into words you understand. Words are only symbols for people, objects, and events in the outer world because they are only descriptions for a more fundamental reality.

I've only had one encounter with the bilingual phenomenon, which presented itself when I was teaching in Germany last year. Now, I do not speak German. When I brought one little crabby old dachshund out onto the stage, I asked her the color of her bed. "Grun!" I heard. "Green? Are you sure it's green?" I asked. "Like my leash, stupid!" I looked down and found that I was indeed holding her on a green leash. When I asked her what her boyfriend looked like, she said, "Shefferhund!" I said, "Your boyfriend is a German shepherd!? But you're just the size of a potato!" I argued. "I said he's a Shefferhund!" she snapped haughtily. The human guardian confirmed that this little dog, so full of piss and vinegar, did indeed have a boyfriend who was a huge German shepherd. (I guess size really does matter.)

Do Animals Lie?

Again, I'll let a student answer this one because this story speaks volumes about animal intelligence. This comes to us from Susan Schebler:

> I took your seminar in San Diego in July and have been talking to animals since — even to a dog from England. So I thought you might enjoy this story. My husband's friend at work wanted to know if his horse, Ginger, was pregnant. I used your gestalt method to scan her, and when I got into her brain, she was fantasizing about running through the mountains with her mane and tail blowing in the wind. *Wow!* She told me she couldn't do that anymore because her owner moved her to a different pen and she now couldn't see the mountains. She felt she'd been "demoted." When I told the owner, he confirmed that Ginger had just been moved. When they went out and

walked through her old pen, they noticed that there was about a three foot section where you could see the mountains between buildings. Happily, Ginger is back in her "view" pen and the owners say that she seems happier. By the way, Ginger wasn't pregnant, but she said her owners were feeding her better, thinking she was, and asked me not to tell them. Gotta love these animals!

Okay, so it means if you get to eat better, any lie is worth telling. If you recall, I used to have four kittens. When I asked them who started a fight, they'd all yell, "Not me! He did!" And once I found a dead squirrel in my workout room. When I asked who killed the squirrel, all four cats said, "I did!" Mr. Jones used to tell me he was all right when he wasn't. Butch men do that. And if I asked, "Are you not feeling well today?" he'd say, "Don't worry your pretty little head." So, yes, of course animals lie. That's why it's best to not only listen to their Animalogos but to actually look at the holographic records inside them. Sometimes, as with people, we have to dig deeper if we want to find the truth.

Now I've responded to a few of the questions I get asked most often, and some of these answers, like those on death and reincarnation, are a taste of things to come in my final chapters. Let's turn our focus now to how to send commands.

ALWAYS USE POSITIVE STATEMENTS

LET'S SAY YOU HAVE A DOG who is too aggressive toward other dogs. Every time you pass another dog in the park, your dog goes after him. Let's say your reaction to this is fear and anger. The minute you see another dog, your body freezes up, you yell, "No! No!" and you envision exactly what you don't want — your dog attacking the other dog. This is not how to say "heel."

Your thoughts must always match your words. Send only thoughts of what you *do* want, not thoughts of what you *don't* want. Words such as "won't," "can't," "shouldn't," "not," "couldn't," and the like are negative concepts and should be dropped from our conversations as much as possible. We should only visualize the positive part of the statement. Thus, a negative command like, "Don't bite!" becomes positive with "Keep your teeth in your mouth!" or "Keep your jaws shut!"

The words "No!" or "Don't!" mean "Stop what you're doing!" But when you couple it with another word, you make it a negative concept. "No bark" or "no bite" becomes a command to do the exact thing you *don't* want. If you send the thought "Don't bark!" your dog will hear, "Bark!" He won't register the "don't." (Even some human behavioral psychologists teach that the subconscious mind doesn't understand "no." You tell yourself "Don't be afraid!" and your mind hears "Be afraid!" But if you tell yourself "Have courage!" your mind responds the way you intended.) To make matters worse, you are probably sending pictures of what you don't want. This is just our natural tendency as human beings. We project our fears into the world, so our animal and human friends act them out. When this happens, you might think you had a premonition that something bad was going to happen, as in, "I just *knew* that dog would try to bite me," but in actuality, the thought you sent was received by that dog and it *encouraged* him to do exactly what you did not want. This is where we get the notion that dogs respond to fear.

Here's another example: Imagine that you give your cat a command like "Don't scratch the couch!" With this negative command, you automatically send the picture of the cat scratching the couch. The cat thus receives the command "Scratch the couch!" There's anger in your voice, so he knows you really mean it. He waits until he has your full attention, then he attacks the couch and scratches with vigor, just to accommodate you, all the while wondering why the hell it's so important to you that he scratch the couch.

When he proudly does it in front of you to prove he understood your command and is willing to comply, you yell at him and chase him around the house, clapping and screaming, "No!" Then, you corner him and toss him outside. He lands with a thud. "Well, that's a fine how-do-you-do!" he thinks, baffled.

Of course, the cat thinks you're nuts. He deduces that humans are a bunch of knuckleheads. He needs to scratch, and you just told him to scratch the couch! Then, when he scratched the couch, you threw him outside! When you send this kind of mixed message on a number of issues every day, the cat resigns himself to the fact that you can't be trusted. He vows to tune you out completely and ignore everything you say. Why shouldn't he? When he does what you *want*, you explode, yell at him, and chase him around the house.

It's not fair to your animals if you send a mental command of what you *don't* want and then punish them when they act on it. Remember that whatever you send, be it positive or negative, will be what the animal acts upon. Get into the habit of telling an animal only what you *want* him to do. Because we picture all we think or talk about, you will then automatically picture the correct action with the correct response. "Don't jump!" becomes "Stay down!" and then you add the sensation of gripping the floor under your four paws. Sending the picture or feeling of what you want strengthens the command.

To help you get going, here are a few examples of negative commands changed to positive alternatives:

"Don't claw the couch!" becomes "Only claw your scratching post!" (Make sure your cats have one.)

"Don't bite!" becomes "Keep your teeth in your mouth!" or "Keep your jaw shut!"

"Don't pee on the rug!" becomes "Only use your box!" (Or "Only go outside.")

"Don't jump!" becomes "Keep all four paws on the floor!" (Send with this the feeling of having all four feet connected to the floor.)

"Don't bark!" becomes "Keep silent."

"Don't chew up my slippers!" becomes "Only chew your own toys!" (Make sure they have toys of their own.)

"Don't lie on the counter!" becomes "Only sleep in your own bed!"

You get the idea. Use your imagination to reverse negative commands and send the opposite imagery of the negative action. Although most animals do understand the word "no" when it is isolated as a command, they do not understand it in a sentence. To them, "No biting!" means "Biting."

Thinking only in the affirmative takes a wee bit of mental retraining.

Be patient and honest with yourself. And it may take a good deal of time and patience to gain ground with your old animals because they might be accustomed to your mixed messages. If you've got a dog, you must establish yourself as the authority and send out calm, assertive energy at all times. Dogs like pack leaders. They *need* you to be in serene command. But please don't despair when you get ignored or are told "no" by a cat. Aunt Flo tells me "no" all the time, but I always try to see her point of view. If we don't treat our animals as toys or indentured servants, treating them instead as 50-50 partners in our relationships and honoring their wishes, they are much more likely to honor our wishes because they want to. (In fact, I'd give Flo 80-20 in her favor.)

SENDING SEQUENCES: THE PSYCHIC SANDWICH

IN MY LAST BOOK, I coined the term "psychic sandwich," and now that people are making psychic sandwiches all over the world, we're going to continue to use that name. The psychic sandwich is an extremely effective three-step process of sending the negative sandwiched between two positives. I'll explain it with a story about Gidget, the cat who kept ripping out her stitches:

First, I sent the image of the behavior I wanted: the cat sleeping peacefully and walking around with her mouth as far from her tummy as possible.

Next, I sent an image of the behavior I didn't want: her ripping out the stitches with her teeth and having to take another grueling trip to the vet to get sewn up again. With this I sent the word "No!"

Finally, I sent a reinforcement of the behavior I wanted: the cat happily ignoring the stitches, with the incision healing without interference. Gidget took the suggestions and healed beautifully, without nipping at the stitches.

Now, remember, this was the method I used in contacting Harry, the ferocious German shepherd attack dog mentioned in chapter 5, even while I was still in my car on the way to his house. As I drove, I mentally contacted him and sent the image of the dog curling up at my feet, docile, with his mouth shut. When we met, he obliged me by keeping his jaws shut and rolling on his back to show me his tummy.

However, this kind of success is not usually the case with barking dogs; some have a job to do and won't stop barking at a stranger no matter how hard you try to pacify them, so please don't judge your progress by your communications with unknown dogs. Silencing dogs is perhaps the hardest feat you could attempt.

Psychic sandwiching requires you to begin to watch your fears. If you think you will have a terrible time getting your cat into her carrier, you probably will. If you're sure your dog will bite the groomer when he gets a bath, he probably will. If you're sure your horse will shy on a particular trail, he probably will.

If you are facing a dreaded situation with your animal, mentally run through the entire scenario of what you *do* want to happen — and *only* what you do want to happen. Your positive imagery will bring around the desired result. And I reiterate: be patient! This training takes time. Our animals are so accustomed to receiving mixed messages from us that when we reorient our thinking in this positive way, they will need some time to get acclimated to it.

Here's one of my favorite success stories. For those of you who read my book *Straight from the Horse's Mouth*, you know of the infamous Mr. Jones. As you know, for eight years the big gray-and-white, emerald-eyed Maine coon cat was my sun, my moon, and my stars. One day in Mr. Jones's later years, our vet, Karen Martin, had sent us home with one of those little urine sample cups — you know, those stupid lidded cups that sit in your cabinet and collect dust, only to remind you of what a nincompoop you are for ever even thinking you could get a urine sample out of your cat. Well, Mr. Jones was no easy cat. Equal parts spun sugar and barbed wire, this cat was Clint Eastwood in fur. He was a big, mean killing machine, the kind of man that was going to take a pee when *he* felt like it, not when *I* wanted him to. Well, one morning I got out the cup. "Dr. Karen needs a urine sample," I said. He looked up at me and rolled his eyes. He really did. I swear. "If you do it for me now, I don't have to take you back to the vet and let her squeeze it out of you." (That was my attempt at a psychic sandwich, but as you can see, I hadn't finished the finished my bribe/threat with another sweet-tasting bribe yet.) When he didn't respond, I said, "Okay... I'll give ya some swordfish." "Oh, for Chrissakes, Amelia!" was what I heard telepathically, but all he said out loud was "Gahrrrarahrahrahh!" Then, with a disgusted "Harrumph," he sauntered over to the litter box. He crouched in the sand with his tookus held up high, so I could slip the cup under him. He peed in the cup, I snapped on the lid, and that was that. He got his fish. Karen got her pee. I got what I wanted, and everybody was happy.

When I volunteer at animal shelters, I medicate many, many a pussycat. When the other volunteers turn around and say, "This one needs her..." I say, "I know. I did it already." The pill or syringe goes in the mouth like lightening, and in a flash it's over. Here's how you do it: Send the thought to the animal, "Relax your body and open your mouth," then move gracefully and quickly. You don't have time to be clumsy or flounder. If you're nervous, spend some time telepathing with the cat first. Tell her everything you're going to do so that she can anticipate your every move. And when you're ready to move, move *fast* and the medicating will happen smoothly. Cats hate a klutz.

ALWAYS PROVIDE SUBSTITUTES

PLEASE DON'T SAY to your dog, "No! You can't have that!" and then not give him something else. Animals steal, chew, or destroy our things when they don't have things to claim as their own. Give your animal his own possessions. This is very, very important. Aunt Flo has an array of scratching posts, blankets, pillows, ribbons, perches, bandanas, bowls, glasses, and stuffed animals. These are her things. She doesn't destroy *my* things, but we share almost everything, including a rare and occasional flea. When she goes to the vet, I put a pillow and a sweatshirt with my scent on them in the cage. She often sleeps with her own brush in her arms, clutching it and using it as a chin-rest, and she also has access to her kitty carrier, which is always left out and sprinkled with catnip. These two "instruments of torture" should not be brought out only when you're ready to do battle with your cat. If your cat's carrier and brush are at her disposal at all times, her attitude toward them will be different.

If you provide wonderful substitute items, your problems will diminish. If your cat likes to scratch the couch, get him a scratching post that is similar to the color and texture of your couch.

If your dog is chewing your things, it's because she doesn't have her own things. Go get her some more chew toys and say, "These are *yours*. This shoe is *mine*. This pillow is *mine*, but this rubber porcupine is *yours*." I gave this advice on a radio show recently and the deejay said, "But if we get our dog things to chew on, they'll be gone in a day. He just chews them all up." And I said, "Right! So? Go get him new toys to chew on every day. He's a *dog!!!*" Dogs experience the entire world with their noses and their mouths. That's the way they are. We're not going to change them. But we certainly could change our behavior to make them happier, right? Rawhide bones and rawhide pig ears are tasty and inexpensive substitutes for favorite house shoes.

Here's an interesting way to look at this: Let's say you're a sculptor, you like to cook, and you enjoy reading books like this one. But you're the slave of some foreign species, say, a Shrek-type troll. Your master is bigger than you, doesn't understand a word you say, and controls your every move. If your master didn't like who you were, he would say, "Ugh! This person likes to make sculptures I can't understand and bake foul-tasting cakes I can't eat and read worthless books about animals! Make her stop! It's *disgusting!!!!!*" And then he would take your modeling clay and all your pots and pans and your copy of this book and throw them all out into the street. That wouldn't be very nice, would it?

Chances are, you'd resort to stealing *his* stuff when he wasn't looking. His resistance to understanding your wants and needs would make you even more defiant, and your tactics would go covert. You'd start digging up his yard and making sculptures out of the mud, stealing the hubcaps off his car to make pizza pans, and because you'd have no books to read, you'd try to snail-mail letters to me and all your friends. Then, when you got caught, you'd get in trouble for destroying the yard, vandalizing his car, and stealing all of his paper, envelopes, and stamps.

Wouldn't it be nicer if your Shrek-like master went out and bought you some modeling clay, cookware, maybe some recipe books, and told you to spend all the time you want sculpting, reading, and cooking? Wouldn't you stop stealing his stuff? Wouldn't you stop digging in the yard? And wouldn't *that* be better than the troll trying to erase your natural behavior?

Your dog needs to chew, and your cat needs to scratch. Your cat needs to hunt. Your dog pulls on the lead because you're not running fast enough. That's how it goes. We didn't design them; God designed them. But we certainly can find ways to accommodate their needs.

You've Got to Accentuate the Positive

Here are two more success stories. These come to us from Jamie Greenebaum in Boston, who shows us how beautifully you can master nonverbal commands.

Moving the Barn

A late-night call came in from the owner of the farm where I kept my beloved horse, Jeepers. She said we would immediately have to move all the horses out of her barn tomorrow — eleven horses and everything associated, lock, stock, and barrel! I was in a panic about Jeepers and how she would react to the move. If there was a lot of tension and excitement, she might not load onto the trailer willingly. And if she acted up, would the other horses protest, too? I had just gotten her settled into a stall next to her boyfriend, and I didn't know if that arrangement would work out in the new facility. How would she feel?

The woman who owned the farm where we were renting was difficult enough to deal with, but recently her forty-something son had moved onto the property. He was facing charges of child pornography. The entire atmosphere at the barn changed overnight. My husband asked me to promise that I would never be at the barn alone. Fathers began to pull their young daughters out of the riding program; horses left, lessons were canceled. What had been a wonderful safe haven, a place to unwind from the demands of daily life, a place to forget everything but me and my horse, became a place where I was looking over my shoulder.

I knew all the horses had been feeling the increased tension. The horses had held many late-night heated discussions about what we would do if we had to move. These arguments took place in the aisle of the barn in front of the horses' stalls. The air was charged with uncertainty. Would we be able to find one facility where we could all go?

Friday would be utter chaos. Mentally I got into contact with Jeepers and told her what to expect, then I asked her to tell all the horses in the barn that we were moving and that everyone would stay together and be safe.

When I got to the barn early the next morning, the horses had all just been given their morning grain and flake of hay. As I walked down the aisle I sent the thought that this would be the last time we would all be here. When I reached the far end of the barn, I looked into a stall and saw that one of my favorite horses, Floyd, was contently eating his hay. "Floyd," I said, "there will be a lot of disruption and chaos today. I want you to know that we are all moving to a new barn. The herd will stay together." I again sent the image of everyone in the new barn. When I first said his name, Floyd picked up his head from the hay and walked toward me to give me his complete attention. I next went to Lexus and gave her the same message. I worked my way through the barn, back and forth across the aisle, to Merlin, Honey, Faith, Fizz, Christie, Gully, Jeepers, Timmy, and finally Seekret. Each horse lifted her head out of the hay and came over to me, listening intently. By the time I was done, the barn was completely quiet except for the sound of horses munching hay.

Later that morning, I had to go to my office to get some paperwork regarding the move. While driving back to the barn, I got to thinking about how each and every horse had lifted her head out of her morning hay. Normally, I would expect most of them to keep eating and ignore me. But not a single one did. They all came over to me and listened to every word I said. I thought about the message I had sent to Jeepers last night and wondered if she had indeed passed it along, as all the horses seemed to know what I was saying.

Suddenly, there was an interruption to my thoughts and I heard a soft, mature voice resonate in my head. " I told them," she said.

With all the disruption to their normal routine, all the people running into the barn, anxious and worried about getting off the property without a confrontation, I was still afraid the horses would pick up the nervous energy. When it was time for the horses to be loaded onto the trailer, there was voiced concern about whether they would load quietly.

We had one two-horse trailer, so that meant six trips. The two most likely to protest were loaded first. They just walked right on, and then right off into their new stalls! All the horses loaded quickly and quietly! There were no problems. They settled into their new stalls and were soon back to munching hay. Afterward, I heard my friends say, "The horses moved so easily, with no loading problems, and they all settled right in! It didn't seem to be such a big deal for them after all!" And I smiled to myself and thought, "Because I told them!"

Where's the Kitty?

Bluenose and Firebelly, seven-week-old Siamese kittens, total savages with no manners, joined my family on December 21. On December 25, I got Amelia's book as a Christmas present from my husband. I began reading it and was immediately so focused that I didn't talk to anyone for the rest of the day.

The kittens' first visit to their vet, Dr. Terry, had been a total disaster — full of growling, snarling, clawing, and biting. Before we left for the vet, they played a naughty game I now call "Where's the Kitty?" They disappeared right when I wanted to put them in their carrier. So I began trying Amelia's exercises, tentatively at first. I focused on the kittens, working on sending images of how to behave while going to see Dr. Terry.

Now fast-forward to two weeks later. I put the carrying case on the floor and opened the door, and they both walked right in. No "Where's the Kitty?"! No fighting kittens who had to be stuffed into the carrier! They sat quietly during the drive — no cowering in the back of the carrier. They allowed me to take them out, one at a time, and let Dr. Terry examine them without clinging for dear life to the inside of the carrier, and *no* growling, snarling, clawing, or biting Dr. Terry! It was all as I had envisioned! I stood, stunned, as they were examined — such purrfect kittens. What had happened here? Had someone switched my kittens?!

"Oh my God, Amelia is *right!* They can hear me!" I thought. At this precise moment I realized I *had* to meet this woman who had turned my life upside-down. My Siamese boys could hear me, and I wanted to hear them! *Now!*

In less than a month, I found myself flying off to Memphis to take a workshop with Amelia. I cried and sobbed my way through the guided imagery meditations — my emotions totally overwhelming me. In a church filled with women who loved animals, with Amelia guiding us, I was more aware and in tune with life and love than I had ever been.

When Amelia asked the first dog a question, the answer "blue" appeared in my mind. I wrote it down. Could it be this easy? I could not doubt or fight what was happening. With each question, thoughts, words, colors, and images raced into my mind. And when Amelia turned to the human guardian to verify the answers, I was left with my jaw dropping into my lap. I was afraid to breath or move for fear that the magic would disappear.

Immediately after the workshop, my doubts returned. Not about what had happened in the workshop, but about whether I could ever do it again, on my own. I decided to test myself. As I was driving back to my hotel on dark, unfamiliar roads in an unfamiliar car I said to myself, "Okay, let's see if I can talk to the kittens." Before I could even get the thought completed, I heard laughter! Peels and peels of laughter! It was the high-pitched laughter of kids, so pure and joyous; it just filled my head and heart to overflowing. It was like I was inside the laughter. It was like I was the laughter. And then I heard, "We're here! We're playing and having fun!" Then they sent a picture of themselves, rolling around play-fighting with each other. I felt so overwhelmed, so connected with my boys, filled with so much love, and so thankful to Amelia. With tears streaming down my face, I missed my exit.

When I got home from Memphis I could still hear them, their young crystal-clear voices, each distinct from the other. They are not chatty, and they use their words sparingly.

I always check in with them when I'm not home. I think of each one and send my love, asking them how they are. Firebelly, I discovered, likes to speak emphatically, like a petulant two-year-old. One day I heard him say, "He brought in others!" I was startled and confused, but then I remembered my husband, Rob, had invited a friend and his young son over to see the kittens! Firebelly has told me: "She's HEEERE!" (referring to Jenn, the cat-sitter). And once while Rob was crumpling a piece of paper to throw but got distracted by talking to me, Firebelly interrupted with: "*Throw it now!*" I am always jolted out of my usual mind chatter by him, and I always have to laugh.

Bluenose's voice is softer, and he has a very different style. Once Rob and I were going away and leaving the kittens for five days. This was the first time we would be away from them for longer than one night. I spent hours counting with them the number of days and nights we would be gone, showing them a wonderful homecoming, telling them Jenn would be staying in the house. They appeared calm about this; I was a wreck. As I was finally walking out the door, I glanced back one last time to see Bluenose trotting toward me. "We'll be fine," he said in his soft voice. These three little words filled my eyes with tears and removed an enormous weight from my heart.

CONNECT IN A FLASH!

ONE OF THE MOST COMMON QUESTIONS I'm asked about dogs is "What is he afraid of?" Let's address this in a short exercise: you'll practice creating Resogenesis instantly and effectively and try a psychic sandwich. Here's the turbo-charged version, so once you've practiced slowly you can kick into high gear and fly through these steps.

- Quiet your mind.
- Put your focus in your heart.

- Send the Lumensilta. See a silver bridge of light streaming out of your heart to connect with his body. Quantum information is going to travel back and forth on this bridge of light. Love, joy, fear are all frequencies, like sound waves that carry data. Your Lumensilta will light up the holograms you want to see.

- Start by asking, "What do you love? What makes you happy?"

- Hold your focus in your body and listen.

- Get quiet, be patient, and use your body as an instrument. What do you see? What do you feel? What do you hear? What do you taste? And for a dog, the most important question is, What do you smell?

- Send him the thought, "I'll wait forever right here until you tell me. I will be nonjudgmental and you will be safe in sharing your feelings."

- Start with the positive questions (frequencies of love) first. Tell the dog, "I love you, I love you, I love you," and then only ask questions that bring joy, such as questions about who they love, what they like to eat, what kinds of activities they enjoy.

- Once you've got the love pouring back and forth between you, send the frequency of fear.

- Now pretend you are in his body looking out his eyes. In order to see yourself as a puppy, you would imagine that you are young, vulnerable, and scared.

- If you're looking at the dog's past, pretend you can roll back in time as many months or years as you wish. Now you are the age when the trauma occurred.

- What do you see? What are you afraid of? What do you hear? What's under your paws? Why do you feel powerless? What do you want? What would make you feel secure? Where do you want to be? What are you afraid is going to happen?

Never start the conversation with negative thoughts. Always bombard the animal with love and joy, then ease into the troublesome issue. Remember, the speed and the quality of the thought are different from your normal thinking process. You receive imagery faster than you produce it. An incoming message breaks the rhythm of your thought process because it comes in like lightning; it feels like it's coming in from left field. When it surprises you or is too "weird" or funny for it to be something you would have guessed, you know you did not manufacture it. You heard it.

And unfortunately, confirmation is your only benchmark. That's why I ask basic questions before I ask abstract questions. Start with confirmable things. Lock down some verifiable details first:

- Favorite food
- Favorite activity
- Favorite person
- Favorite toy

Then, when you move into the fear, just listen. Chronic fears are almost always a result of post–traumatic stress disorder. Additional traumas trigger the old hurts and remind the animal of the painful memories. Thunderstorms are a common object of fear for dogs. But if you get something totally bizarre and unexpected, that's how you know you've actually tuned in. I've had a dog in a workshop who was unusually afraid of thunder and went into wild panics at the sound of fireworks. When the group tuned into her past, they all saw images of her being forced to work as a hunting dog, when this was not at all what she wanted to do with her life. Her guardian confirmed that it was true. Her former owner was a hunter who made her retrieve ducks. Now the sound of what she perceived to be a gun shot sent her into a wild panic. In another workshop, our guest teacher was a cat who was terrified to be alone, which is a very odd dilemma for a cat. When we all tuned in, we saw the sad situation of this kitten being orphaned and left to die. We all felt that she was the only kitten who survived in her litter and that her mother simply disappeared one day and did not come back. When I tuned in, I could see that her mother had been hit by a car. The human could not confirm that, but she did say that she had found this one feral kitten and there were no other kittens in site that day.

If you can confirm the information with a human, then you know you're definitely right. And even if you can't confirm what you receive, perhaps your new understanding of the animal can help your friend heal from his fears, if only because you now see him through more compassionate eyes.

When you absolutely can't find out the history of an animal, one way to gauge your success is to see if another psychic receives the same information. The perfect example comes from something wonderful that happened recently in a workshop in Germany. Once again, this comes from Marcel, the stunning tracker in Switzerland. First I had the group ask a dog where he was from. I heard only the words, "Down south!" but most of the group heard "Spain!" When we asked the dog about his puppyhood, Marcel saw the dog living in tents, in a traveling circus in Spain! When I tuned in, I also saw the tents, and I heard the words, "I lived with clowns." Come to find out, the dog was born on one of the Canary Islands and then moved to Spain, but the clowns were not clowns at all! I'll let Marcel tell you the story himself.

The Dog from the "Circus"

The group and I asked the dog where he lived before this family took him home to Germany. The dog told me he was a street dog in a very hot country, which he thought was Spain. After this, I heard no more words, but I started to see pictures. He showed me a big place with many people and a big white tent with many flags. In the proximity of the tent, I saw people everywhere dressed in red. Then I heard the dog's voice in my head telling me that this place was a circus with many red-dressed clowns. During the next break, the new guardian of the dog came to me and showed me a real photo of this tent and the "clowns." They were not clowns at all but Buddhist monks! Mentally, I said to the monks, "Excuse me! But it was the dog calling you clowns! Not me! I am not guilty." But we all had a really good laugh.

In the next chapter I focus on animals as healers and how their tremendous healing abilities have blessed the humans in their lives. I also explore how we can energetically heal animals and learn to contain any of our own negativity that might be contributing to their problems.

CHAPTER EIGHT

Intentionality and Healing

Nobody has an explanation for how consciousness helps
you move your little finger when you want to, let alone
how it might operate at a distance to bring about healing.
The mysteries are far deeper than we want to acknowledge.

— DR. LARRY DOSSEY

THERE ARE COUNTLESS STORIES about how animals heal our hearts and
even our bodies. My most intimate encounters with animal-healers have
all taken place with my cats. I once injured a knee and felt a warm buzz
on that aching knee in the middle of the night. My cat, Rodney, who had
never slept on my knee before had settled himself right onto my throb-
bing knee. How did he know? This process is twofold and even more
revealing than what the telepathic perception suggests. Yes, he knew I was
in pain, but that's only the beginning. He also had the desire to comfort
me and knew that his warm, soft, furry presence would help alleviate the
pain. That generosity is a luxury we human beings rarely offer to each
other.

One of my favorite people in Los Angeles is a homeless woman named
Stephanie, who sits in front of my favorite Chinese restaurant. People
don't stop to comfort Stephanie. They simply step over her. The impulse
to help each other has been squelched in many human beings. But my cats
not only perceive my pain in my times of need, but they have the confidence of knowing that they can vanquish my pain just by a kiss or a touch

of the paw. One of the most memorable moments I've ever had with my beloved Aunt Flo took place one night only days after I came home with her three years ago. She was still skittish and reticent to be touched. I couldn't pick her up and she'd refuse every cuddle. But late one night I woke suddenly with a monstrous sore throat. I didn't move or call out or even fumble to turn on the light. I simply lay there staring into the dark, feeling the awful pain, and thinking, "Uh, oh. I'm in trouble." Suddenly the bed shook as a nine-pound "nurse" landed on the mattress and tip-toed up my body. I felt one marshmallow paw reach out and touch my throat. She held her paw on my throat for several minutes as I gazed into her tiny face. Her emerald-green eyes were transfixed on mine as she worked her magic. She didn't touch any other part of my body but just anchored her little white paw onto my aching throat. The pain quickly subsided and she walked away. That was the moment I knew my new roommate was a very special lady and it was going to be my greatest honor to share my life with her. Not only did Flo know I was in trouble, she knew she could do something about it, and she put forth the effort to do it. That's more than anyone has ever done for Stephanie. Animals aren't stingy with their love. They don't rationalize about which humans are worthy of love and which aren't. They even love humans who are abusive to them because I think they understand on some sublime level that the only way to melt an icy heart is with warm, patient love.

I had a very special doctor work on me once. His name is Dr. Shen and he lives in Atlanta, Georgia. His human guardian Leslie Connell, a wonderful masseuse, had to write the story for him because he doesn't have opposable thumbs. Dr. Shen is a shih tzu.

Dr. Shen

Before Shen ever appeared to me, I could feel his presence and power for healing. The day I adopted him, I took him straight to my office to work. He entered as though he'd been there many times.

From the first day, he has demonstrated an observable phenom-enon when I'm working with clients. As soon as the massage session begins, Shen lies down, regardless of the level of energy he has exhibited just prior to the commencement of the table work. He settles immediately and goes to sleep, as though he knows that it's time to work. Many times during sessions, when I am working with a person on a bodily area of physical holding and energetic contraction (a part of the body that is knotted, painful, or just blocked), Shen will begin whimpering in his sleep.

Frequently, this escalates into other vocalizations and bodily jerking that subside only when the energy is released. He rarely barks or whines when awake, so hearing his voice seems significant. When I first witnessed this in Shen, I thought that he was only dreaming, for I know that such motions and sounds aren't unusual when dogs are sleeping. However, his activity seems precisely timed with the work of releasing the knot or tension in the person's body. Many clients have commented, "He must be having a dream!" I would say that he might be having a nightmare — theirs! Either way, I've had a strong sense that Shen is actively assisting in the release process.

Amelia gave us the gift of confirmation with her experience with Shen, so I'll leave it to her to comment on this as an "expert witness." I also must say that this does not happen with work on every tight area of everyone's body. It remains a mystery how or why Shen assists — I don't know if he even has any control over that. I have always felt that he knows what he's doing, though, and can safely work in this manner without "taking on" undesirable energies.

Here's my account of what happened: This little dog appeared to be like any other little dog: he greeted me at the door, all business, and ushered me into the massage room. But when Leslie put me on the massage table, Dr. Shen quickly lay on the floor directly under the table beneath my body and fell asleep. Now, I've always had problems with my right hip. When Leslie worked on the rest of my body, boy, it felt good, so we decided to do more. We decided to "go for it" with my right side and lower back. As Leslie started digging into my sore spots, I was in enough pain to shed a few tears. Suddenly, Dr. Shen started acting strangely. He began to let out piteous sobs, and I could see him thrashing around, even though he was sound asleep. When Leslie moved her hands down to my feet, Dr. Shen stopped howling. When she moved back to my right hip, he started whining again. My neck — silence. Back to my hip — whining. And the little dog never woke up for a second. We did some deep release work and when it was all over, Dr. Shen woke up as if nothing had happened.

I said, "Leslie, do you realize that your dog is a...um...er... a healer?" I told her that he took my pain into his body, transformed it into catharsis, and helped shoulder my burden. Leslie said she'd always suspected this but had never gotten it verified. To this day, Dr. Shen's picture is on my refrigerator and there it will remain. He's wearing a Santa hat, and every time I see his luxurious little face, I am reminded of a line from the song, "Santa Claus Is Coming to Town," but I change the lyrics from, "He sees you when you're sleeping," to "He sees you when *he's* sleeping!"

WHAT IS "HEALING" ANYWAY?

IN MY MINISTERIAL TRAINING, I studied the writing of Dr. Ernest Holmes, the founder of the Church of Religious Science, a philosophy based on positive thinking. As a practitioner of Religious Science, we are taught how to pray for each other and remind each other of the "truth" of our being and our own personal power in any situation. The "truth" is that we are God individualized, not helpless victims lost in a sea of random events. God operates in us, as us, through us, when we stay on point and lovingly fulfill our destinies. In his textbook *The Science of Mind*, Dr. Holmes writes, "Let us take into consideration the ideas of love and compassion. We cannot speak what we do not know. Remember, we are speaking and feeling — something that is alive — into a form that the intellect has consciously created. But have we enough love to cover every sense of fear? Do we have enough love to cast out all the hate in our patient and alleviate his every feeling of not being wanted or needed or loved? There is enough love to cover it, but do we have enough to cover another person's? If we do not have it, we won't heal him."

We have enough love to counterbalance other living beings' sense of lack only when we operate from our absolute highest Power Source, which allows other beings to "cohere" with our more stable frequency. Some forms of healing may be the product of a property in quantum physics called "coherence," which I described in chapter 5. The perfect illustration of how coherence works is demonstrated through the behavior of a tuning fork. Gregg Braden explains coherence with finesse in his book *Awakening to the Zero Point*:

> When two electronic modules are placed near one another, with one vibrating quicker than the second, something interesting begins to happen. The module of lower frequency will have a tendency to match, through resonance, that of the higher pitch. This process is identical to that of the human energy system, which may be considered a module of composite frequencies reflecting individual cell and organ complexes. This module, our mind-spirit-body complex, when placed within the fields of another module will have a tendency to move into resonance with the higher vibration. In the human energy system, however, the process takes on an additional component: the willingness of the conscious mind governing the body to adapt to the new range of vibration.

What on earth are we talking about? The frequency of the most divine expression of Universal Intelligence, in all its calm, beauty, and peaceful dignity, is not only measurable, it is contagious. Other people are literally changed and transformed when they are exposed to a higher frequency; it anchors them to a more joyous expression of life and centers them back into their own soul, but on a higher rung than where they last left it.

Simply put, your animal may have a higher vibe than you. If you allow her to lift you up, your dog can cheer you; your cat can calm you in as much as you are willing to heal and cohere to his energy. Can your animals completely transform you so that you'll be free of your cancer, depression, or illness, or let go of your anger, frustration, and guilt? Can they lure you into the present moment, where their joy is so great they overpower any feelings of suffering? Are you willing to let them teach you how to completely let go of the past? Can you just be here now, with someone who really loves you, even if he has four paws or hooves? Yes! Can your animal get the same kind of healing from you? Yes!

Coherence is the root of all healing. And in order to heal you will need three things:

1. Freedom from the past and your own limiting belief systems. This will get you out from under whatever got you in trouble in the first place.

2. Sovereignty over other people's agendas for you and the collective belief system, so that you can learn how to think and feel for yourself, maybe for the first time.

3. New direction, so that your life can move forward after your purpose and your passion are not at odds with each other but are one.

Applied to our studies of animal communication, "coherence" is the word we use to describe a chain reaction of spiritual advancement, the magical moment where a sick vibration "logs on" to a healthy vibration and harmonizes itself. Let's say it's not you that needs the healing, but one of your animals. How do we heal other beings?

Bestselling author and spiritual teacher Wayne Dyer tells us that all energy is calibrated. What that means is that all energy is measured in terms of frequency, lower to higher, like the notes on a piano. The verb "to inspire" means "to in-spirit." When you are inspired, dormant forces, faculties, and talents come alive and you discover yourself to be a greater person than you once thought. This raises your vibratory rate and inspires all the living beings around you — two and four-legged — to elevate their energy levels as well. Your emotions are your compass, your God-given inner guidance system. And on this new adventure toward the source of our power, ordinary states of consciousness keep us from becoming "sorcerers" (living from the *source*).

Wayne says that if we want to live more joyously and create more abundant lives, we need to "Make your opening statement, 'How can I serve?'"

You can make things dissolve; you can make things appear; you can manifest things, solely by the frequency in which you vibrate." Now once we ask, "How do I serve?" we're inviting a Universal Power supply into our bodies and minds that becomes amplified by the purity of our intention. Can good intentions alone heal animals? Well, I'm going to tell you a story about an incident where a few good intentions transformed the life of a woman and a horse. But first let me introduce the star of the show.

Every now and then, I have a student who's so outrageously good, he or she almost scares me. One of the most hair-raising students I've ever trained is named Yvette Knight, and it's just a matter of time before this belly-dancing ball of fire sets the British media on its ear. Yvette lives on the beautiful Isle of Man, and we met there during one of my workshops at Brightlife.

In the midst of our workshop, I decided to throw the participants for a loop, but I was the one that got thrown instead. I said, "I've got a man on my mind back in L.A. What's his name?" The crowd made a few tentative guesses, yelling out the name of my ex-boyfriends and ex-husband. Finally, when they were all finished, I turned to Yvette and really put her on the spot. "What's his *name*, Yvette?" I demanded. I can always tell when someone is "tuned in." They get this wild look in their eyes, staring at me with such velocity of spirit that I think they're going to burst into flames.

"Jeffrey!" she screamed. "His name is Jeffrey!" I almost fell down, but I didn't want to stop pushing her. "That's right, Yvette, his name is Jeffrey. And what does he look like?" "He's six foot, brunette, green-eyed, big guy. Whoa, he's sexy, hot-tempered, has a black belt in Karate..." "That's right, that's right." As you'll see, the rest of the group was really intimidated.

Of course, I snuck Yvette into my room that night to pick her brain and needle her into telling me my future, just like everyone in the world does to me. She gave me a dozen details that no one could possibly have guessed, and she predicted an ugly breakup between me and my Jeffrey. She went on to tell me exactly what was going to go wrong and why. When I got home and things turned out just as she had told me, I might have been more upset if it hadn't been for Yvette's prediction. Instead, rather than crying, I smiled slyly to myself. I had just trained an incredibly gifted psychic. There are lots of other Jeffreys in the world, but there's only one Yvette Knight. Here's her story.

The Horse Who Cried

Michelangelo is a beautiful chestnut gelding, standing tall and majestic with a pure white star on his forehead. His coat is the deepest copper you could imagine, and he shines like a new English penny in the sun. He stood in a field that I often passed, and I knew his owner. I tried to send healing to him because he was desperately lonely and misunderstood. He was a dangerous and unpredictable animal when ridden, and this was the sole reason for his partial abandonment and his owner's inability to bond with him.

One day I stood in the field, crying for no apparent reason, feeling an overwhelming sadness emanating from this horse. I began to realize that while this was normal to me in a mad way, something was different this particular afternoon. I started feeling and hearing things I didn't understand. The reaction I had to Michelangelo was the shove I needed to make me sign up for Amelia's workshop at Brightlife.

This is what happened at Brightlife the night after I got the name "Jeffrey." I was sitting at a grand dining table on the last evening of Amelia's workshop, having dinner with Amelia and the group, when a large, studded, leather dog collar landed beside my plate. "This dog has crossed over! See what you can do with this!" one of the other students snapped as she stalked off to the other end of the table. The collar had a near miss with my dinner, but I was actually polite to her, which was totally out of character for me. I told her I would do it after dinner.

By the end of the meal, I had really pissed off this woman by having two puddings. So I tuned into the collar and the beautiful doggy that used to wear it. The dog was insistent that I say, "Montana! I go to visit Montana!" I wondered why the dog would possibly want to go to the American state called Montana, so I told the woman that the dog loves to go visit Montana. Then I asked her why. The woman looked stunned and replied to my question with tears in her eyes. "Montana is my daughter! Oh my god."

After Amelia's Workshop

The first day I worked on Michelangelo upon returning home, I did everything Amelia had taught me. I was working on him in secret at the request of someone who felt sorry for him. As I stood in the middle of the field with the wind blowing up me knickers, I concentrated for a while on Michelangelo, sending him love and white light. To my amazement, he stopped eating and approached me from the other side of the field. It was a bit unnerving to see this huge horse making a beeline for me. He stopped about thirty feet in front of me, looking at me as if to say, "Well, I'm here! What do you want?"

I walked over and stroked him gently. I knew we were in tune with one another when he laid his huge head against me. I asked him why he was troubled. He told me he had taken a bad fall and had injured his former rider. She didn't ride him again, and he was sold several times after that. The physical pain he felt was nothing compared to the pain in his heart; he missed his rider, a young lady called Karen.

The fall had left him with a spinal problem. As I was communicating with him, I had had my eyes closed, so I had failed to notice what was going on around me. When I opened my eyes, I got quite a shock. I was surrounded by all the other horses in the field! They had formed a circle around us! Suddenly I realized it was not a wise position for me to be in. But all the horses stood completely still without bickering or snapping at each other. I was a little freaked out, but at the same time I felt safe. I promised Michelangelo I would come back again and speak with him.

The next day, I walked over to work on Michelangelo. The sun was warm and the air was still, but he was so sad that I was finding it difficult to concentrate. As I looked up at him, a huge teardrop rolled down his face and onto my hand. I checked to see if there was dust in his eye or the sun was making his eyes water, but it was neither. Just then, another one fell and another, and another. I began to realize that this horse was actually crying (me, too, by this time). We stood for a while with his huge head cuddled into me. I reassured him he would be okay. Mentally, he told me it was a relief that he could be understood, and his burden could be shared. He knew I couldn't alter his situation, but he started to feel easier, and I felt his huge body relax. As I walked away, he started to eat grass and seemed much more at peace.

Later that day, I took a walk with my dad and brother Jon up to the field. When the horses spotted us, the whole herd started full gallop to the gate. I think dad and Jon were expecting trouble, but instead they all slid to a halt and Michelangelo put his big head over the gate and shoved his muzzle against my face. He blew gently several times. I knew he felt so much better. I would never be as presumptuous to think I had cured his sadness, but he was thanking me for listening and loving.

Now, I think Yvette is being uncustomarily mild-mannered when she claims that her therapy session didn't cheer up Michelangelo. I can't even think of Yvette, the hilarious British psychic belly dancer, without getting a huge grin on my face. Apparently, neither can the horses. Even if her healing session seems mild to you, I've had the exact same thing happen to me on many occasions: a head-shy horse that no one else could touch will bury his nose in my chest and cry. And I've had many a vicious dog or feral cat crawl into my lap — the first human lap they'd ever come near — and collapse into my arms for a long nap.

No other outward signs of healing seem to take place on these occasions, except that I allow them to tell me their stories and express their pain without judgment or agendas from me. These animals simply need to be heard, and once they air their complaints, their behavior magically changes in the twinkling of an eye. The horses go back to jumping, the dogs stop attacking, and the feral cats allow themselves to be caught and taken to the vet. Being a therapist for animals is no different from being a therapist for humans, except animals often respond and heal more quickly.

Here's another tale from another superstar from this same workshop; again our focus is using animal communication to promote graceful psychological healing.

Tales of Fishes and Dogs

My name is Elaine Downs, from Lancashire, England. When I got home from Amelia's workshop on the Isle of Man, I started practicing on a photo of my dog trainer's dog, with amazing, if somewhat sad results. My trainer's dog was expecting pups when I attended the workshop. When I got back home, my trainer asked me to speak to her dog and tell her to stay calm during the birth, as she got really stressed on the previous occasion. When I made mental contact, the dog told me her favorite food was chopped liver. I received an overwhelming feeling of gentleness and also got the impression that this dog was a prankster. My trainer confirmed all of those facts to me as well. I have to say that at this point I was quite stunned by this confirmation because I didn't consciously know anything about her dog.

The sad part of this story is that during a meditation, I contacted this dog again, and she told me that her pups would be born but would die shortly after birth. She said that it was okay because that was how it was meant to be. Very sadly, this is exactly what happened. (I had hoped that I would be wrong about that.) I have spoken to her since, and she is really struggling with her grief; she has said to me that no one knows how she feels, and I got this overwhelming feeling of sadness. But I know how she feels because she told me, and I pray in some small way I made a difference by being her confidante.

But here's a funny story to cheer you. I was in a garden center where they have an aquarium, so I decided to try to talk to the fish. I approached a tank full of colorful fish and started to send thoughts out to them. One of them came straight up to me and stayed at the front of the tank, staring straight into my eyes, while the others carried on, swimming around. I asked him which country he came from originally, and he told me, "Africa." I then asked if he was bred in captivity, to which he replied with great indignation, "Of course I was, stupid! Do you think I swam here?!?" Well, that told me, didn't it? I made a quick exit after that, thanking him for his attention.

I've shared Elaine's dog story for two reasons. The first is that animals have a mysterious capacity to tell the future even when humans cannot. I never met a human woman who told me her baby was going to die. But I've worked with many, many pregnant animals who could tell me the number of babies in their litter and, on rare occasions, could predict if one of the babes was not going to make it. Animals are far more in touch with their own bodies, thus their own unborn babies, than we humans are.

HOW TO COMFORT A GRIEVING ANIMAL

I HAD A TALK RECENTLY with my friend Linda Sivertsen (the ant goddess from chapter 7) about her dog, Adobe, a gorgeous female shepherd who seemed to be sad for no reason. Adobe told me that she wanted to have babies, but now that she was fixed, that could never happen. In order to cheer her with a substitute, I asked Adobe to show me her favorite thing in the world. She sent me the picture of a rural landscape absolutely hopping with bunny rabbits. Linda confirmed that Adobe had chased a multitude of wild rabbits in their previous home in New Mexico. Just as with the image of puppies, Adobe sent me a huge wave of pain and longing attached to the rabbits.

"She misses her rabbits, Lin. And she wants puppies," I said. What to do? Instantly, I had an "aha!" moment. "Linda," I said, "Go to a toy store and get Adobe five or six dark-colored 'puppies,' in the shape of stuffed bunnies, and see if you can find some as close to Adobe's coloring as possible." Linda protested that Adobe had never liked toys and refused to play with stuffed animals. I begged her to give it a try. Low and behold, when Linda came home with all the "puppies," Adobe was delighted. Every single night, she gathers them all up with her mouth, heaps them in her dog bed, and sleeps on top of them as if they were nursing.

We tried this solution again when a little Jack Russell terrier named

Tinker, my "assistant teacher" on the Isle of Man, lost a litter of four. Two were born alive, but one then died suddenly. The last survived for a while, but eventually even this precious one joined the angels. Poor Tink was devastated. Her human mom, Jane, went out at my request and got Tinker a litter of "puppies." Jane gave her three tiny stuffed bears — one black and white and two brown and white, with the same coloring as the pups. Jane said the look on Tinker's face when she handed her the "puppies" was the most remarkable thing she'd ever seen in her life. Tinker sniffed the "puppies" and buried them under her. Of course, the stuffed pups couldn't replace the real thing, but the look of comprehension and appreciation in Tinker's eyes — the look that confirmed that Tinker *knew* her human friend was trying to comfort her in whatever clumsy way — was enough to make the trip to the toy store worthwhile. And it elevated their relationship to a new level of love and trust.

Then I had a caller on the radio whose five-year-old child had just died. Her daughter had epilepsy, and the night she died, her seizure-alert dog, Charlie, had frantically guided the mom into the room. Now the poor woman wanted to know how to help Charlie. She said that when Charlie found the child dead in her bed, he came out of her bedroom with eyes dripping with tears — real tears, just like Yvette's horse friend. And since then, he's refused to go into the daughter's room, having fallen into a terrible depression.

In cases such as these, where your friend, human or animal, has experienced a great loss, there is nothing to do but know that time will heal all wounds. We can funnel love into our friends and hold them in our arms. We can pray that God will replace their pain with peace, and we can honor their process for as long as they need. After a period of a few months, get another animal companion for your animal. A new boy or girlfriend is a wonderful way to leave the sad memories in the past.

COLD-BLOODED LOVERS

Now, as for Elaine's sassy fish, I just did a flurry of over one hundred radio interviews here in the United States that gave me a new perspective on how people view cold-blooded critters. A shocking number of the deejays wanted to know if fish, reptiles, and insects have thoughts and feelings. It's a compassionate question. I told one that in one of my workshops in Germany I was assisted by a gigantic tarantula who was much larger than a mouse. I asked, if we were to hold the mouse and the tarantula up for closer examination, what is really the difference between these two sentient beings? Size, mostly, and a few (well, maybe a lot) differences in structural design.

Just because an animal is cold-blooded or lives in the sea doesn't mean it can't telepath. As Elaine showed us, not only could she talk to a fish but the fish actually told her off! I bring this up because the majority of fish I see in tanks are utterly miserable, just as are the birds I find in cages. Yet they respond beautifully to love and telepathic contact. One of my most memorable call-ins on these numerous radio shows came in from a gruff man who kept one single Japanese fighting fish in a tank. Every night, when the man got home from work, the fish would swim to the surface of the water and allow himself to be petted. For several minutes every evening, this man pets his fish. Every living being can think and feel, and we all respond to unconditional love. And a pat on the head never hurt, even if you're a fish.

A Walk to a Miracle

Now here's a healing of a different nature, not a psychological one but an actual physical metamorphosis. This dramatic success story has come to us from Ronda Holst, who is now incorporating animal communication into the veterinary practice where she works in Northern California.

One of our clients brought her nine-month-old female cat into the vet's office where I work. Little Misha was a small, cream-colored cat with lilac points on her ears and a heart-shaped face. This cat was absolutely gorgeous, but her back legs were paralyzed. As we started to examine her, her crystal-blue eyes looked up at me pleadingly and tugged at my heart. Dr. Neal, the vet, said the problem stemmed from a blood clot that was blocking the blood flow to her legs. The medical description of this condition is "cardiomyopathy with a thromboembolic clot at the aortic bifurcation also involving the femoral arteries, resulting in coldness and paralysis of both rear extremities due to a lack of blood flow." Dr. Neil said that usually a vet attempts to dissolve the clot medically. If a doctor can keep these cats alive long enough, blood flow may be partially restored and they may survive. In this case, he offered to perform surgery, but the client couldn't afford it.

The client took Little Misha home, then brought her back a week later. But by now Little Misha was completely paralyzed in all four legs. She could move only her head. Dr. Neal said she would last only two more weeks. She was eating a little but having no bowel movements. The client brought her back two weeks later to have her put to sleep. Since there was no improvement, she didn't want her to suffer.

I was holding Little Misha and crying. When she started trying to rub her face on mine, we all just looked at her and agreed she wasn't ready to go. I started to perform some animal communication with Little Misha. I found out that she was missing a young human boy who used to live at their house. And she told me she had not yet fulfilled her life's purpose — to teach her owner that she, too, could heal and feel for animals. Misha told me to have confidence in my abilities.

I also did my Theta healing technique on her, which means I visualized my spirit lifting up out of my body and connecting with our Divine Creator, where I asked what needed to be done. When I practice this, I wait in silence and listen. Within seconds, I'm "shown" what needs to be done. I see the healing occur in my mind's eye, but it happens in many different ways.

With Little Misha, I saw the blood clot breaking up and dissolving into God's light. I visualized a beautiful warm golden light entering the cat's body and healing her legs. Then, I instructed her subconscious mind to accept new energy and demonstrate the directions. After I witness a healing happen in my mind's eye, I release it, knowing it is done. Misha's owner agreed to take her home and wait to see if there was any improvement. I worked on Misha several times a day from a distance, visualizing all of her veins and arteries functioning perfectly, with the blood flowing effortlessly.

Slowly, the beautiful cat started showing signs of improvement: A twitch of her tail, a flexed paw! I communicated the idea to her that she must do her part in helping herself heal, and she agreed. She had lost too much weight, so I told her she needed to eat even if she didn't feel like it. She listened to me and started to eat again! Over the course of the next few days, there was more and more movement in her pretty little body. Within about four weeks time, she started walking again! She was wobbly, but she was walking! The last time I saw her, she had gained all her muscle tone back and she looked great! Her person said she was even climbing trees again!

FEEL FIRST, THINK LATER

RONDA WASN'T MAKING a blanket statement when she decided this cat wanted to live and could heal. Some animals cannot or do not want to heal. And in those circumstances, it is not our job to let our ego take hold and try to keep animals hostage on earth who are ready to leave damaged bodies behind. It is our job to have the wisdom to know the difference, and that takes tools.

If we use logic where instinct is needed, or vice versa, we are crippled. Most challenges in life are complex and involve both of these things, but most of us are lopsided. Most people go through life putting their intuition in the backseat or the trunk, where they hear it knocking and pounding to get out. Let your intuition (right brain) work *first*, then let your critical mind (left brain) come in to measure and organize the information. You don't need to pit these two parts of your brain against each other. They can get together later and meet for a drink.

A related idea comes to me from what you might consider the least likely source, my art teacher, the resplendent Karl Gnass. Believe it or not, all these concepts apply perfectly to animal communication. Karl teaches his students to synthesize first, analyze later. In Western civilization, we've been trained to use our logic first and deem sight as king. So there's great difficulty in breaking the habit of observing only shape. We don't see what is really there. We see what we've been trained to see. Instead, don't describe the surface. Learn to "see" in different ways — not with the eyes, but with the sensations. Sense the animal from within, then let your courage take over. First comes an impulse, then comes evidence.

Sight is nothing more than a visual analysis, a way of organizing complex material. But it is a form of shorthand. Sight does not do the entire language justice. None of our abstract feelings, for example, have objects to represent them. That's why it's so difficult for us to agree on what love is, or what good parenting is, or what it means to be driven by "God's will," or how to ascertain when an animal is ready to die. All those things are subjective, and so are the assumptions we make about our animal's happiness.

The truth of an animal's condition may not be upfront, center stage. Reality is often backstage, behind the curtain. And the animal's body is just the costume he's wearing. For instance, let's say I meet your dog and you say, "He's a beagle." That's what you see, so you'll try to get me to see that. "See? He's a beagle," you might insist. But I won't see a beagle. I won't see a dog. I'll look at your "dog" and see a matrix of frozen light, an energetic field held in place by complex relationships and dynamics. That's why I can see inside animals' bodies, because my perspective may be completely different from yours. I'm retraining you to see not outer form but *content*, whether it's aesthetically pleasing or not — pleasant or not. Suspend your judgment about what you may find there, and with each new animal, put aside your preconceived notions. Let's dare to go where no human's gone before: inside your own heart and body.

Learn to feel your own feelings. The answers to your questions will come from inside you. Your body has an intelligence within its own center — not located in the head or brain. Your cues will be given to you from your own body; then your brain can come in with a cleaning crew and put everything in order. We default to "logic" when we don't have the courage, patience, or discipline to actually connect with the animal and feel her pain. If Ronda had been lazy or acted like a coward, Little Misha would be dead right now, not climbing a tree with four healthy legs.

This is not to say that healing does not involve the mind. It does. To a layperson, Ronda's Theta healing might look like "magic," but remember, a good healer has a full menu of cerebral skills that are so well integrated that they look spontaneous. Distant healing is not a "talent." The ability to heal someone without touching them is derived from a set of well-honed skills, working in tandem so quickly that they look effortless. Ronda and Dr. Neal used the wisdom of traditional Western medicine as well as animal communication and Distant Healing to make a diagnosis and execute the treatment.

When you meet with a sick animal, do everything in your power to research the medical condition at hand so that you bring to the table all the factual knowledge your logical mind can uncover. I don't want you to get stuck with only two or three skills, regardless of whether or not they have always gotten you where you want to go. When I'm working with a sick animal, I don't rely only on my communication and Distant Healing skills. I want to know every herb, every vitamin, every medicine, every type of food, and every type of physical therapy and every possible surgery that might improve the condition. Then I ask the animal which one *he* prefers.

Spiritual growth comes with the ability to shift into new skills no matter how uncomfortable, to invent the tools you'll need to travel in a new direction. The old tools might drag you down into what's comfortable within your own limitations, but it is only through healing others and being challenged to explore new methods that we truly grow. You won't grow by sitting on your living room couch and sending "white light" to everybody. You've got to get in the game.

INTENTIONALITY: HARNESS THE LIGHTNING

WE CAN INFLUENCE THE WORLD around us, perform healings, and access nonverbal information through a fundamental quantum process called "intentionality." Think of intentionality as desire driven by intense concentration. Fueled with the knowledge that your intentions are loving and righteous, you can wield this force with surprising strength.

Intentionality is the new term for the engine driving an old concept called psychokinesis (the ability to move objects without touching them), or PK for short. Most of the studies involving the power of prayer and PK were funded by the Institute of Noetic Science, founded by our champion, Dr. Edgar Mitchell. Doctors such as Deepak Chopra have participated in these experiments. One of the other pioneers of this revolution in the mind-body-spirit connection is the maverick Dr. Larry Dossey, who was a combat surgeon in Vietnam and went on to head a hospital in Texas. Dr. Dossey has spent the last twenty-five years investigating the roles that faith, religion, prayer, and attitude can take in the process of human healing. In a multitude of studies, the data overwhelmingly favor the controversial notion that prayer, positive attitude, creative visualization, and a strong belief in the Divine Creator help patients recuperate quicker. What's more, this research even shows that surgery patients who pray or are prayed for are less likely to go into shock or have complications after surgery. Some studies have shown that prayer can even diminish the amount of blood loss.

Likewise, Dr. Bernie Siegel speaks of medical studies that have compared the health of animal owners to that of patients who do not live with animal companions. The presence of animals has been known to lower blood pressure in humans, give terminal patients the incentive to have remissions and leave the hospital so that they can get home to their furry loved ones, and even lengthen the life span of the elderly. Giving love and care and receiving love, even if it's from some little whiskered critter whose salty tongue is wildly licking your face, is a terrific impetus to go on living a happy life, especially if you live in a retirement home.

One breathtaking case involved a woman in a home for the elderly who was unable to speak and had apparently lost her will to live ... until a dog was brought in. The nonverbal patient started speaking again, and for good reason. She revealed that in her youth, she had been a dog breeder for this exact type of exotic dog. The appearance of the dog ignited a flame in her heart no one else could kindle.

What a travesty it is that every year our pounds kill millions of dogs and cats who could be lifting spirits and even saving lives in retirement homes, orphanages, children's hospitals, prisons, and office buildings all over the world. Can you imagine the difference in corporate morale if every office worker in every cubicle on earth had a cat in her lap and a dog sleeping at her feet? What a wonderful world it would be, for two and four-leggeds alike. We can change this situation by intending it to be different, and then doing the work that will manifest this new reality. Yes, it will ultimately come to pass through nothing but hard work, but in the beginning, we need to start with confident positive intention.

TICKLING THE MACHINE

HERE'S YOUR SCIENCE LESSON about prayer and intentionality — a real lulu, I promise. Some of the most fascinating university research on paranormal phenomena was conducted by one of the most unsuspecting scientists. Robert G. Jahn was a professor of aerospace sciences and Dean Emeritus of the School of Engineering and Applied Science at Princeton University. As a former consultant for both NASA and the Department of the Defense, his passion was deep space propulsion, and he authored a book called *Physics of Electric Propulsion*. In 1979 he was minding his own business, being a genius egghead and skeptic about anything metaphysical, when a student named Brenda Dunne, a clinical psychologist, approached him about a little experiment. The obscure project became very famous and so did the Princeton Engineering Anomalies Research Lab, known later simply as the infamous PEAR lab.

In one series of experiments, they employed a device called a random event generator (REG) to see if people could actually affect the behavior of the machine by using nothing but their minds. The phenomenon under investigation was PK, an ability that I possess out the wazoo *and* the yin-yang. The REG was designed to produce a strand of binary numbers, like this: 1, 2, 1, 1, 1, 2, 1, 2, 2, 1, 2, 1, 2, 2. Think of an automatic coin-flipping machine. As you may know, if you flip a perfectly weighted coin one thousand times, chances are, you'll get nearly a 50-50 split. Similarly, the numbers produced by the REG were fairly evenly weighted.

Well, the goal of the experiment was to have volunteers sit in front of the REG and have it produce an abnormally large number of heads or tails. What they found in thousands of trials was that not only were people capable of affecting machinery in ways that had previously been considered mathematically impossible but that certain individuals had a unique ability to jinx machinery and make equipment malfunction using only their minds.

Sometimes, when a volunteer would focus on a particular result, she would get the opposite of what she wanted, but in such abundant proportion that it was highly unlikely that the incident had been "pure chance." Whether these effects occurred through the "gremlin effect," the frustrating gift of making machinery go against your will (which yours truly also has in abundant supply), or the positive abilities of PK, which would allow a human to nonlocally affect a machine, Jahn and Dunne's experimental results stunned the scientific world. Our minds can and do affect the world around us, and if they affect nonliving machinery, imagine the effect they have on animals!

Here's my point: Apparently when the volunteers in the PEAR lab were in the process of changing the way machinery operates without even touching it, they were using their consciousness in its "wave aspect." We could say that they sent out a wave of intentionality and the energy affected the machine; or to take it a step further, their consciousness may have merged with the machine so that they *and* the REG became one big field. This is exactly what I do with animals. I don't simply reach out with a wave of energy and touch them. I enlarge my energy field to *include* them. But in order to make this expansion work, we have to kick into overdrive and put our minds into motion, in *waves*.

Michael Talbot, in *The Holographic Universe*, tells us, "Since all known physical processes possess a wave/particle duality, it is not unreasonable to assume that consciousness does as well. When it is particlelike, consciousness would appear to be localized in our heads, but in its wavelike aspect, consciousness, like all wave phenomena, could also produce remote influence effects. They believe one of these remote influence effects is PK."

ASKING THE RIGHT QUESTIONS IS 50 PERCENT OF THE GAME

So let's say you can shoot these energy beams of light out of your heart and third eye and expand it outward to include the world around you.

How can we determine when and why to use this ability? Well, for starters, it really comes in handy when you're faced with a barrage of information, first from the animal's guardian and then from the animal himself. When you're troubleshooting a problem with an animal, there is often too much data, so you need a way to focus. You need to become aware of the internal emotional action of the animal, not the end result of the problem behavior or illness. Remember the cat who ate sheets? His humans asked me why he liked to eat bed sheets. His behavior had nothing to do with his feelings toward *sheets*. It was about his need for security. It was about his feelings toward *them*.

Wonderful Leeza Gibbons has invited me to be a guest on her talk shows many times over the years. On one show, the dog I was working with had stolen all the doormats in the house and piled them up in front of the front door, where he would sleep on top of the pile, guarding them stubbornly. Of course, his human parents asked me why he liked doormats. I had to see through the bizarre behavior with the doormats to discover what he was feeling. First I got hit with a wave of fear, then pain, then intense love for his young human couple; next I felt his anger and his desperate desire to keep them with him in the house. Those emotions were the landmarks that would guide me to interpret his story: he figured that if he collected all the doormats in the house and lay on them, then his humans couldn't use the doors to exit the house and leave him all by himself. The behavior had nothing to do with doormats. It was about loneliness and abandonment.

The sheets, the doormats, whatever object the animal is using, may have nothing to do with the core of the behavior. We're not just looking at what animals use to express their needs. We want to see past that. And when we look at their bodies, we're not just investigating the outer edges of things. That's Explicate Order. That's kindergarten. We want to look inside, to add a fourth dimension to the visible three, so that we can sense the content and meaning beneath the physical world.

Now, when I'm on a talk show and I bust out with the big epiphany, it seems to the audience like magic. But I am simply using my tools to create a map to the truth. You, too, have got a toolbox full of techniques at your disposal. When one tool doesn't work, another will.

YOUR GIFTS OF PERCEPTION WILL DANCE

WHEN YOU'RE ASKING A SERIES of questions and receiving a variety of intuitive hits, a rhythm will form in the way these elements interlock, like a dance or a flow of musical phrases. You could receive a picture, a feeling of fear, a wave of pain, a picture, a word, a flood of joy; or your own personal process may repeat itself in a myriad of ways. If you have the endurance to stay in the dance long enough to feel the pattern it takes, you'll find that your intuition has its own unique choreography. Learn to dance in your own recital. It takes courage, discipline, and energy to stay on the stage. It's easy to revert to self-doubt. We have a tendency to default to our strongest characteristic and shirk our weaker attributes so that we remain safely in our comfort zones. But instead, invest the currency of your time and your energy into self-trust.

A thought disconnected from intuition leads us nowhere. A *feeling* is a tool that helps us engage with more focus and perspective. Feelings create a treasure map leading you to the answers you seek. The real issue with the animal is probably something you don't readily see, something you couldn't think up yourself. As I've said before, if the answers surprise you, this may be the flag that indicates you're on the right track. Every time you get a strange hit, that's a landmark that will function as an anchor point on your journey.

Parts of the story the animal shares may appear conflicted. The gems of the treasure hunt are in that conflict. Remember in chapter 6, when Chloe/Lowie told me, "Yes, there's a pool in my backyard," but then, "No, I'm not kept in the backyard with the pool"? She was trying to tell me that she could dig her way out of her yard, and thus didn't *live* in it. Often, like humans, animals also hide the shameful details they don't want to admit for fear of punishment. Pride, too, comes into play, like when Dusty failed to mention to Marcel that he had a broken leg and tried to pawn off his injury on an old woman in a yellow dress. But the rewards in the revelations bring healing and joy. The animals have no other way to speak to you except through your own patient listening, and the patience lies not only in piecing their stories together but in learning to trust your own process.

CULTIVATE YOUR FRUSTRATION

REMEMBER THIS WORK takes time and practice and it is invariably frustrating. You might get angry at yourself and want to throw this book off a pier. You might get really discouraged with the ebb and flow of your ability and say to yourself, "This is too hard. This hurts. Is there a pill for this?" In this make-it-easy, make-it-quick consumer society, we're getting awfully used to having things handed to us on a silver platter. We've grown accustomed to being able to simply purchase anything we want, take it home, and expect it to work. But this isn't one of those things. You can't buy this. You have to struggle for it, but if you do, the rewards are endless. After you've developed a sense of this new geometry, don't lock it down and polish it. Keep learning. Continue to allow something spontaneous to move out of your sense of order. You will grow in your own time, and your rhythm will turn into a consistent procedure. But have the persistence to allow things to get difficult again. It is in struggling with difficulty that we learn.

If you didn't feel the inertia, you wouldn't feel the awesome liftoff when your consciousness takes flight. If you didn't know the pain of isolation, of having your heart shut and your third eye closed down, you wouldn't feel the euphoria of making contact for the first time. Remember Marcel in the coffee shop, minding his own business, more than likely being frustrated with himself and cursing me, when suddenly he hears, "Hi. I'm Nora, and I'm going to the vet at 3:00." He looks down and realizes the "voice" he heard came from a dog! That's what I want for each of you. But I want it even more for all the four-legged Noras everywhere.

Here's another account, not about Nora, but about another heart-stealing dog named Reagan. This lovely account was written by one of my workshop coordinators and students, Lisbeth A. Tanz, who lives and practices in Saint Louis.

Reagan the Australian Shepherd

When Reagan first came into my life, she was a tiny bundle of white, black, brown, and gray fur. But most striking were her eyes — a steely gray blue. They seemed to look right into your soul. My first experience with her was when she spotted me across her yard and made a mad dash over to me yelling, "I'm in the wrong house, I'm in the wrong house!!! I want to live with *you!*"

Needless to say, things became uncomfortable between me and my neighbors because Reagan listened to me, came over every time I was outside, and would wait for me at my kitchen door if our garage door was open. I finally had a firm talk with her, explaining to her that she would have to learn how to deal with the situation she was in and that she couldn't live with me. She was so dejected, she avoided me for quite a while after that conversation. Then, not surprisingly, she began to show up on my deck and at my kitchen door again. I became resigned to the fact that she considered herself part of our family — even if she slept, ate, and pooped next door. I also had a nagging feeling that Reagan was not going to be around for long, but I had no idea why.

Ultimately, Reagan lived to be only two years old, departing from life after being diagnosed with leukemia. Weeks before her diagnosis, I noticed she was watching me from her usual perch in her yard. Uncharacteristically, she didn't approach me. Out of the blue I asked her, "Are you sick?" The message back was swift and stern, "Yes, but don't tell!" She turned her back to me and wouldn't respond further. Her people didn't seem to notice she was moving more slowly, her beautiful coat was looking more ragged, her breathing was labored, and she was losing weight.

I didn't know what was wrong with her, but I knew she was dying. Each day her energy slipped a bit more, until her people finally noticed. I kept my promise to her not to tell, a decision I sometimes question. The leukemia had spread quickly, and there were no treatments available that would have helped. When my neighbor told me this, I asked Reagan just how sick she really was. The answer stunned me. "Only days left," she said.

I sat on the grass stroking her once-silky coat and asked if she had the strength to come visit us on our deck one more time, to say good-bye to Katie, Bogart, and Miko, my family of dogs. "When you come, just let me know." A bit later, as I was working in my office, her message came through "I'm here." I raced downstairs to find her at our gate, waiting to be let in, just like old times. Katie and Bogart were thrilled at first. Then, amazingly, they became very deferential to Reagan. They were subdued and respectful of her — not trying to get her to play as they usually did. They sniffed and touched noses, and then Reagan lay down. Katie and Bogart retreated to the other end of the deck, leaving us alone.

As she lay in my lap, the love and gratitude she exuded was almost palpable. She was so connected to us. We were her port in the storm that was her home life. With her head in my lap, she let me know that she felt her life was complete, and could I please let her people know that she's ready to go? And could I let John, one of her guardians, know that she loves him, and to thank him for trying to give her a good home? She then relaxed fully and sighed. Breathing had become quite difficult, but for the moment she was comfortable and content.

After a while, we walked back to her house and I relayed her requests to John. If he thought I sounded nuts, he didn't say so. He was so upset that he was losing "his girl" that he started to cry. On a whim, I gave him a pet stepping-stone kit that I'd bought a couple of days earlier to use with my animals. "Do this tonight, do not wait!" I instructed. Thankfully, they didn't, and now they have that permanent memory of her. Reagan died two days after my last talk with her, but I know she's free and at peace now. She's come back to visit more than once — even appearing for a brief moment on the hill above our houses where she loved to lie in the shade. It *was* only a moment, but I could see her beautiful silky coat and her steely gray blue eyes — those eyes that even in death seemed to look right into your soul.

HOW TO MAKE A DIAGNOSIS

LISBETH HAD TO MAKE A TOUGH CALL. She chose, as I would have, to keep the confidence of the animal. All that mattered was what Reagan wanted, and Liz had the courage to honor her wishes. Unlike Little Misha, Reagan had chosen to join the angels. It is not our job to send healing to those who don't want to be healed. As I said before, it is our job to develop the wisdom to know the difference. Every case is unique. It will be up to you to fine-tune your "inner compass" so that you can make the right choices.

I'd like to give you the flexibility to be your own teacher in this. Here are a few keys. When you're attempting to heal a medical or behavioral problem, always ask these four questions.

1. Is this trait native to the species?
2. Is this problem common in this breed?
3. Is this problem specific to the individual?
4. Is this issue specific to the situation?

For instance, let's say our client is a purebred dog named Barney who has attacked a human child. Working with the four questions above, this is how I would approach the situation. Notice that my focus is starting large, then zeroing in:

1. Species: Is this behavior normal or abnormal in dogs in general? Perhaps this child is approaching the dog from behind the back of the neck, which causes a reaction in all dogs because they can't see what's coming up from behind. After I've determined that this has nothing to do with species, I look at the breed.

2. Breed: Could this dog be high-strung because of inbreeding? Is this particular breed not the best dog to have around children? If there is nothing particular to the breed that might cause this behavior, I assess the animal himself.

3. Individual: Next, I investigate Barney's personality, his history, and his medical problems. Let's say Barney has a wonderful personality. He's has never bitten a child before and

has a perfect track record of good behavior in his six years with this family. Because his personality has always been gentle and easygoing, this new behavior is out of character for his docile personality. I may deduce he must actually have a good reason to be acting out his anger in such an obvious way. I look at his diet and may put him on raw fresh meat and real bones, which will calm down the most aggressive dog, and add a vitamin and mineral supplement to his food to nourish his nerves. But to make sure I have the behavior diagnosed correctly, I also examine its context.

4. Situation: Next I look at the situation. Is Barney jealous of the human child? Has the child impeded on the dog's territory? Is the child hitting or pulling on the dog in a way that upsets the dog? Or perhaps the issue has nothing to do with the child. Perhaps the dog doesn't see well, or the humans act in ways that aggravate the dog; therefore, attacking their child is a way to vent his frustration and get their attention.

Now, numbers 1, 2, and 3 are not psychic stuff. That checklist is pure logic you can use as a process of elimination for every single animal you try to help. But you'll need to use your intuition for number 4, to assist in the integration of the various bits of information you receive in going through the checklist. And you should let Barney speak for himself, in a flood of emotion and visual images. Remember, the family will only see the problem. "He's doing *this*," they'll say, with horror and disgust. It will take every ounce of your strength to isolate yourself from their expectations and listen to the animal without judgment.

Now, in order to intelligently grasp and assess the problem of any animal, you need to take in a pile of intuitive information. Allow your brain to absorb a flurry of impressions and *not* figure it out. I personally write pages and pages of notes that are just stream of consciousness, then I go back in with my critical mind and start troubleshooting with questions. If you don't get a lot of impressions, be patient with yourself. Your instrument may not be state-of-the-art because you've never picked it up and used it purposely. You've used it only by accident, but you will develop it over time.

The checklist is one of the tools you'll use, but the true revelations come from the actual communications with the animals. For example, logic said that Little Misha should have been put to sleep on the spot. This situation was not common to the species, the breed, or the individual. It was specific to the situation. This particular cat did not want to die, and for some strange reason (just as with my paralysis patient, Chloe) the animal knew she had the fortitude to heal. I am not promoting sustaining the life of all paralyzed animals. In a thousand other cases, the humane choice would have been to have Little Misha put to sleep. But in this particular situation, that would have been the wrong choice.

Now, when you're under pressure, you've got to have a certain mental selectivity. Too many opinions cause utter confusion. If someone comes to me with pages of medical records, and the conflicting diagnosis of a half a dozen vets, all that data only get in my way. I don't want to hear other human's opinions before I make a diagnosis. I want the animal to speak for himself. Go at it blind and take in the intuitive data raw, then you'll learn to refine certain tools and concepts so that you can articulate them better. If you don't know how to do it, do it anyway. Stay on it.

When you smooth out what's bumpy and traverse this new road over and over, it becomes a well-worn pathway in your brain. This means you've built a teeny-tiny freeway for your neurotransmitters. It takes time. At first, this telepathic business is crude and frustrating. But as your successes start to accumulate and your self-confidence builds, eventually you'll get comfortable taking risks. Don't stop and ask, "How do I do this thing?" Get going, keep going, keep going, and then ask.

Eventually you will realize you've become skilled. Whether you've got a sick cat and your intuition keeps telling you, "My cat doesn't want to die yet. My cat doesn't want a vet," or the opposite is true and your intuition keeps telling you, "My animal is suffering. He needs some help," you'll find that the consistency of the message is key. Some information that is hiding will reappear later and when you get the same intuitive "hit" over and over with the same animal, that's how you know you're feeling the truth.

OSMOSIS ILLNESS

IN ALL THE YEARS I HAVE SPENT TALKING to sick animals, two things have reappeared so consistently that I want to speak about them now because I believe one day, in the not too distant future, both of these forms of healing may become accepted.

I discovered a shocking phenomenon when working with sick animals. The opposite of coherence is also true: we can share our negativity and disharmony, to the detriment of our animals. I've seen humans share diseases with their pets in ways that are no less than parasitic. In our present world of modern medicine, few recognize the evidence of the psychosomatic transference of disease, but this is a phenomenon I have come across hundreds of times. When an animal has a liver or blood-sugar problem, I've often found a human diabetic or alcoholic in the family. When there is cancer in an animal, there is all too often a history of similar cancers in the human family. When there is an animal who has problems with food, there is frequently a human mother who is dieting or bulimic.

I have seen humans and animals share inexplicable problems with their blood platelets, and I, too, have shared intestinal disorders and arthritis with my cats. The disease in the animal is not always traceable to the disease in the humans, so I'm not asking you to blame yourself for the illnesses that befall your animals. But I have encountered so many cases of what I call "osmosis illness" and have heard about so many thousands of others all over the world, that I think this topic bears mentioning.

My first case of osmosis illness was with the golden retriever I mentioned in chapter 7 who was scratching off the skin on the side of her jaw. She told me that her human father had just had surgery on his lower left molars, the same side of the jaw that the dog was scratching. I was stunned when her guardian confirmed he had just had his wisdom teeth removed and had had complications with this one particular tooth. The dog felt her guardian's pain to such an extent that she was bloody and raw from all the obsessive scratching.

Because our animals live with us and are susceptible to our energy fields and thought patterns, they often come down with the same disease their human owners have, even if those diseases are by modern definition not contagious. It's possible that symptoms and perhaps even diseases are not contagious in the way we presently believe them to be transmitted.

The most tragic of these cases was for me the most memorable. Years ago, I did a reading for a woman who had lost nine dogs to cancer. On closer questioning, I discovered that the woman had lost her mother, her father, and almost every one of her family members to cancer. What made this woman a cancer magnet, when she herself did not have it . . . at least not yet? I don't pretend to understand it, but I feel obligated to speak out about this mysterious phenomenon because I have seen it so many times with a myriad of diseases. I feel that humans are like energy cup vessels of some sort that are filled with emotion, patterns, and beliefs, and when our cups are full, our emotional debris spills over into our animals. If humans are cups, then the animals who live with us are sponges. They absorb whatever we are full of and mirror it back to us. Often the emotional trauma that they absorb from us is a part of ourselves we don't want to deal with or are not even aware of, and the issue has been subconsciously suppressed in our shadow side. If this is true of animals, the implications for humans are astonishing.

What we accidentally project onto our pets, we must certainly project onto our human families as well. Dr. Mitchell's explanation of this phenomenon would be that both humans and animals are caught up in a quantum entanglement, an energetic union shared by beings living in contact with each other. You might recall my discussion of this phenomena in chapter 4. A related term is "family constellation." Some tremendous research is being performed in Germany on the effects of family constellations, where one family member enables another by holding a particular role in a pattern. These studies have now been extended to include animals so that we may see if our behavioral patterns are getting projected onto our animals. I think the scientific revolution of the future might entail the discovery that germs alone are not responsible for disease. Germs are available in abundance everywhere at all times, but I believe it is only through a compromised immune system that we will get attacked by a disease. I think our susceptibility stems from stress and negative belief patterns that incubate in the mind, or unresolved pain that we carry in our hearts. Sometimes the only way to heal our animals is to heal ourselves.

HOW TO PRAY FOR YOUR PET

Let's put these ideas in practice and see how your animal responds. Distant Healing is easier that you think, and even if you've never tried it before, you can direct your "chi," the life force within your body, to gently comfort the aches and pains of your animal. With some animals, you can gently massage them as you direct healing energy to pour out of your palms. If the animal is severely injured, you might just want to hold your hand over him and not touch their body. Some people envision colored light radiating out of their hands, and often the color that the animal needs will intuitively present itself to you. But no matter what the problem may be, you can never go wrong with white, gold, or baby blue. In the following meditation, I'm instructing you to not touch the animal, but if it is more appropriate to pet them gently, let your spirit guide you to touch the animals in the ways that they will find most comforting. Place your hand about six inches above your animal and say along with me this truth:

I believe there is but one Power in the universe and that Power is God. This Power created every person, every pine tree, every body of water, every tiger, every rose, and every star. I know that this Power created my animal's body — each molecule, each cell, each atom — and this Power knows how to operate and sustain my animal's body with its Infinite Intelligence. I reach deep within my soul into the most silent sacred space of my being, where I effortlessly unite with this Power, the Source of all my supply. God works through me as me in all I think, say, and do. I know that God has designed my animal's body to heal itself and that all I need do is step out of the way and allow God's most elegant design to realign with its own perfection. My animal's body is a self-healing expression of God, and its physical form is always seeking equilibrium. I trust that the Divine Creativity that designed my loved one knows how to maintain my animal's health. My animal now enjoys perfect, radiant, dynamic, energetic health. I let go of the past and any memories that no longer serve us as I peacefully bring my focus into this divine instant. I am fully present in this sacred moment, where I only feel the joy, the power, the flexibility, and the energy flowing from God into my animal's body. I acknowledge that my friend's body is a vessel that joyously serves her Divine Purpose and carries her effortlessly through life with great freedom and ease. I step forward into new adventures with my animal, knowing that the excitement I feel about our future together is contagious. I am grateful for my animal's new vibrant health. I'm grateful that her body has been restored to balance. I give thanks for the recuperation of my loved one, and I release these thoughts into Divine Mind, knowing that God's Great Good is already so and that these blessings will go forth to bless other animals and people everywhere. And so it is.

CHAPTER NINE

Open the Gates to Heaven

You will grow strong in all the broken places.

— DR. BERNIE SIEGEL

"DID I DO IT RIGHT?"

A COUPLE OF YEARS AGO, I attended an event to hear my friend Alan Cohen speak. We were going to coteach a workshop together on his native Maui the following summer, so I knew he'd introduce me to promote our event. Just before he took his break, he had me stand up so he could introduce me.

He started with: "This is Amelia, one of the world's most gifted animal intuitives and the author of a book that's a national bestseller..." I waved cheerily to the crowd as I thought, "Gosh, Alan, you're laying it on a bit thick." Then he said the words that made my knees buckle: "...so Amelia will be available to answer all your questions during the break."

I smiled through clenched teeth and looked around to meet over a hundred pairs of expectant eyes. Some of the people with beaming faces were already rising up out of their chairs toward me. "Dammit," I thought. "There goes my potty break."

I had come that day as a participant, not a visiting expert, and I was really hoping to just relax anonymously in the audience. As I tried to sneak out the door and into the bathroom line, I was waylaid by a dozen exuberant interrogators. I tried to answer all their questions succinctly but found myself immediately getting pulled into their stories. A bright-eyed blonde made beds for police dogs, a bubbly redhead needed to tell me of her dog's phobia to buckwheat pillows, a silver-templed retired schoolteacher had just lost her cat and had only begun to grieve. Tears filled her eyes as she pulled tattered pictures of a beautiful Siamese out of her purse. I tried to silently urge the long-winded and ever-increasing crowd to shorten their stories as I glanced woefully toward the growing bathroom line. But they all, as always, had dams inside them that had been longing to break; they had few people in their lives who could understand their pent-up passion. Their pain and their joy and their rarely shared humor poured from them in rivers of unstoppable words. "At last!" their eyes seemed to say, "Someone who *understands!*"

Without wanting to seem indifferent toward their heartfelt stories, I tried to nudge them toward the door because there was a dam inside me that was about to break too, but it was a dam of another nature! Just as I had finally broken free and was weaseling my way toward the bathroom door, a heavyset woman with soulful brown eyes touched me on the arm. Something about the gentleness in her touch compelled me to stop in my tracks.

"Excuse me, I'm so sorry to bother you," she began, "but I only have one quick question." I took a deep breath and prepared to hear her out.

"See, I have six Labrador puppies," she said awkwardly. "Their mother died. And I . . . uh . . . they're eight weeks old. . . ."

My face must have betrayed me and showed my impatience because she stumbled to hurry her story, not wanting to hog up the time of the "famous" author, but the more she tried to hurry, the more dizzy the stumbling got.

"You see . . . I have these . . . um . . . six puppies . . . and I . . . er . . ."

"I'm sorry I can't take any more animals," I said quickly. "And no, I don't know anyone who wants any Labrador puppies." Everyone who knows I work with animals for a living seems to think I'm the depository for all the world's rescued animals or that I will magically know someone who wants their orphaned dogs.

"No, you don't understand. I can find them all homes," she said, getting more flustered. "I won't have any trouble finding them all homes." She was staggering over her words, visibly frustrated with herself. "You see, one of them was sick and I was...um...nursing it with a bottle. Their mother died just after they were born, and one of them was just not doing well no matter what I did...."

I remembered the advice of the famous intuitive Dr. Judith Orloff, who had told me what to do when I'm overwhelmed: "Refer out! When you really need to, refer new clients to other experts!"

I cut this woman off to say, "I know of someone in Memphis I could put you in touch with who runs a Newfoundland rescue. Even though she doesn't work with Labs, she knows more about newborn puppies than anyone I know."

"No, that's not what I meant to say. They're all well now," the woman said, growing flushed in the cheeks. By this point, I wanted to shake her and yell, "Well, if you don't need the dogs *placed* and you don't need the dogs cured, what on earth do you want!?"

"You see...um..." she struggled along, "I was holding the sick puppy, nursing him, and I'd been up all night. I'd done everything I could do. I'd nursed him with a bottle for four days and I was just exhausted. It was obvious this one little one was...not going to make it. Well...he died in my arms and I just wanted to know: did I do it right?"

"Did you do it right?" I asked, bewildered.

"Yes. I mean, I held him and petted him like this." She cupped her hand over her shoulder and pantomimed gentle strokes down the back of what was once his potato-sized body. "I just petted him like this...until he died. I didn't know what else to do. So I just held him against my shoulder like this. Did I do it right?" she whispered.

She was still cradling and petting the invisible puppy when I reached out to hug her. My eyes misted over as she gave me a stiff quick hug. I get a lot of these nervous hugs. I'm averaging a few thousand a year. There's a profound dichotomy of feelings when someone reaches out to hug a total stranger whom they've just entrusted with their most intimate secrets — secrets so dear, they don't dare breathe a word of them to anyone else for fear of ridicule. First they look at me with searching eyes full of awe and tears, eyes that seem to say, "Is my secret safe with you, Amelia?"

This is followed by a moment so tender, it defies all definition, a moment where they know I know and I know *they know* I know. Without words, our hearts connect, and in that warm rush of pain, like saltwater washing over a freshly scraped knee, we share the recognition of the unspoken: There is nowhere to take this pain. There is nowhere to get this information we need. But we experience this pain. And there's no one to turn to when we need to ask, "Did I do it right?"

"Yes," I said, as I pulled back from her chest and put my hands firmly on her shoulders, instantly ashamed that I'd been such a bitch.

"Yes. You did it *right!* You just pet them and love them and talk to them until they take their last breath." All the anxiety drained out of her face as she said, "That's what I did because I didn't know what else to do."

"You did it *right*," I assured her. "You did it *exactly right!*" I could see the compassion in her eyes and in her embrace I had felt the gentleness of her heart. I knew that if I were a dying puppy, in this woman's arms would be a very good place to be. As she gazed into my brimming eyes, she knew I knew. A tear rolled down her reddening cheek, but it was a tear of relief, not pain.

When our beloved humans pass away, we can consult our ministers, priests, and rabbis. But when our nonhuman loved ones pass away, where do we go for advice? There are no puppy priests.

SILENCE IS NOT ALWAYS GOLDEN

WE'VE ALL HAD LITTLE ANIMALS go to heaven in our presence. We often bite our tongues and turn our backs on these memories in hopes that our forced oblivion will banish the pain. From where does this disassociation stem?

We don't have far to go to find the answer. What child on the planet has not said, "But Mommy, a baby bird fell out of its nest!" The more compassionate parents let these children usher the chick into the house to die in a shoebox under young watchful eyes. Children less fortunate are told: "There's nothing you can do. We're in a hurry! Now, come on!" or "Nature is cruel. It's only a bird."

Our parents, siblings, and schoolmates may have spent years trying to build calluses on our hearts, but this toughening-up doesn't shake the truth. We all have moments that crack the armor. A puppy dying against all hope at three in the morning had ripped off this woman's suit of armor and thrown it into a kiln. When we melt our armor in the fire of undiluted feelings, we feel sorrow and loss because this little nonhuman being *mattered*. This warm little life had meaning even if its spirit was housed in a body with paws or whiskers or scales or wings. The loss is real, and the pain is real, and these beautiful beings deserve our reverence in their moments of sacred passage.

When this truth is honored we can melt the armor in fiery surrender and achieve a kind of alchemy in which the steel in our hearts turns to gold. This is the very metamorphosis that allows us to hear the thoughts of other living beings as well as feel their feelings because we have first been brave enough to feel *our own*. In order to establish Resogenesis, we must find the courage to be fully present, braced and ready to discover whatever our friends are truly feeling.

This fearlessness is born from a restructuring of belief systems, some of these systems so old we recognize them as truth without question. This love of baby-beings is one of the most universal experiences all children encounter, and the squelching of that love is one of the wounds all humans share. So if we were to deconstruct a belief system that functions as an interference pattern in our ability to connect with other living beings, this "bug in the system" may be one of the most primal blocks that impedes our ability to establish Resogenesis. Let's rewrite the program.

THE RECIPE IS ON THE BOX

A RELATIVELY ADVANCED WAY of establishing Resogenesis is through realizing that you and your animal are already one, parts of a larger puzzle.

One tiny, individual puzzle piece does not need to strain to connect with another tiny puzzle piece. When you recognize the entire puzzle, you become larger and expand your consciousness to include the animal as part of yourself. If you are all of life, all of nature, all of love, then all of creation is part of you. Expand your awareness, and *shazam!* — you know more than you thought you knew!

When you master God-awareness, even for a minute, you realize that you are not alone. If we can acknowledge that God is everywhere present, in an expanded state of consciousness, then we can be everywhere present, too. If God is all-knowing, and we are simply individualizations of God, then we have built into our spiritual program the ability to know much more than we think we know.

Our physics lesson today revolves around the physicist Dr. David Bohm, who was a master teacher of most of our master teachers. For a few years immediately after World War II he was on the faculty at Princeton University, where he was a colleague of Einstein. Now, don't doze off, because this rocks! As the story begins, the hot new idea among eggheads was the brainchild of an extremely smart dude named Niels Bohr who had conceived the principle of complementarity. This principle proposed that items could have several contradictory properties; for example, light can be both a wave and a stream of particles. Bohm became dissatisfied with the orthodox approach to quantum theory and started scrambling the yolk of his own magnificent cranial egg to set out to create his own approach. In the process, he had a few famous chats with Einstein. Maybe they met for breakfast and shared an omelette. Who knows?

Bohm began by developing a theory whose predictions agreed with the nonlocal quantum theory. He also assumed that there is a deeper reality beneath the quantum world, a subquantum level not yet discovered by science. Bohm called his proposed new field the "quantum potential" and theorized that, like gravity, it pervades all of space. However, unlike gravitational fields and magnetic fields, its influence does not diminish with distance.

Dig it. "Does not diminish with distance!" What this means is that if you want to track a lost cat in Russia, you can surf the Zero Point Energy

(ZP) field to find him just as easily as if he were down the street. This inter-galactic subway system we're learning to zip through has no relationship to time whatsoever. You think a thought, an animal thinks a thought, and bang. There's no time passing between the two of you — no interchange in time — because in this sea of quantum potential, you are connected to the animal, even if the animal has gone to heaven. When you expand your consciousness to the ZP level, you are no longer you. At this point you are all of creation, all of Divine Intelligence, and the entire world as you know it is inside your mind, including the mysterious land over the Rainbow Bridge.

Back to our eggs: Michael Talbot in *The Holographic Universe* helps us crack open a few new ideas: "Classical science had always viewed the state of a system as a whole as merely the result of the interaction of its parts. However, the Quantum Potential stood this view on its ear and indicated that the behavior of the parts was actually organized by the whole. This not only took Bohr's assertion that subatomic particles are not independent 'things' but are part of an indivisible system one step further, but even suggested that wholeness was in some ways the more primary reality."

The behavior of the parts is organized by the whole! What does that mean? Nature has a mind, and it wants us to succeed. This means that God is rooting for you! You can employ this enormous new paradigm shift, you can use this new recipe for success, to actually change your life and the way you relate to animals. Living beings aren't just a bunch of mismatched ingredients lying around God's kitchen. There's a system to how we all relate to each other in order to create universal harmony, and the recipe is on the box!

The notion of quantum potential also explains how electrons in plasmas (and other specialized states, such as superconductivity) could behave like interconnected wholes. As Bohm states, such "electrons are not scattered because, through the action of the Quantum Potential, the whole system is undergoing a coordinated movement, more like a ballet dance than like a crowd of unorganized people." He notes that "such quantum wholeness of activity is closer to the organized unity of functioning of the parts of a living being than it is to the bind of unity that is obtained by putting together the parts of a machine." Hot diggety dog!

For our purposes, let's lift from this wisdom three newly coined ideas. First, "superconductivity." Groovy word. Fabulous concept. It means that you and your animal can engage in a dance where energy flows with no resistance, not disjointed, like two old broken-down cars up on blocks beside each other in a field — you're an organized unity. We are functioning in this world in a coordinated, synchronized effort for the good of the whole, in tandem with each other, with zero electrical resistance, supervised by the Divine Orchestra Leader, even though we are usually unaware of our connection to each other. As cells in the body of God, we are as coordinated as the cells inside our own individual bodies. It is as if you and your animal were the two ends of a barbell, or the two wingtips of an airplane. When one end moves, the other *must* move because you both are part of the same organism. The connection is fundamental. Our attention creates the bridge through which the information can flow.

For our second idea, let's turn to the Hindus. They call the Implicate level of reality "Brahman," the formless birthplace of all forms in visible reality. Everything appears out of Brahman and then enfolds back into it in endless flux. Bohm says the Implicate Order can also be called "spirit," and similarly, the Hindus say Brahman is a fundamental level of reality composed of pure consciousness.

Thirdly, let's surf the ZP field and go Down Under, okay, mate? Like Bohm, who says consciousness always has its source in the Implicate Order, Australian aborigines believe that the true source of the mind is in the transcendental reality of the Dreamtime. This state of consciousness could be accessed in trance by their medicine men and offered a window to eternity where all the members of the tribe and all living things mentally communed in blissful harmony. Most Western people do not realize this communion is possible, believing their consciousness is rooted in their bodies. But Australian shamans also know about more transcendental states of awareness, and that is why they're able to make contact with the subtler levels of reality.

I want you to become well versed in the geography of these subtle realms. You may end up being the tour guide for future generations. Western culture has devalued the mystical realms by defining reality strictly in terms of the material and in the process has sold the animals to the devil. I want you to right this wrong. I can't do it by myself. I need your help. People and animals everywhere need your help. Here's a story for you that illustrates these ideas, showing how I glimpsed the level of Brahman, where all consciousness is made visible.

WHEN LIGHTNING STRIKES

WHILE TEACHING A WORKSHOP in a vet's office in Northern California, I asked the participants to exchange photographs of their animals. Using the photographs as "coordinates," the students partnered off in twos to flex their intuition and learn how to communicate with each other's animals nonlocally. As the group worked silently, I walked around the circle of people, watching them concentrate. One woman started to shake. Her cheeks were wet with tears and she was going into a total meltdown. This is not unusual in my workshops because many of the students offer up photos of their beloved pets who've crossed over, and the work can get highly emotional. But there was something about the intensity in this corner of the room that drew me over. Apparently the woman working with the photo had established a strong resonance with the animal in question and was very gifted, because only authentic telepathic connection can bring such a blast of pain. I could tell by the searching look on her partner's face — her eyes also stinging with tears — that the women were getting in over their heads. I peered over their shoulders to get a glimpse of the animal who was causing such a deluge of tears.

"Uh, oh...dammit," I said as my knees went weak. The photo had captured more agony and remorse in the eyes of a horse than I had ever seen in my life.

"What the hell happened?" I silently asked the horse. I knew in that instant that the rider had been killed. I slammed on the brakes and pulled back so that I wouldn't get sucked kicking and screaming into the hologram. I locked eyes with the horse's friend. She knew I knew.

"Oh, my God. I'm so sorry," I said. I tried to swallow the lump in my throat and shake it off so that I wouldn't "lose it" in front of the entire class and be unable to teach. At the break, the owner of the photograph, Sue, walked up slowly behind me.

"I know you aren't doing private readings," she whispered, "but my niece..." I turned to face her and saw the vision of a bright-eyed teenager with long, curly, blonde hair standing behind her. "...was killed on the back of this horse," she continued, "and I just need to know..."

I saw the girl in spirit vehemently shaking her head "no." Then she showed me her heart. Suddenly, I saw the heart pumping inside her body. As if I were a camera zooming in for a close-up, I saw a valve in the heart that didn't close properly. The "lid" had an irregular shape, and the malfunction caused the valve to misfire.

"It was a birth defect. I had a heart attack. Please tell her it was not my horse's fault," the beautiful spirit pleaded. The speed and clarity of the vision absolutely took my breath. I reached out and grabbed the desk to steady myself.

"Did your niece have long, curly, blonde hair?" I asked Sue. She nodded. "Jennifer was only nineteen and she had long blonde hair down to her waist," she said.

Suddenly, I was in Jennifer's body, reliving her ascension. I could feel a shockwave move out of my chest and down my spine. I could feel the warm, sweet weight of the horse between my thighs as my body went limp. I could feel my spirit slip down and enter the body of the strong swift horse as she desperately tried to carry me to safety. Then, suddenly, I was lifting skyward. I was filled with a wave of bliss, and I didn't want to come back down to the earth. I switched positions and found myself again in the body of the horse. The horse never faltered, even for a moment. She gracefully tried to counterbalance the body falling limp on her back.

"I tried to take her back home as fast as I could!" I heard the horse say. I felt the horse's horror when she realized what had happened, and I felt her guilt at not being able to rescue the girl. Then I was torn apart by the sense of heartbreak and frustration at not being able to tell the humans what had happened. I could sense the pressure of accusation and blame directed toward the innocent horse.

"Please help us," Jennifer begged.

"Listen, I'll make an exception and do a private reading. God brought us together for a reason," I whispered to Sue. "Your niece wants her family to know she had a heart attack and it was not her horse's fault."

I asked Sue to mail photographs and a list of questions to my home in Los Angeles. The following week, while discussing the tragedy over the phone, Sue confirmed many of the details I had picked up from Onyx, the horse. Jennifer had told me that Onyx tried to save her and did not contribute to her death in any way. Sue confirmed that when Jennifer's body was found by the side of the trail, she had no broken bones or signs of impact that would indicate she had been thrown. Onyx told me she went for help, to try to find any humans who could assist Jennifer. Sue agreed that Onyx ran alone toward home, but along the way she stopped at a farm, where she was found trying to get the attention of the people who lived there. Jennifer relayed that her little brother had never been fond of horses, and he blamed Onyx for his sister's death. Jennifer said he felt it was his older sister's "stupid obsession" with horses that had led to her death. She begged me to help her little brother forgive horses and understand that she would have had the heart attack anyway.

Sue asked me if Jen had "known" it was her time to go. Jennifer told me that on a deeper level, she had already decided to cross over, and given the option of dying behind the wheel of a car, where she could have endangered other people, or in public, where people would be traumatized by her passage, she chose to die in her very favorite place, on the back of her horse. She didn't want to be with anyone who could have tried to stop her, especially her mother. Jennifer showed me the vision of joyously riding her horse from earth to heaven as she galloped up into the stars.

Sue confirmed that Jennifer had said unusual things the week before she died, like telling everyone how much she loved them, and she completed some important unfinished business. I've heard these stories often about people tying up loose ends before their accidental deaths, as if unconsciously they knew they were about to leave this earth. Sue confirmed that Jennifer's mother was utterly shattered by her daughter's death, and that Onyx was Jennifer's most beloved being. She had been a "horse-crazy" girl from the time she was born.

Sue told me that after our meeting at my workshop, she checked Jennifer's medical records and discovered a birth defect in Jennifer's heart called a mitrovalve prolapse, a condition where one of the valves is misshapen. This confirmation helped the family forgive Onyx and understand that the horse was in no way responsible for Jennifer's death. In her communications with me, Jennifer named her mother, Carol, and little brother, Sean, by name, and she asked me to say hello to her best friend, Allison. But she kept repeating a name Sue couldn't identify: Danny. With this, the dead girl showed me a young man who was such a dear friend that at first I scrambled his name with Sean's. I got the name "Danny" superimposed on the vision of her little brother. Sue couldn't register a friend of Jennifer's named Danny, so the name remained a mystery until a week later.

Sue called to say she had discussed our conversation with Jennifer's grief-stricken mother and relayed Jennifer's message for Sean to "forgive the horses." Then Sue went out to Jennifer's grave to try to talk to her herself. She noticed for the first time that a grave next to Jennifer's belonged to a young man who had died shortly before Jen. Sue's voice broke with excitement when she told me the name engraved on the boy's tombstone: Danny. They were about the same age when they died. Apparently, Jennifer had made friends with Danny in heaven. I got even more confirmation a few weeks later, when Sue told me she had contacted Danny's family. They told her that Danny had died almost a year before Jen on the very same property where she died. Danny was nineteen at the time of his death, the same age as Jennifer. He had been stringing Christmas lights on a roof and had fallen off the ladder. Two sudden tragedies involving two beloved teenagers enabled them to form a celestial friendship.

HEAVENLY HOLOGRAMS

WHEN I MADE CONTACT with the horse and the dead girl in Northern California, I located first the signature frequency of Onyx, then of Jennifer.

Through my intentionality (will power), I adjusted my own vibratory level so that I would be in Resogenesis with both, first the horse and then the girl.

The feeling is somewhat akin to that of watching a great movie. Immediately, you lose yourself, you forget about your own identity, and if the film is compelling enough, you might even lose track of time. As you identify with the characters and get caught up in the story, you begin to laugh, cry, and feel their feelings along with them. You experience their drama as your own.

As we've discussed, I believe that the holographic information logged by every being on earth is stored in a vast cosmic warehouse called the ZP field. Although many scientists would not agree with my ideas about life after death, many physicists do agree that the memories of animals are stored in this cosmic warehouse of holograms. These images I perceive as animals and spirits may be electromagnetic fields, or perhaps even more subtle structures, like echoes of fields for which our modern scientists have no definitions.

I do believe that the spirits of animals survive the grave individually and remain intact after death, and that they can also reincarnate back into our lives again and again. This is, however, strictly a subjective opinion, based on feeling, not reason, and it may be subject to my own interpretation. We will explore these ideas in depth in the next chapter.

PAW PRINTS ON THE RAINBOW

I NEED TO SHARE A STORY with you about a conversation I had with an angel. She was a little butterscotch cat named Lillie, and from the minute I saw a picture of her face and felt her human mother's loss, I felt a freight train roar through my heart. Lillie had just gone to heaven when her human mother, Ronda Holst, whom you met in the last chapter, sent her photograph to me.

When I saw the photo of this little golden ball of fluff peering down from between two branches in a treetop, I started to cry and couldn't stop. While establishing resonance with Lillie, I experienced a cascade of sensations I'd never encountered before. At first, I saw the fresh grave of my own Mr. Jones, buried under his baby apple tree, as if I were doing a flyby and sailing through the air above the tilled soil. I knew what this analogy meant. It was the Spirit's way of showing me that Ronda had just lost the love of her life.

Then I heard music. The song was Don Henley singing: "I'm learning to live without you now, but I miss you sometimes. The more I know, the less I understand . . . I try to get down to the heart of the matter, but the flesh is weak and the ashes will scatter, but I think it's about forgiveness, forgiveness. . . ." The serenade was crystal clear inside my mind, and the emphasis on "forgiveness" was unbelievably strong. When I got hit with a sinking feeling of remorse, I knew something terrible had occurred and that someone left on earth was to blame.

As I downloaded the holograph of Lillie's death, a sense of impact hit me so hard from behind my neck it nearly knocked me off my chair. Then I was baffled by a phrase I will never forget. Lillie kept showing me a painting with the words, "Paint! Color! Tell her to *stream the beauty in to bridge the worlds*." This message, too, came with a distinct visual film clip. I saw a scene from one of my favorite movies, *What Dreams May Come*, in which Robin Williams suffers a tragic death and leaves behind an inconsolable wife. His wife is a painter. He tries to talk to her from the Other Side, but her grief is so overwhelming she can't hear him. He reaches across dimensions in a fierce act of intentionality and makes the paint on a canvas in her house physically "weep." Similarly, Lillie showed me rainbows of color soaring across space and time to penetrate our world and literally build a "bridge" to heaven. This vision of paint came to me with such clarity and velocity that I assumed Lillie wanted Ronda to paint, but Ronda's answer totally confused me. Then Ronda revealed the connection that absolutely stopped my heart. But I'd best let Ronda tell you herself.

Lillie: Earth Cry, Heaven's Smile

I feel compelled to write my story now because I'm living through a tragedy and looking for answers. While driving to work today, a huge revelation came over me; it was so huge that I almost couldn't breathe. I realized that by writing my story I could help other people who are going to go through their own tragedies. So here we go.

My sick little kittens came to me when they were about four weeks old. Someone had abandoned them at the veterinary clinic where I work. I had lost my old cat, Sam, some months earlier, and my husband and I had decided "no more cats!" When I brought the little kittens home, I reassured him I was only getting them healthy so I could find them good homes.

Of the three kittens, a very small, cream-colored female with absolutely no tail was the ugliest and the most sickly. She didn't have much hair; her little tummy was all bare. In a short time, she seemed to take most of my attention.

I hadn't named any of them because their new homes would name them. As time went on, I started to think about which of the kittens I would offer up first to a new home, but it became increasingly hard for me to make that decision. Then names started coming to me. As I named the last cat, I knew they *all* had found a home with me. Charlie, Shy Boy, and then Lillie. I named her Lillie because she was the ugly duckling who would turn into a beautiful swan. Every day she blossomed. She started growing hair; her little eyes cleared up. They all became so special to me, but Lillie had captured my heart.

For the first few months, I took them back and forth to work with me. All our clients looked forward to seeing the kittens in the veterinary office, but Lillie was a favorite. Often she would sit on people's laps as if she wanted to comfort them. And even more amazing, she would comfort the cats and try to calm them, as if to say, "You're safe here. We're here to help you."

Okay, here's where the tears come: One of our good clients, Janet, came in with a female rottweiler she had rescued several months before. Janet and I were by the counter, chatting, as her daughter was leading the dog around. I wasn't paying much attention. Dogs came into the clinic all the time. The dog came back behind the counter and up to the chair where Lillie was sleeping. Lillie hissed at the dog, and that was all it took. That dog had Lillie in her mouth before any of us could stop it.

It seemed so dreamlike — as if time stood still. I remember the dog shaking Lillie like a rag doll. Janet was yelling at her dog to let go. I tried to pry the dog's mouth open to release Lillie, but it's true that a dog's jaws are incredibly strong. I remember crying out, "She's killing her! Please, no! Not my Lil!" Then somehow the dog released Lillie, and I grabbed her. I held my precious little girl in my arms, but she was growling. Janet quickly got her dog out of the clinic. I checked Lillie out: there were no open wounds, but I knew shock and internal bleeding could kill her.

Suddenly Lillie's breathing changed. She started to pant. I needed to get her to an emergency hospital! As I raced out of the clinic with Lillie, I heard Janet yell, "Don't worry about a thing! I'll close up here and pay for Lillie's doctor bills." I drove so fast to the ER my heart was pounding in my ears. I promised God I would do anything if only He would save her. After what seemed like an eternity, I finally got there and ran into the ER. They checked her out, gave her pain meds, took x-rays, and started an IV solution. She seemed to be stable. Lillie needed to stay in the hospital, so I had to leave her there for the night. Feeling fear and not being able to do anything about it is crippling. The thought that she would die, that I wouldn't be able to see her sweet face again or smell her breath, was drumming through my head like a locomotive.

The next day, the doctors at the ER said Lillie was stable enough to go home, so Janet met me at the hospital to settle up the bill. We both waited for Lillie to come out, almost like two expectant mothers. When they brought her out, I was so happy to just feel her in my arms again. Aside from being very sore and quiet, she seemed like her old self, just resting. I took her home and she seemed fine.

But in the middle of the night, I sensed something was wrong. When I found her, she changed so quickly before my eyes. Her breathing grew rapid and she started letting out moans of pain. Her gums were turning pale. "Oh God, I need to get her back to the hospital," I yelled. My husband and I dressed quickly and got into the car with Lillie. How slowly time can pass when you desperately need to be somewhere fast!

As we drove, I knew I was losing her. She was gasping for air and then letting out long howling sounds. Her little body was in spasms, and her legs were tight as her body was dying. In the few moments before the hospital opened their doors to us, Lillie took her last breath. She was gone! Lillie, my angel, was a *real* kitty angel now.

As we left and I was carrying her little body to the car, I felt an explosion of emotion building up in me. As I got into the car with Lillie on my lap and my husband closed the door, I started to wail. Somewhere deep down the agony lifted into my throat. I rocked back and forth in my seat as my husband drove, feeling all the pain of the loss, so deep and raw.

I started to rub Lillie's head and her little paw, still warm, but she didn't stretch it out to me like she used to. Back at home, I laid her on the counter and kissed her face. Just for a split second I thought she was purring. Maybe I did hear her because she was happy to be out of pain and in her new angel body. I said good-bye and covered her up with a towel. I walked to my bedroom feeling as lifeless as her dead body. I knew it would be a long few hours before daylight, and I knew it would be a long road to recovery. I even dared to hope that maybe I wouldn't wake up at all.

For the rest of the night I couldn't stop questioning, "Why? Why Lillie? Why didn't I watch that dog more closely? Why didn't I get to Lillie faster? How come I couldn't get her away from the dog? Why didn't the vet fix her? If I had been able to get her to the hospital in time could they have . . ." I prayed to God every second to give me an answer — a little answer — anything just to stop the pain.

The next day I was back at work. I knew it would be a hard day, with everyone asking, "Where is Lillie?" What could I say that wouldn't set me off, crying? Janet waited several days before she came in to the clinic. We held each other and wept. We had both lost. But as I stood looking at her, I realized something new was developing: a friendship. Instead of anger and resentment, I felt love and compassion.

Janet and I started spending some time together, and I discovered she was a very talented artist. I boldly asked her if she would paint Lillie's portrait, and she said she would be honored to. I picked out my favorite picture of Lillie, and in just a few days Janet had finished. When she brought me the painting, I cried. Lillie was so beautiful! Janet had captured her perfectly. I believe in my heart that the circle of love had been completed. My Lillie had come back to me through the love of my new friend, Janet.

Some time earlier, I had ordered Amelia's book. I had put it aside for awhile, and I literally stumbled across it the morning after Lillie died. I read it cover to cover in one day. I sent Amelia a package of questions and several pictures of Lillie.

When I called Amelia, she described the violent impact she felt on Lillie's neck in her final moments, and I knew she had connected to the right cat. Amelia said that Lillie crossed over to be with another cat, a cat who was her soul mate, and that Lillie was happy. Amelia went on to say that Lillie wanted to come back but that she would come back with her "husband," and that when they were born I should take them both in. Lillie also told Amelia about my mom, sister, and husband, and named them all by name. Amelia talked about Charlie, Lillie's brother, as if she knew him personally.

But here is the most amazing part of the reading: Lillie kept trying to tell Amelia about painting and color! Amelia said Lillie must want me to paint because she kept showing her a painting. I laughed because I don't paint! But Lillie was insistent. She said to Amelia, "Tell her to stream in the beauty to bridge the worlds." When I told Amelia about Janet's painting, she put it all together. I was astounded! Lillie knew about her portrait! And when Amelia said she kept hearing the words to a song about "forgiveness," I knew Lillie was talking about Janet and her dog. She wanted me and Janet to be friends — to hold no blame or anger.

After the consultation I was exhausted, but for the first night in months I slept well. Amelia had told me that Lillie likes to sleep by my head, so that night I was comforted to know that she was still there sleeping with me.

The next few days were amazing. I started to feel a strength and purpose grow in me. I kept wondering if Lillie had a message for me through this harsh lesson. If Lillie was my teacher, what was I to learn? I felt that from the Other Side, she was urging me to try something new, but I didn't know what it was. I tried to quietly go inside myself and listen. I asked a friend of mine, Sherry, about meditation, and suddenly, with that one question, the haze in my mind cleared. Suddenly I could perceive Lillie's message for me. Information started coming from everywhere. I started taking meditation and healing classes every week, and I attended several of Amelia's workshops. People have been coming into my life with new techniques to share. All I had to do was ask and the universe just opened up. It was always there, but a beautiful cat had to show me the way. Lillie's greatest gift came in her death. Only that kind of tragedy could push me hard enough to get clear. This is Lillie's message: The possibilities of life are endless, and miracles can come out of tragedies. Love can heal, even from the Other Side.

When I apply the animal communication techniques and healing methods I've learned at the veterinary clinic, the animals really respond! Recently, an older cat came in and he was not happy. We needed to draw blood out of his jugular vein and send the sample to a lab. I telepathically explained to the cat what we needed to do, and why, and asked for his cooperation. He agreed. He calmed down immediately and allowed the needle to be put in his neck. The doctor could get only a small amount of blood out when he withdrew the needle. The doctor changed needles and tried to reinsert, but the cat jumped and would not stay still. I got the message from the cat: "You didn't say anything about having to be stabbed *twice*." He literally took me at my word. Since then I have been careful about my wording when communicating with animals!

Healing vs. Inertia

Lillie's death could have prompted Ronda to make a number of negative choices. She could have decided that God was punishing her, that dogs can't be trusted, that animals would be in danger in her care, or that she would never love that way again. She could have moved into anger and blamed Janet for Lillie's death. She could have used the pain to victimize herself and further shut down her heart, intuitions, and growth.

But she chose none of these things. Instead, she transformed the pain into love, and this alchemy sent her catapulting into greater spiritual heights. She used it as a means of expanding her awareness, rather than closing herself down and cowering within the walls of her mental box in an effort to protect herself from future anguish.

We can reprogram ourselves when we grant ourselves the power to create our own healing. You are always at a point of choice. If you think of yourself as a computer and the thoughts you carry about yourself and your life as programs accumulated from the past, then the painful and negative holographic memories are virus programs you incorporated into your own system, either by absorbing the negativity of others or by making judgments about your own limitations based on past failures. If you don't believe you can perceive "dead" animals, you may be in for a big surprise. But before we can install our new psychic software, we need to excavate your authentic spirit, see what psychological programs you're running, and make some new choices.

Someone with a Halo Says "Hello!"

My workshop coordinator in Scotland, Lorraine Kenyon, is now teaching not only animal communication but spiritual clearing workshops. These workshops help her students get their emotional blocks out of the way before they try to tune into their animals. Lorraine has a marvelous success story to share about a conversation with a cat who phoned home from heaven.

> I had been asked by Lynn, Sam's guardian, to communicate with him, as he was ill and would not eat or drink enough. The minute I saw Sam's picture I knew he was special. Wee Sam was a beautiful cat. As I gazed at his photo the first thing I noticed was his extremely confident posture. An air of great wisdom surrounded him. His beautiful soft fur was a delicate ginger color all the way down to his gorgeous white sox. His lovely green eyes held such a warmth, and his mouth almost smiled.
>
> I contacted wee Sam, and he gave me some information he thought was important for his mum. I knew he had more to say, so

I thanked him for this info and advised we would speak again. A few days later I was in my kitchen when Sam suddenly leapt into my mind "Call my mum, she needs your help!" I smiled and said, "Okay Sam, I'll tune into you in a little while, I am busy just now."

"No," came the reply. "You must call her now! She *really* needs you!" This was too strong, I could not ignore it. So I went upstairs and called Lynn. The moment she heard my voice she broke down in tears. Sam had passed away that morning.

"Well, Lynn, I can assure you he has not left you; in fact, he is communicating loud and strong from the other side." Then information came flooding through that Lynn could totally connect with. He told me that she wore something blue and coral around her neck. This turned out to be a necklace that she wore whenever she was feeling good. He wanted her to wear this necklace more often. He told me she had recently had her hair cut and said how beautiful she was. He loved her so much. Then he told me that I had to call a friend of mine and get the name of a book that he wanted Lynn to read. I passed this information on to Lynn and advised I would call her later in the day with the name of the book.

As I went to call my friend, Nadia, about the book, Sam came back into my mind again. He told me that Nadia was having trouble with her throat. "Her glands are up on the left hand side," he said. I called Nadia and got the details of the book for Lynn, then asked "Is your throat sore, Nadia?"

"Yes, how did you know?"

"Your glands are inflamed on the left hand side."

"Yes, they are," she said. Being a psychic herself, she was not fazed when I told her it was Sam who had told me.

A few days later Nadia called me and asked me to send her some healing, as she had a terrible pain in her kidneys and was about to leave for a four-day holiday in Tenerife. She didn't want to miss the holiday, because she and her sister went twice a year and always fed the local cats.

"I really want to go; the cats will be looking for us," she said. I promised to send healing, and then, clear as day, Sam said to me, "I will help, too. Tell her to go, she will be fine." She called me the following week to say she had had a lovely holiday and was able to feed the cats. One of the cats came up to her, and she felt he was very special. As she described him I knew it was a messenger from Sam in heaven.

A few weeks after Sam's passing, I had the pleasure of meeting Lynn in person when she attended one of my courses. She was wearing her blue and coral necklace, and she was as beautiful as Sam had described. He was with us during the course, offering love and support to his beloved Lynn. He even asked me to take her a special cheese. When I gave this to her, she beamed a huge smile. It was a cheese she had eaten when she lived in America many years before, which was a happy time for her.

It has only been a few months since Sam crossed over and Lynn misses him terribly, but she knows he is with her. He won't let her forget, as he always lets me know when she needs to hear from him and then I call her. He is devoted to helping Lynn on her spiritual path and continues to bring her great happiness!

MEDITATION: A VISIT FROM HEAVEN

Here is an exercise for doing a little psychological housecleaning of your own, which may enable you to better contact your departed loved ones — both two- and four-legged. Try it and let the emotion sweep you away, let the tears flow. Cleaning out your emotional blocks may be the only way you can learn to see into Heaven. Remember, nothing really ever dies; it's all there for the asking. Life forever goes on being life. And love forever goes on being love.

Relax your body and become aware of your breathing. Feel the steady rhythm as your reliable lungs fill your body with sweet breath. It is this breath that fills our bodies with glowing life, with pulsing power, as a galaxy of stars spins within our bodies in a celestial firmament of busy, self-repairing cells and dancing electrons.

Focus on your spinal column. Feel the soft pillows between each vertebra. Sense the flow of life in your spine as the spinal fluid drifts up and down this column of light. This brings you back to your center — to the neutral place where you are deep inside your body, feeling balanced, in command, and at peace. Now we are going to go on a journey together, a relaxing adventure where you can find healing and lighten your heavy heart.

You find yourself on a deserted beach at midnight. Feel your bare feet sink into the silky sand, lit from above by the translucent light of the moon. You see a gondola floating toward you across the quiet ocean. Its silver prow curls majestically above the blanket of mist on the surface of the sea. This boat will take you to a distant island where you will find healing. You feel your heart skip with excitement as you climb into the gondola and sit comfortably in the floor of the boat. Magically, it drifts away from shore. It glides on its own inner guidance system. You don't have to do a thing. You have only to lie back and gaze up at the stars while the boat drifts across the water under the light of the moon. You enjoy the ride as the boat bobs rhythmically, peacefully, up and down on the waves in synch with your own breath.

Finally, the boat reaches the shore of a distant island, totally uncharted and untouched by humans. You climb out of the boat and walk across the sand into the jungle. Here you find a cave. You duck expectantly into the tunnel opening, knowing that what you find here will bring you great healing and joy. The floor of the tunnel slopes downward, so as you walk forward, you find yourself descending into the earth. The cave walls glow with a subterranean light, and the ceiling of the cave is illumined with the twinkling of a million multicolored gems. You descend into the tunnel with a growing sense of curiosity and anticipation, aching to see what beauty awaits you behind every turn.

At last the tunnel opens up into a wide breezy cavern. You breathe easily and explore the walls with your eyes. The walls and high ceiling are studded with gold, rubies, emeralds, amethysts, and diamonds. As you're gazing up, not watching where you're going, you stumble into a hole and feel a pleasant sensation of falling down, down, down into the center of the earth. You surrender and let yourself freefall, feeling exhilarated. You laugh and let out a scream of joy as you fall from the past into the future, leaving the entire known world behind you.

You land with a gentle thump in a soft pile of sand. You feel someone reaching out to you to help you get back on your feet. You look into the face of a kindly old woman and gladly take her hand in yours. You see she's smiling at your not-so-graceful arrival. Her eyes twinkle with humor. You smile, too, laughing at yourself and feeling relieved to have found her once again. She tells you she's delighted to see you and she's so thankful you "dropped in." You hug her in a warm greeting, and here in her arms you realize she is your oldest friend.

She guides you down another corridor into her own home. She explains to you that her name is Hecate and she is Grandmother Nature, the soul of the earth. She tells you that all the animals on the planet were her creations. You look into her ancient eyes and see her pain. Her creations are in jeopardy. Ask her these questions: "How can I help you, Divine Grandmother? What can I do to heal your world and shield your animals from suffering?"

Pause for a few moments and listen to her words. Now ask the goddess, Hecate, to remove your burdens, to help you dispose of all the emotional debris that keeps you from functioning with your optimum power. She asks you to show her your pain. Suddenly, your arms are holding the weight of your suffering. Your emotional baggage has moved out of your own body and taken shape in front of you. It may manifest as brown, sticky sludge or ugly objects. It may even take the form of evil animals. Hecate asks you to tell her what it represents. Hold it in your hands away from your body so that you can separate yourself from everything that hurts you. Describe the sorrow, anger, pain, weariness, or limitations you've been carrying with you for so long. Now you can take your tragic past and see it as something separate from you. You can take all your painful memories and actually hold them in your hands. Grandmother Hecate asks you if you're willing to give this up.

If you're holding the grief you carry from the death of a loved one or past abuse that has crippled your self-esteem, it may take some time before you're ready to make this resolve. When you're ready, tell Hecate that you're willing to give up your pain and heal. Now she leads you into another cavern, where you find a huge chasm in the floor of the cave. As you peer over the rocky edge, you see molten lava glistening red and gold far below you. It churns like a fiery volcano. She tells you to throw your burdens down into the abyss, where the negativity will be burned and return to pure spirit. Take a deep breath and hurl your burdens into the crack with all your might.

Now Hecate leads you into the den of her inviting home, where you find a waterfall splashing into a huge round pool. You wade out into the warm, healing water. Then you swim over to the waterfall and let the refreshing water crash down over your head. As the rivulets cascade over your body, the healing waters wash you clean of every last bit of pain and sorrow.

When you're ready, step out of the pool, feeling like a child again. You are young and new and free. You find a big, thick robe by the side of the pool and wrap it snugly around your body. Explain to Hecate that you want to be able to communicate with her animals. Tell her you'd like to be able to see the spirits of those who have gone so that you might better comfort those left on earth. Ask her if she will lift the veil.

She hands you a huge golden chalice and tells you it is full of the nectar of the Goddess, the magic elixir that promotes clear visions. She tells you the drink will heighten your psychic perception and help you see spirits. She explains that her intention for humans was that they would guard and cherish all her creations. By drinking of this chalice, you will be bestowed with the gift of mediumship, the ability to see the souls of humans and animals who have crossed over to the Other Side. But in return, you must promise to devote your life to her service and to use this gift wisely to foster healing between humanity and the animal kingdom. Tell her how much you adore her and the planet she created. Promise her that you will champion her animals.

Now you drink deeply of this magic nectar. Feel its power pulsing through your body, all the way into your toes. You are replenished. You are renewed. This fluid heals every wound. It soothes every ache. It erases every scar. "Behold, I make all things new." Give the chalice back to the Goddess and promise to visit her often and learn all the wisdom she will offer. She tells you she has one last gift for you.

Suddenly, you see that someone you love is running toward you — someone you haven't seen for a long time. Here is the beloved animal that you miss so much. Touch him and feel him and look into his eyes. Understand that this is real — not an illusion your mind is creating but a real state of consciousness where you can actually see him. Tell him how much you love him, how grateful you are for the time you shared together and how happy you are to see him once again. Ask him where he's been and who he's with and what his life is like in heaven. Spend as much time as you wish petting and kissing your lost loved one and understand that there really is no such thing as death. Love transcends all space and time. Tell him that you'll be back soon and that now you understand he is alive, healthy, and happy but simply living in an alternative dimension. Your heart is lighter now because you realize that your animal is in the Goddess's loving care. He runs back to her and with a warm kiss, she takes him into her embrace. You know he's safe and happy here with her.

When you're ready to say good-bye for now, Hecate claps her hands and suddenly you find yourself above the ground on the sand at the beach. Step into the boat and embark on the journey back across the water. Now you feel younger. You are relieved to finally be free from emotional bondage. Now you can get clear. Your mind is filled with exciting new plans about how to serve the earth and help the animals. You look for the pain you've always carried with you, but you can't find it. It's gone.

CHAPTER TEN

Reincarnation

Ti Shazi Jenjo — A Wink from Heaven

Something unknown is doing we don't know what.

— SIR ARTHUR EDDINGTON
(REFERRING TO THE HEISENBERG UNCERTAINTY PRINCIPLE)

TAKE TWO!

SEVERAL YEARS AGO I WAS SUMMONED to a home in Beverly Hills to meet two little animals named Corey and Daphne. The conversation made such an indelible impression on me that I'll remember it for the rest of my life. The human guardian, Pam, was very distraught that both of her beloved animals were acting strangely. Daphne wouldn't eat and Corey refused to be picked up and would run from Pam as if terrified of her.

Pam had sent me photos in advance, so I had tuned in before the house call. When I had asked Daphne her favorite food, she had said, "Zucchini." Before I left my apartment, I packed a baggie with five little treats that I thought Daphne might like to eat. I packed the to-go bag with a cherry, a grape, a butter cookie, a piece of cheese, and a big chunk of fresh zucchini. When I got to the house and told Pam about Daphne's request, she protested that Daphne had never tried zucchini and she argued hotly that Daphne could not possibly know what zucchini is. She had never had it in her entire life.

After a quick chat and an introduction to the animals, I emptied the baggie onto the coffee table and put Daphne down next to the pile of loot. Daphne rifled through the treats. She threw the cherry aside, flung the butter cookie in the air, tossed the cheese with disgust, and singled out the zucchini. She hadn't eaten in several days, but she devoured most of the huge chunk of zucchini right there on the spot, then took off with it in her mouth and made a beeline toward the bedroom. I caught her before she ran under the bed and settled her onto the couch so that I could have a long talk with both of the sick girls.

Corey didn't run from me like she did from Pam. She let me pick her up, and she snuggled comfortably into my hands. I was delighted. I had never cuddled one of these animals before, and here was one smiling up at me with shining, intelligent eyes. Daphne crawled onto the couch and joined her sister, so now I had two of these little critters staring up at me with glee as if they had climbed into Santa's lap. Corey said their human father worked on a computer for a living and laughed a lot in front of the screen. Pam called her boyfriend into the room, who confirmed he was a computer programmer and created comic video games. He joined us and excitedly pulled up a chair so that he could hear his two little girls "talk." Corey said the "round blue beads" were the only food that could cheer her. Pam ran to the kitchen and pulled out a bag of round blue cereal from the cabinet. She said it was the only thing Corey would eat in her time of grief.

Corey told me she was mourning the loss of her dark-colored partner, who had died of a terrible illness. Daphne gave me the name "Terry/Teresa." Pam confirmed that Corey's dark-colored sister, Tessie, had recently died. "Pam killed my sister," Corey said. Pam agreed that Tessie had been put to sleep. That explained the fear. Then Pam gave me terrible news. Tessie had been born with a deadly disease called mycoplasma that Corey also carries.

"Tell me it's not going to happen to me," said the radiant little being, trembling in my hands. I couldn't, but I could tell her that her life had meaning, that she was dearly loved, and that if she could summon the strength to survive this pain, she would know joy again. Corey had been in such anguish, grieving the loss of her sister, she had refused to be touched for the last five months. But after she spoke to me, she fell asleep on my chest. She sat in my cupped hands for an hour and a half, snoozing sweetly while I funneled warm energy into her small body. I telepathed with her while she slept.

Corey told me Tessie's spirit is now living with Pam's grandmother, Suzie, on the Other Side. Pam ran out of the room and came back with a framed photo of her grandmother, Suzie, who had passed away the year before. With tears pouring down her face, Pam said that this was impossible.

"Tessie can't be with Grandma! Grandma always hated them! Suzie was always afraid of them! She's a neat freak! She thinks they're gross!"

"Well, not any more!" I argued, with a sly smile. "Tessie reformed her in heaven! She's made a rat lover out of your prim little Grandma!" That's right. Here's the punch line: Corey and Daphne are rats!

Now, this was one of the clearest conversations I've ever had with any animal in my life. What can this possibly mean? There is no spiritual food chain. Can it be that all other animals, no matter how great or small — be they elephants, horses, cats, dogs, parrots, gorillas, or yes, even rats — think and feel the same way we do? They love, they laugh, they hope, they dream, they fear, and they grieve. Daphne's life is no less significant because she's a rat. Corey's anguish is no less painful than yours.

Even these most tiny and underprivileged animals are articulate, emotional, tender beings who have complicated thoughts and loving relationships. What does this say about every rat being injured and maimed in research laboratories all over this earth? I don't know what it says to you, but I'll tell you how I see it. God is not watching from heaven. God is beating inside the trembling heart of every agonizing animal in every confining cage, as they frantically try to open human hearts so that we will stop spreading suffering.

These animals are literally dying for the day that a scientist says, "Oh my gosh. I'm hurting someone. I should stop this." Wouldn't that be nice? Who knows why humans feel the need to create an arbitrary pecking order and decide that small, helpless animals do not suffer? Are you one of those people who doesn't like rats or spiders or snakes? Perhaps you might need to look within yourself at those aspects you'd like to cast out. What is it *in you* that is not worthy of compassion? Of attention? Of time? Of quiet, gentle acceptance? This is where we begin.

And this is *why* we begin: The dazzling upshot of this story is not that I could talk to a rat. Pam asked me if Daphne had ever been "with her" before in a previous life. Daphne showed me the body of a little black and white puppy who had been the love of Pam's life. Pam told me between breathless sobs that she had suspected all along that Daphne had been this very dog. The spunky dog had died shortly before Pam adopted Daphne. And to top it all off, it was this *dog* who loved zucchini! The sneaky pooch would steal the zucchini off the vegetable plate every time Pam had a cocktail party and run to devour it under the bed! Daphne was not describing to me only what she ate *now*. She was telling me about her favorite food in her previous life, and when I gave it to her now, she still liked it! She had changed species, but her tastes remained the same. Could this be an example of quantum memory?

I meet thousands of people who feel they know beyond the shadow of a doubt that their new animal is their old animal in a new body. There is no name for this, a reincarnated animal, so I decided to create one. It's called a Ti Shazi Jenjo. That's Zulu for "a wink from heaven." Look with your heart, not with your head. The journey of love opens all doors. Then let me ask you this: if you knew your dog or horse could come back as a rat or a snake, would that change the way you look at rats and snakes? If you remember we are simply one of four types of primates and thousands of mammals and hundred of thousands of vertebrates and millions of invertebrates, it helps us eliminate our sense of separateness.

ONE OF THESE THINGS IS NOT LIKE THE OTHERS

BY NOW YOU COULD PROBABLY GUESS that I dare to disagree with the common belief that animals have a "collective soul" that gets absorbed into some sort of cosmic mishmash after death and that their spirits lose their individual characteristics. I have spoken with far too many deceased animals who have given me facts about their lives and guardians long after their deaths: names, dates, causes of death, changes of residence, and the comings and goings of the humans left on earth, all in intricate detail. They often tell me the names of the human spirits who keep them for us in heaven, and these spirits are always departed family members (usually grandmothers). Usually, the human spirits talk to me, too.

Because most animals' lives are usually so much shorter than ours, we can have the same animal more than once in our lifetimes. These same spirits can come back to us over and over. There is one form of cosmic super glue in the universe that seals our friendships together for all eternity: Love. There is only one force so strong that it transcends space and time: Love.

The Lumensilta you form with your animal creates a bond between you that keeps you connected on a silver cord of light. Like a needle and thread sewing in and out of a tapestry, the spirit leaves the material world and then comes back, again and again. If you're facing the death of one of your magnificent animals right now, I want you to say this out loud: "I surrender all my past mistakes into an ocean of love that is bigger than I am. I shall sleep in peace and wake in joy. I am secure in the knowledge that good governs." All you need do is pray that your animal returns to you, and your intention will take root in the Universal Mind. So your pact is not just with the animal; there are three beings involved in this negotiation: you, your animal, and Universal Intelligence. How can we expect an infinite mind to be concerned about our little affairs? Because divine guidance is always available to those who dare ask.

If you're facing the loss of an animal, be buoyant, be peaceful, be hopeful. You can discuss with your animal how she wants to die — when and how — and whether or not she needs the assistance of a vet. I know it's hard to stay centered when you're overwhelmed with emotion, but these are the times your animal needs you the most. You can negotiate particular behavior, like asking a dog to put his head on a particular pillow when he wants to say good-bye or to bark at you loudly if he needs the assistance of a vet. If your animal is having intense panic attacks at four in the morning, this is usually an indication that heaven is near (unless that animal is diabetic, in which case, it simply means their insulin isn't lasting through the night). I once asked a horse to lie down and not stand up when she was ready to go, and the morning after I saw her, after months of standing on three legs (she had terminal cancer), she refused to stand up. We can ask our animals to give us signs indicating whether they need to be euthanized or they'd like to go on their own, and we can agree on what the signals will be. Then we can negotiate the particulars if our animals want to come back to us — God willing — when, where, and what form they will take.

Yes, I believe that heaven is simply jam-packed with animals, and your animals will be reunited with both the animals and the humans they love. There are also dimensions that resemble vast, cosmic animal sanctuaries, where there are no humans. This is where the spirits of elephants and cheetahs can live undisturbed. But spirits travel in packs. You and your four-legged loved ones will enjoy life on earth together many times, and the stories I've heard from all over the world are absolutely endless. Here is the tale of one my favorite Ti Shazi Jenjos. This amazing story was written by Laurie Anderson after she came to see me a couple of times. If you have a box of Kleenex in the house, go get it, but know that if the tears come, you'll be drying tears of joy.

"I'll Meet You in the Garden of Eden"

One April morning almost ten years ago, my boyfriend, Larry, gave me the greatest gift of my life. It arrived in a Korbel champagne box, mewing loudly. I opened the box to look into the eyes of the most adorable kitten I'd ever seen. I knew at first glance, this was no normal cat. This was a gift from heaven. I named him Seth.

At that time I was a dance teacher and had recently completed the construction of my new two-story Performing Arts and Gymnastic Center. The center was wonderfully successful, and Seth came to work with me every day to sit in the receptionist's lap and get petted and kissed by all the children as they poured in and out of their dance classes. Our first year together was idyllic, and I fell madly in love with this little seven-toed angel cat.

But in the flash of an eye, my entire life changed. I had a terrible car accident and my life as I had known it spun wildly out of control. Within three months, the Performing Arts Studio was closed. Pride had kept me from telling anyone the real truth about how badly I was internally injured and how much pain I was feeling. A blood clot had formed in my brain from the impact, and I had taken meds to thin my blood. I had endured a ruptured eardrum from an experimental procedure performed to restore my hearing. Infection and fever set in, and I began to bleed through my right ear. I never chose to share my agony with anyone, and I drifted deeper into darkness and pain each day. My business was a huge part of my life, and now it was almost gone. I could not imagine being able to dance or be happy ever again. Healing seemed so impossible. Almost overnight, the students were gone, the money was gone, and I owed everyone. To make matters worse, my boyfriend left me. It seemed best to just give up.

Treatments were not working, and I began to slowly bleed to death. Deep depression overtook me as I disconnected myself from all people and locked my doors and unplugged the phone. I had decided to die at home in my own bed, as I was feeling so very unloved.

The Creator uses what He has, and all I had was my little kitty, Seth. Seth was not about to let me die. He wrapped his body around my head in bed that night and licked up my blood as it trickled from my ear. I would start to drift off into what I knew would have been permanent unconsciousness, but Seth would simply pull me back time after time. He purred so loudly that the noise alone kept me awake. Every moment was so painful that it seemed to last for years. I wanted so badly to die, to be out of this anguish, but I knew there was no one who could really take care of Seth. Who would love him if I died and left him all alone?

Somehow he "spoke" to me and told me to get in the car and drive to the hospital. And somehow I did. I gathered him in my arms, wrapped my head in a blanket, and made it to the car. I ended up in the emergency room, where I actually did die on the table for six solid minutes. Meanwhile, Seth was locked in my car in the parking garage and no one knew he was there.

This is what I remember: When my spirit left my body, I felt a pop and a surge of pure energy. "I" rose to the ceiling above the surgery table, feeling light and free. The pain was gone, and I was filled with a sense of unconditional love. I felt a magnetic pull as I continued to rise upward. Immediately, I could see the thoughts of everyone around me. Suddenly, I had an intense desire to have all of my questions answered about my life. Just as quickly, I was filled with a consciousness and intelligence that already held all of the answers. I have never felt such peace and tranquility! There was no doubt in my mind that I was in the presence of my Creator.

I allowed myself to be pulled upward by a tornado- or hurricane-like wind. I went into a tunnel and knew I was traveling at speeds that are not measurable by our earthly minds. I felt my body healing and restoring itself to its original perfect state. Love filled me and became me. I saw a light in the distance, and I wanted to fly toward it. The desire was stronger than anything I had ever felt before in my life.

As I entered the light, I recognized two figures. One was my grandmother, Becky, and the other was my horse, Bonfire, both of whom had passed away. I experienced an utter explosion of joy and outpouring of love from them. I knew I was home again, and it felt so incredible! I felt the love and presence of our Savior Jesus Christ within this light. He stayed with me as together we reviewed my earthly life as if it were a movie. It was holographic, and I was allowed to see, feel, hear, and become the experiences of every moment all over again. This experience was so profound; there are no words on earth to describe it.

Jesus gently rocked me in his arms and explained that my death was premature and by my own hand, not God's. It was not yet my time. He said everyone's death comes by divine timing, and only when it is right and perfect. I was shown that each person and every animal has a unique and wonderful purpose to fulfill in the overall plan of Creation. At that moment, I was filled with the memory of the complete plan for my individual life. You might say, my pure potentiality was revealed to me.

But then I became filled with an intense sadness! When I was told that I was going back to earth, I begged in my own manipulative way to *please* be allowed to stay! I knew that coming back to earth after being in the presence of my Creator would be the most difficult thing I would ever have to do.

But suddenly, I saw Seth fitfully sleeping in my car in the parking garage at the hospital. No other person knew he was in my car, so no one on earth would ever come to rescue him! Then I had a vision of his purpose for coming to earth. He came in the form of a cat to keep me alive, and he could bring forth a message of love through me for everyone in the entire world to hear, if they so chose! The animals are here to facilitate our enlightenment through their unconditional love. For a split second, I saw his true spirit: an ancient soul and a healer in the higher realms. My gratitude for his existence and sacrifice swelled. In that moment, I realized that if I didn't return to earth, he would die. I had to come back and find the resolve to finish my work on earth.

After returning home from my near-death experience, Seth continued to play the role of my personal angel. He went everywhere with me, never really leaving my side for more than a few minutes. We slept together, ate together, and traveled back and forth to various hospitals and doctors' offices. The next three years were very painful for me, as my immune system began to shut down. As a result, many different diseases and infections ravaged my body. My right ear continued to be a source of much pain, which led to infections and fever. Seth continued his work with me as an incredible source of love and healing energy. He became psychosomatic and took on the same symptoms of whatever infection or disease I was suffering. I remember that when my ear was painful, hot, infected, and oozing, Seth's ear would also become infected as he transmuted the energies for my weakened body and immune system.

I began to realize that we were sharing thought forms and consciousness. One day we were lying in bed together and Seth had wrapped his body around my head on the pillow. I remember feeling so guilty when my thoughts turned to the overwhelming debt that I was facing. I was wondering how would I ever pull out from under all of these bills and how would I ever get well enough to work again. Seth loved me through those hard times and the very sight of him helped me banish some of my fears.

It took me the next three years to really decide to heal and live again. I can honestly say that I would not be here today if Seth had not stepped into my life and just loved me. His love was like a bright and beautiful light that shined into every corner of my life. He simply refused to let me feel pain or be lonely. It was almost impossible to be depressed in his presence. His personality was so cuddly and bubbly that it became increasingly difficult to hold sad thoughts or to spend time feeling sorry for myself.

I began to realize that I was communicating telepathically with Seth on a regular basis. He helped me first to observe and then to be truly grateful for the simple things in life. We began to enjoy sunsets together, birds flying over, lying on the grass, cloud formations . . . and to simply give thanks for the sunshine. By sharing his love with me, Seth brought me to a place where I was also able to feel the love of our Creator within myself. I began to see that through loving my own life and myself, I had opened an energetic flow straight from God.

When little Seth passed away, I was devastated. I knew that I had to come to terms with why he had been allowed to leave the earth plane while I was still here. Since my near-death experience in 1994, I was always just a little bit jealous when I heard that someone died. I felt joy for the soul who passed over, but my own ego would get in the way and I would plead with God to tell me when I would be returning "home" again, too. Now I knew in my heart that I had to go on without Seth and that he had never really left me. I talked to him every day, especially at night while lying in bed. Our telepathic communication continued, as I would feel his gentle presence and wisdom come into the room when I spoke to him from my heart. On many occasions I would drift off to sleep while seeing his gentle face hovering over me. But the pain was still there. I didn't want to live without him.

One day, I was walking into a little market and I picked up a *Learning Annex* magazine. As I flipped through it, my eyes settled upon an advertisement. The class was called "How to Talk to Animals and Get Answers." I registered for the class, knowing I had been doing it for years unconsciously.

In October, I attended Amelia's first class in San Diego. Listening to her talk made me feel like I was with a family member I had known forever. I remember having to leave her class early to go to work, so I approached her with Seth's picture. She spoke the most amazing words I'd ever heard. She said this cat loved me so very much and that he was coming back in the spring! I knew she had contacted him mentally because she mentioned he had seven toes on his paws even though his paws were not showing in the picture! She went on to say that he was an ancient being and a healer of the healers in the spirit world, just as I was told in my out-of-body experience! She said he would be born again on March 1 or 2, but at the moment, he was helping me from the Other Side more than he ever could have from his little cat body on earth. She said that when he returned, he would be gray and white again and look very much the same and that I would recognize him right away.

Then I experienced a wash of love flow over me in a way that is hard to verbalize. In two minutes Amelia had told me more than I had ever hoped to hear. I was absolutely thrilled at the thought of Seth coming back in just a few short months. Instantly, life on earth was happy again and I was filled with joy! During the next two months, I was so elated to know that my friend was coming back, I told everyone and began practicing telepathic communication daily with birds and other people's animals.

That December I registered again for Amelia's class, and when it was over I approached her once again to show her at Seth's picture. I knew she did not remember me from the class I had attended in October, but I just wanted to hear Seth talk through her one more time. Once again, she gave the same reading, almost word for word. The only real difference was that she said Seth would be born in the "Garden of Eden" on March 1 or 2. I wondered what that could mean as I rejoiced once again at the thought of having my beloved Seth back again in just three short months.

As the time of the prophesied birth approached, I began to search for pregnant cats in the neighborhood. I lived part time in Baja, Mexico, so there was a lot of territory to cover. I was so anxious to find the kittens once they were born that I had forgotten that Seth was going to come to me, and that I did not need to search for him. On the eve of March 1 I was in San Diego, and I knew in my heart that the moment of birth was very close.

That next week, my friend Riua in Mexico called. She had found a wild cat and her newborn kittens and had brought them inside her home. The kittens had been born on March 1. I was so afraid to hope that this could be the litter. Was Seth actually back and living in Riua's house? Then it hit me. Riua lived in a big, beautiful botanical garden called *Eve's Garden* in Mexico! Wow!

I was so excited to get to Mexico and drive over to see this beautiful mother cat, Gata, and her newborn kittens. When I looked into the box of five beautiful baby kittens and saw Seth's brand new shining face, I was overjoyed. He looked almost exactly the same, except my beautiful boy had returned as a baby girl! She was just three days old and had the most innocent little rosebud face. When I picked up this delicate little angel cat, we instantly recognized each other. My heart sang out to the entire Universe as I gave thanks for this precious gift.

I was floating on air that first night as I went home after holding baby Ophelia in my arms. It was only a couple of hours before I was on the phone with Riua, asking for permission to take Mama Gata cat and all five baby kittens home with me. Seth had only been away in heaven for six months. But I had missed him so much and did not want to spend one more moment apart. I realized that part of the gift of his return to me would be having the pleasure of raising all of these kittens almost from birth.

Riua delivered Gata and the entire family of kittens to my home in San Diego the next day. Now I didn't have just one gift from heaven. I had an entire family of angels, and we created our own Garden of Eden!

BEHOLD, I MAKE ALL THINGS NEW

IF YOU ARE NOT CHRISTIAN, I don't want you to be put off by the fact that Laurie saw Jesus. The fact of the matter is that whatever your religion, when you die you will be greeted by the deity you consider the most divine. I introduce the deities of other cultures only because many of us have attached limiting patterns to the gods of our childhoods. For example, when we prayed for something and didn't get what we wanted, our trust might have been broken with the archetypes we were taught to worship. Yet there is tremendous power in the collective unconscious allotted to Jehovah, Moses, Mohammed, Jesus the Christ, Buddha, the Beloved, and the Great Spirit. And I honor them all. I personally work with Ganesha, Sekhmet, Quan Yin, Isis, and all the Archangels. I don't care what you call your god. Just call your god.

We can think about this in physical terms and that might be helpful. In order to renew our relationship with the divine, we often need to start over. We have the ability to create new neuropassageways in the brain that greatly increase its potential, a process that I call "Superradiance" — the ability of your brain to become such a powerful generator of energy that it can actually move your intentions into your outer world. First, however, we need to create a feeling of newness. In this clean, pristine state of consciousness we can scrap everything that hasn't worked for us in the past and make a definite, aggressive commitment to start over. In Christian theology this is called being "born again." Then we can find, among other things, new or renewed images of the divine to key into.

In our Judeo-Christian society, nothing is more sorely missed than the concept of the Divine Mother. Although Christianity honors a Mother Mary, the powers of healing, creativity, and omniscient wisdom were allotted to her son, not to her son's mom, who started the whole darn thing. Other more ancient cultures do not put the cart before the horse, but honor the Divine Mother first and foremost. And as logic would indicate, and history books will verify, many of these have been the most peace-loving societies the earth has ever known, and cultures where animals were honored as sentient beings.

In her lively book *Jambalaya*, a rich anthology of African mythology, Luisah Teish introduces the goddess Yimayou, the African equivalent of Venus.

When I lost Mr. Jones, the Maine coon cat who had been the love of my life for eight years, I found myself drowning in a grief for which I had no words. Mr. Jones had been the sanctuary for my heart and my fortress against the assaults of the world. When I was groping through the darkness, I reached, as I always do, for a book. I found the wise words that would give me something to cling to. I copied this passage from Luisah's book, and to this day it remains taped to my desk where I can see it daily. Of the African Mother Goddess, the creatress of the ocean, Luisah writes:

> There is no mountain of trouble that Yimayou cannot wear down,
> No sickness of heart that She cannot wash clean,
> No desert of despair that She cannot flood with hope.

If we believed that, I mean *truly* believed it at the very core of our being, it would mean that we can trust both life and death. We have the intrinsic ability to heal ourselves. We inherit this ability simply by being born into this world where God has created order, which means that we and every process — including death — are part of Yimayou's divine plan. The macrocosm (the universe) is a self-organizing, living organism seeking expansion. Therefore, all of us, as cells in the body of God, have psyches that are constantly seeking equilibrium. Healing and growth are our true nature. When we eliminate all the diseased patterns we've accumulated, we'll find that the very essence of our being is a shining sanctuary of love that craves only to share this love with other beings. Its expression promotes a joyous, exciting evolution of our universe.

LOVE NEVER ENDS

LET'S TAKE A LOOK at what I was doing when I first saw the photograph of Seth, the seven-toed kitten. You already know that you live and breathe and have your being within a universe of gravitational forces. You aren't these forces, but you use them. There are also other forces at play in this world. You could call them divine, or you could call them quantum. All we know for certain is that our science has yet to uncover them, to document, measure, and name them, but that certainly doesn't mean that they're not here. It was not so very long ago that the entire European world thought that the world was flat and that if you fell off the edge, you'd get eaten by sea monsters. But no amount of belief in a flat earth would ever flatten the round world. I use the other forces of nature, too, just like gravity. When you're asking an animal to come back to earth, you're coconducting with the Divine Orchestra Leader. I think these principles would fall under the categories of intentionality and coherence.

I wasn't "predicting the future" when I looked at the photo of Seth's beautiful little face. It was, instead, a lightning-fast negotiation in which I asked him how much time he needed on the Other Side before he came back, what he would like his body to look like when he returned, and where he would like to be found. When I deliver this type of news, I do it as though I'm making a prediction, but that is really not the case at all. In this case I said to Seth, "How much time do you need?" and he named the number of months, so I said, "How about by March 1?" He said, "Okay." I asked, "What would you like to look like?" He said, "The same. She likes me like this, and I love my extra toes." I said, "Where would you like to be found?" To which he replied, "Eve. The Garden of Eden." I asked, "How will she know you?" and he said, "Tell her I'll find her. I'll make my way back to her." That's how it works. I say to the animal, "Do you promise? So we've got a deal?" and if he says yes, it's set in stone.

There have been cases, unfortunately, where last-minute snafus occurred and the returning animal was aborted or died in the womb. But if the first attempt doesn't work, they simply come back again as soon as they can.

Remember, I'm not the only one who can do this type of communication. I want you to listen to one of my students as she has her first huge breakthrough in talking to animals on the Other Side, so that you'll understand that you can learn to do this, too. Here's the success story of Kathryn, who lives in London and works as a healer. Kathryn shows us that her contact with a marvelous dog was not broken by his death.

Sammy on Earth and in Heaven

A friend gave me Amelia's book, which I found mind-blowing. I thought, "How much I'd love to go to a workshop with her," but dismissed this as an impossible dream, since she is based in the States. I was then amazed and excited when, a couple of months later, the same friend emailed me to say Amelia was coming to the UK to hold a workshop on the Isle of Man. We both signed up on the spot. I am building up a practice as a spiritual healer, working with both animal and human clients, and I wanted to work with Amelia so I could communicate with animals alongside the healing.

I practiced a little before the workshop, following the instructions in Amelia's book. I seemed to be able to get through and get information that checked out, at which point I had to pinch myself again and again. I could scarcely believe it. But the confidence wore off quickly, and I became convinced that getting through to the animal had been a fluke and that I would not be able to do it again next time. I so much wanted to be able to do it, but I was convinced that I would not be able to contact any animals at the workshop, that what I got would be shown to be rubbish, and that I'd make a complete fool of myself.

What I did find was that I *could* do it, but that it took extraordinary levels of focus, concentration, and discipline to stay with an animal and get consistently good information, so the quality of what I got was variable. I realized I really needed to practice. I also found that in order to get good at animal communication, I had to be prepared to risk making a fool of myself; I had to have faith in what I believed I had gotten from the animal, even if it sounded crazy. In fact, the crazier it sounded, the more likely it was to be true. The following story took place a few months after that first workshop on the Isle of Man.

Louise had a dilemma, and a mutual friend suggested that I might be able to help. Her elderly dog, Sammy, was very ill, but she was not sure whether or not he was ready to go. As the attachment between them was incredibly strong, she wondered whether she was preventing him from moving on, and whether he was holding on for her sake and enduring terrible pain as a result. Louise wanted to explore communication with Sammy further, in the hope of under-standing how best to help him through this difficult time.

I had never met Louise, never seen a photograph of her, and knew nothing about her, her home, or her background. I asked her to send me a photograph of Sammy but not to tell me anything except the most basic information about the present situation, and to give me a list of the questions she had for Sammy. So we had spoken on the phone only once before I tuned into Sammy for the first time.

Having asked Sammy's permission to talk to him, I began, as always, by asking him some questions about food, sleeping places, and favorite people — things that can be independently verified.

I talked to Sammy three times: twice over three days shortly before his death, and then once some time after the date of his passing. Each time, I emailed my notes to Louise, then she emailed back her reactions. The story of my conversation with Sammy is reconstructed below.

I suppose I both longed for and slightly dreaded getting a com-munication request that would be critical for everyone concerned. It was so important to get good feedback because talking to Sammy was crucial for Louise at this point, and I felt both a huge wish and great sense of responsibility to do a good job for them both. So I was both apprehensive and excited. Luckily, I didn't have much time to get too nervous, as I needed to get the photos, communicate with Sammy, and get back to Louise on the same day. She emailed me sev-eral pictures of a gorgeous, wiry-haired dog with a face full of life and character. I took a deep breath, put myself into a calm and focused state of mind, and gazed into his eyes while I asked permission to talk to him. As I did this, I immediately felt incredibly close to him — as if we had opened up completely to one another and there was no separation between us. The connection was immediate and gentle, and I felt his overwhelming weariness straight away.

Talking to Sammy for the First Time

I've reconstructed my conversations with Sammy and Louise in dia-log form: I am "K," Louise is "L," and the images or words Sammy sent me are "S."

K: Sammy, could you show me Louise?

S: Image of a woman of medium height with midlength brown hair, wearing what looked like thick socks and jogging-type bottoms or dark-blue trousers.

L: I have some black trousers with soft material that could quite easily be mistaken for jogging bottoms and a pair of dark-blue leg armers that could also have that appearance if you didn't see them all the way up.

K: What do you like to eat?

S: Image of a plate of what looked like spaghetti Bolognese — with white ribbon-like pieces in brown sauce.

L: Yesterday after speaking to you, I gave Sammy a plate of minced steak and grated cheese with a choice of either rice or spaghetti. He chose the spaghetti! Thanks for the tip! He hadn't been enjoying his food at all, and was eating very little. After a few days of hand-feeding him it was really rewarding to see him eat on his own.

K: Where do you sleep?

S: Image of a shallow, basket-type bed with a dark blanket in it at the foot of a wooden bed frame — with legs and a bottom board (the opposite of a head board).

L: I think this is where he used to sleep when he could get up and down off furniture. He has his own futon chair at the end of my bed, and he would rest his head against the wooden frame. It had a dark denim cover on it. I moved his bed to floor level about two years ago.

K: Who are your favorite people? Apart from Louise, of course!!!

S: Sammy sent two names, Louise and Tom, and an image of a slim, tall male figure — it was hard to tell his age. From the ground he looked tall! He had dark hair and wore dark clothes.

L: Geoff is my ex-boyfriend and Sam's co-owner; the dark clothes and slim build sound like him. Tom is his fourteen-year-old son. Sammy always perks up when Tom shows up.

K: Where do you like to sleep?

S: Image of Sammy lying with his head on his paws in a very warm place, next to a fire or boiler. There was also an old, knitted jumper or some other kind of knitted thing, which he really liked.

L: He always was a radiator hog. The knitted thing could be a pale green, chunky knit jumper I had a while ago. I used to leave it near him sometimes if I went away and I wanted him to know I'd be back soon.

K: How did you come to Louise?

S: Image of Sammy looking young but full-grown. He was looking and feeling scared and lost/alone in a kind of metal run or pen. He was looking round at me and very fearful. Then he is rushing around, jumping up, energetic and happy.

L: When we first met Sammy, we were told that he had been chained up outside his former owners' house and that he used to get beaten by them. When he came to live with us, he was very loving and outgoing and extremely competitive when it came to games, but also extremely nervous, always flinching if you went near him. He lost the flinching after about six months.

K: Sammy, can you show me where you are in pain?

S: I sensed inside his body and felt pain along the spine and stiffness in his legs. His gums and teeth on the upper right side were also very sore and tender, as was his nose on the left-hand side. It felt generally painful to be in his body.

L: The pain was on his right-hand side, where he had a tumor that seemed to have speeded up its growth over the last few weeks. You mention his nose on his left-hand side. He was bleeding there. The vet thought it was caused either by a tumor or a bacterial infection; he had it for over a year and it stayed pretty stable.

The Royal Veterinary College vets, although excellent, were

pretty keen to do some more very intrusive testing and such on him, but we couldn't put him through it. In retrospect I know I made the right choice. What you got from Sammy here, Kathryn, was really amazing; you already knew Sammy was an old dog and so one might even be able to assume he'd have a few aches and pains, but the fact that you managed to tune into the pain in his gums and nose and choose the correct side for each truly blew me away; you were so specific.

ᴋ: Sammy, do you want to go?

 s: "Louise will always be with me." He did not answer this question straight, but his answers were clear. He showed me himself jumping around outdoors, and it seemed he was showing how he looked forward to being able to do this again. I then saw him bathed in a strong, bright, white light. He was calm and alert in the light. Then I thanked him, tuned out, and ended the conversation.

ʟ: I am really moved by this.

After talking to Sammy, I had taken a deep breath, called Louise, and told her every detail of what I had received. I had my fingers firmly crossed that the points about her, the flat, and the other verifiable details were not completely off the mark. If I got those wrong, why should she have faith in anything else I told her? After putting the phone down, I sat in a quiet place and just absorbed the realization that I had been right on virtually everything.

Rather than hold back anything I judged to be unlikely and play it safe, I had stuck my neck out in asking for details about people Sammy loved and so on, and my head had not been chopped off! Tom was the right name, and I seemed to have seen Geoff accurately through Sammy's eyes! It felt at the same time completely unbelievable and 100 percent true, which seemed impossible but was both exhilarating and confusing. This felt like the ultimate confirmation that I am able to communicate with animals. I could find no other explanation for what I had managed to pick up from Sammy. Unbelievable as it still seemed, I had to believe it.

I reflected on how natural and intimate communicating with Sammy had been. I felt transported into a different, very quiet, and sensitive space. I was struck, as at the workshop, at the lightning speed with which the thoughts, feelings, and answers came back from him — faster than my rational mind could get into gear. I could not have answered my own question that quickly. I realized I could also tell what was coming from him by the fact the answers came fully formed — transposed whole into my mind, rather than formed by it.

But that feedback was so incredibly subtle, almost as if being whispered, so I had to concentrate hard not to miss it. The feelings and images floated by like feathers; I had to focus to spot them and then capture them. But once I had spotted them, I found the visual images were clear and strong and stayed with me long afterwards. None of them was familiar to me in any way, so they were not based on my own experience. And I had been able to feel intuitively where in his body Sammy was feeling pain.

Talking to Sammy Two Days Later

I spoke with Sammy again a couple of days later, and Louise emailed her responses a few days after that, the day after Sammy died. I've combined these two conversations her to show both what Sammy said and how Louise confirmed and responded. She and Geoff had both been with him, right up to the end.

K: How are you?

S: "Tired."

K: What could you eat?

S: A feeling of something soft, easy to have in his mouth.

K: Do you want to go?

S: "Louise will always be with me."

K: Can you give Louise a sign if you want to go? She needs to know it from you.

S: Sammy sent the sensation of a lick and/or pushing his head under your arm (hiding it) as possible signs.

L: He pushed his head deep under my arm about an hour before you called me on Wednesday evening. Even at the time I thought it to be slightly unusual. I had one tiny lick yesterday. Geoff had a few.

K: Are you afraid?

S: "No, it's my time."

K: What do you want me to tell Louise?

S: I got a wave of love and understanding from him.

K: Did the healing help? (I sent him healing several times via his photo.)

S: The thought came that it made him feel more peaceful.

L: I noticed something different about him about the time you must have been sending him the healing. It was almost as if he was in a really deep, relaxed sleep. He was really silent.

K: Are you ready to go?

S: "Tell Louise I am going over green fields." Image of a waterfall and Sammy jumping around next to it.

L: This image will never leave me; the words became our mantra after he went and helped us immensely. We all kept telling each other about how much fun he was having now.

K: What would you like now?

S: The thought came that he wanted to turn the lights down, play music softly, and lie together.

L: Which is exactly what we did: one Johnny Cash CD later we were on our way to an enormously peaceful night's sleep. Madonna's *Ray of Light* CD did the rest.

K: What message should I give Louise?

S: "You gave me my life." Then the image came of Sammy bathed in white light again — this time more like he was under a strong spotlight. There were outstretched, welcoming arms all around him.

K: Louise, I wanted to get you this quickly. I hope it is a comfort to you and does not make you feel even sadder than I know you are already feeling.

L: It is wonderful to read. I'm so touched by the depth of some of his feelings. The tears they are causing are both sad and happy.

After this communication with Sammy, I broke down and wept. I felt deeply privileged to be entrusted with such important messages. I felt Louise's pain at the prospect of losing him, and Sammy's pain at having to leave Louise and the others he loved. But I was also so moved by his vision of where he would be going, his excitement at going, and the loving welcome that seemed to await him. "Tell Louise I am going over green fields" is *exactly* what I heard, and it is so specific. I would never have expressed it in that way — those words definitely did not come from me. As a spiritual healer working with energy from Spirit, I am completely convinced that our souls survive our physical death, and Sammy's vision of what awaited him was a beautiful confirmation of this.

So it was natural to me to wonder, a few weeks after his physical death, whether contacting him in spirit would feel any different, and what he would have to tell me. So we tried it. Talking to him in spirit form felt no different — except that he felt well and full of energy. Again I stuck my neck out, asking for verifiable evidence from Sammy that he was still with Louise, and once again I was stunned by what I got back from him.

Talking to Sammy in Heaven — Some Days Later

I knew that Louise was at her summer house in Sweden but that she could pick up emails, so I tuned into Sammy and emailed her what I got back — exactly as I had done before. I first tried to link in to Sammy a few days after his transition. I got a lot of energy from his picture. I then saw an image of him trying to get me or someone to come and play with him. He was coming up close and running away, with his eyes still on me to get me to follow him. Very playful and eager. A few days later I tuned in to him again, and once more I got a lot of energy off his photo.

K: What should I tell Louise?

S: "Don't be afraid to follow." Again he was full of energy, eager and strong. I then saw him doing that other thing some dogs do: he had something in his mouth and he was shaking it (head down) so that his whole rear end was wagging violently from side to side. He was very engrossed in this, but I could not see what was in his mouth.

L: It's probably that stick again, or a wine cork.

K: Sammy, are you with Louise?

S: "Yes."

K: Can you give me some evidence that you are with Louise? Maybe show me something Louise has done recently?

S: Instantly a clear picture came of planking, like a jetty or promenade, with a sense that this was by water. I don't know whether it was lake or sea, but the feeling was of calm water and a serene, sunny day. There were wooden huts and very few people. I could hear water gently lapping. There was a hollow sound of footsteps on the wooden planking — it was very atmospheric.

L: There is a big, old fishing village on the island next to us. There was a very sunny afternoon a few days ago, and we went over there to meet up with some friends who were anchored on a nearby deserted island. We stopped for a few drinks and then made our way to our friend's dingy, walking around the large marina, all the time on the wooden planking over the water.

S: Sammy sent a tranquil, beautiful scene, with a sense of its being very deserted of people — so quiet.

L: There are several bars and restaurants at this place, and it is considered in Swedish terms to be quite busy. But Swedes are about 90 percent quieter and calmer than Brits, so in comparison to London, I consider it to be extremely quiet and very tranquil. It really does depend on your terms of reference!

s: Sammy sent a sense of you there with another woman or girl, with blonde or fair hair.

L: We were with two guys, one of whom has longish, shoulder-length, very blonde locks.

K: I felt that Sammy was showing me somewhere you had been recently, a place that you (and he) really liked. I know you are in Sweden at the moment, but this was different and definitely by water. Then I got a slightly different scene of you on the water in a boat, moving fast with the wind in your face, and that you loved this.

L: The guys took us out to their boat, which they had left anchored on the deserted island. We spent the evening on the island (which is essentially a very large rock in the archipelago), having a barbecue. We sat in very happy silence after dinner, all of us watching the sun go slowly down over the horizon. I thought about Sammy a lot at this time, imagining that he was there with me and enjoying it as much as I was. After we were done, one of the lads took us back to shore in the dinghy. We sped really fast toward the shore again, with the wind in our faces.

K: Lots of love. I hope this helps a little bit to get you through your grief at his physical loss.

L: It really does. Again, you've stunned me with the accuracy and what you have understood from Sammy. And again, it gives me so much comfort.

It is clear that my fear that I may be feeding back rubbish is still with me, and I expect that it will always be there. But I have learned to find the courage to take a deep breath and report back *everything* I get. I find that afterward it is always the bits that I nearly did not include that turn out to have been the clinchers for the client. And these are the bits that give them faith in the rest of what I have fed back. So training myself to ignore the very efficient built-in editor that is my conscious mind is my big challenge for the future.

How It Feels to Receive
Communication from Animals

Here Kathryn shares how she felt as she did the reading:

I tend to tune in to the animal in the picture in the same way I do when giving absent or distant healing. I clear my mind, ask permission to make a connection, and hold my hand over the picture, waiting for the energy to move under my hand. This can manifest itself as warmth, buzzing, pulsing, or any combination of the three. When I can feel a connection between my hand and the picture, I withdraw my hand, look intently into the animal's eyes, introduce myself, and ask the animal for permission to speak to her. Often, at the point when contact is made, I feel a jolt or a wave of feeling or energy wash through my own body, or I feel subtly altered physical or emotional sensations.

I always ask the animal's human to give me a list of very specific questions around which a conversation can be built. Very rarely, I hear the animal's voice (this is something that Amelia assures me comes more often with time). Sometimes I "hear" thoughts from my own cats; usually it happens when I am busy with something else and am not actively trying to tune in to them. I once distinctly "got" the sentence "You love her more than me" from one of my cats, who was lying on my lap when another one came into the room and I greeted her. Trying to tell the first cat that this is not true while avoiding negatives was quite hard on the spur of the moment. (As Amelia teaches, if you say, "Don't get onto the table" to an animal, they are likely to hear "Get onto the table" — they simply don't hear the "don't." Instead, one should try saying, "Stay on the chair or the floor." I usually add "please" because it does no harm to be polite! The same rule has been shown to apply to human communication as well: to make sure your meaning is clearly heard, it is better to describe what you want in positive terms.) On another occasion, another of our five cats was heading toward the open fireplace when I "got" the sentence "I think I'll just go up there." This cat loves to disappear up the chimney, which nearly gave us a heart attack the first time she did it, but she can't go far and always reappears pretty quickly.

The other way information comes across to me is via visual images. I understand that being in one place and seeing in another place is often called "remote viewing." Sometimes I see the animal in its own environment in a lot of detail. This is useful for verifying that I am really in communication with the animal in question, and it is most reliable when I know nothing about the people or home in which the animal lives, since it would be impossible to separate what one already knew from what one is receiving. At other times, I seem to see through the animal's own eyes. These pictures are mostly from a viewpoint close the ground, and they can show an exaggerated scale (such as when a cat I tuned into was trapped in a shed and saw a little girl look in: to him she looked huge). Very occasionally I will get the intense smell of something, or feel how delicious something tastes.

I make detailed notes while communication is going on, which I then type up and send to the human. I generally like to send them before calling, although in an urgent situation (as in Sammy's case) I will call immediately, and then email the notes. I then ask the human to email me back their responses, as a record of the exchange.

"CAN YOU SEE WHAT I SEE?"

This story isn't about reincarnation. It's about where animals go "in between" lives. It sure came as a surprise to me, and I think you might be amazed, too.

I cried myself to sleep Christmas night of 2003 and battled nightmares of convulsions for hours. The "imaginary" seizures traveled back and forth between me and my little cat, Florabelle, who slept sweetly on her pillow by my head. Of course, Ol' Flo was nonplussed and didn't even wake up while I was being tortured. The tremors seemed to be endless. I'd pray myself back to sleep, then it would start again: shaking, shaking, shaking. I had no reason to be crying. Nothing terrible had happened to me. The flurry of tears and hours of night terrors had not been triggered by anything in my outer world . . . at least not yet. Those of you who saw the film *Minority Report* know that being a "precog" is not always fun. I am like a spider on a web connected with all creation, and when that web shakes, even on the other side of the planet, I often feel the vibrations even before disaster hits.

This was my second night of emotional hell. I had been gripped with terror and grief all of Christmas Eve night as well. I was having a lovely holiday in my outer life, so there was no excuse for my inexplicable sadness. Then, on Christmas day, my mystery was solved. I don't watch television and had not yet heard about the earthquake in Iran, where more than twenty thousand people died and up to one hundred thousand were injured or missing. After I got this gruesome news, I received even more sad tidings from one of my dear friends. Beth, my workshop coordinator in Memphis, emailed to say that one of her beloved dogs, Little Girl, unexpectedly died Christmas night after a series of seizures. Ahh . . . more shaking.

Little Girl was facetiously named — not unlike a two-hundred-pound python I once met named Tiny. Little Girl was a Newfoundland and weighed in at about one hundred pounds. She had been a friend of mine, so the news of her death was tragic indeed. This loss caught Beth in the wake of another tremendous loss. Only a few months earlier, the love of her life, a resplendent Saint Bernard named Amelia Talullah, had just gone on to Higher Ground. Now Beth had another agonizing loss to deal with . . . so soon.

The day after Christmas, I sat at my computer and shut my eyes. I "tuned in" to Little Girl to locate her whereabouts. I saw her joyously united with her best friend, Amelia T. Knowing that spirits have "jobs" on the Other Side, I asked Little Girl what she was doing.

"Digging," she said.

"Digging?" I asked.

"Yes," she said with urgency before she ran off to get back to work. Amelia T bounded over to me, stopping only long enough for me to give her a quick pat on her gorgeous freckled face. "I'm sorry I don't have time to talk now," she said. "What are you doing that's so important?" I asked. "Digging," she said. "And I'm helping the children cross over." She hurried back to her post.

Suddenly, a bright-eyed golden retriever ran up to me, her shaggy fur as golden as aspens in the autumn.

"Tell Vickie I'm here, too," she said. Then she ran off.

She was replaced by a rambunctious brown hound dog. "Tell Linda I said hello, and I'm here digging too!"

"When did you know her?" I asked.

"From New Mexico. Tell her I still love her. Sorry, gotta go," this one yelled as she raced off.

Instantly, a little black and white dog appeared, much smaller than all her tall, burly counterparts but no less determined. "I'm here, too!" she said.

"Who was your mommy?" I asked.

"Connie," she said. "Tell her hello from me. Tell her her beagle says hello." This little one, apt to get trampled underfoot, spoke with such authority that she appeared to be the commander of the troops.

"Are you sure you're a *beagle?*" I asked.

Take my advice, readers, because I'm not using it! Despite all the times I've instructed my students, "Don't argue with the information you receive! Trust your intuition," here I was not only arguing with a dog but I was arguing with a *dead* dog! She woofed in disgust. I waited for her to stamp her paw indignantly and yell, "What part of 'I'm a beagle' do you not understand!?" She didn't. She tried to be polite.

"Just tell Connie her *beagle* is here!!!" she said, exasperated. "What are you doing?" I asked the little dog.

"Digging," she said.

"Where the hell am I?" I asked myself, as I looked down the row of five angel dogs digging side by side. I psychically "backed up" to get a more panoramic view. I saw more angel dogs and more angel dogs, all passionately digging. Then I saw what stood in front of this endless army of dogs. Astonished, I "flew" above it all to get an aerial view.

"What the...?" I whispered.

Then...

"Oh, my God!"

We were in Iran. The dogs floated in the air behind thousands of men — men who were bloody, tear-stained, and desperate, so heart-broken and exhausted they could barely stand. With shovels, picks, and their raw bare hands, they attacked mountains of rubble. Each man had an angel dog floating just off his shoulder and whispering in his ear.

"Dig!" the dogs urged. "Dig! Dig! Don't give up! Just keep digging!" Their little spirit paws whirled feverishly in the air.

I saw one man lift a child out of the rubble only to discover the child was dead. The dog off his shoulder was Little Girl. She funneled a wave of golden light into the devastated man, who heaved with sobs and almost fell to his knees as he held the child's body in his arms. Then I saw the child in spirit: she was upset and disoriented until Amelia T came to her aid and ushered her safely into the Light.

I looked down the ranks at the battalion of angel dogs. All of a sudden, I saw what I had not seen before, as if yet another veil had been lifted from my sight. Tunnels of golden light joined every man with his spirit guide as the dogs channeled energy into the men, filling them with courage, vitality, and hope. As I flew higher to survey the terrain, I saw an army of men and troops of spirit dogs spread out in every direction, endlessly. It was the most stunning vision I've ever been privy to in my life. The horror below was indescribable. But the extent of the devastation, the depth of the tragedy, the ocean of pain, was equaled by the beauty of God's cavalry. Heaven had opened her doors and sent to earth her team of "special forces," a battalion of weightless, timeless, tireless crusaders — all canine — each one the very embodiment of courage and good cheer. No human angels could have handled this tragedy better. I didn't know animals did this. I didn't know God did this. I was utterly floored.

I brought myself back to my waking world, wiped at my hot tears, and typed the dog's messages to their former owners. I had the strong sense that Little Girl had crossed over at that precise moment in time just to aid this cause.

As for the other dogs who had messages for their human loved ones, Connie, Vickie, and Linda, I wasn't absolutely sure who they were. Vickie Schroeder and Connie Zimet are two of my best workshop coordinators, but I had no conscious knowledge of the two dogs who came to say hello. Connie is one of my best friends, and she had never mentioned the beagle before (thus my argument with the pint-sized drill sergeant). And Linda Sivertsen is one of my best friends in the world, but I knew nothing of this dog that lived with her back in New Mexico.

Vickie emailed back to say the golden retriever was Morgan Xanthe, one of her first goldens and reddish as red could be. She had rescued Morgan from a divorce. Vickie wrote, "She was the love of our lives. I could see where her love extends beyond all existence."

Beth emailed to say that Little Girl's passion for digging had taken its toll on her backyard for many years. And I knew that Amelia Tallulah had been a therapy dog in life, so it came as no surprise that she was helping children transition into the spirit world.

When Linda called, I told her the brown hound dog looked like a cross between her two present dogs, Adobe and Digger. Linda said Sixdance had been Adobe's sister, and she did indeed live with her back in New Mexico. She added that Sixdance had been "quite a digger!"

But when I got Connie's email, I burst into tears. It was the biggest surprise of all. Connie had spent many joyous years in love with a tough little beagle named Katie, whose air of authority dwarfed her modest height. Connie wrote to say that at first glance, she'd thought I was mistaken. She remembered Katie to be brown and white, not black and white, but when she rooted out her pictures of Katie, she saw that the little Snoopy-model was indeed more black than brown. I called Connie, laughing and crying, and Connie said, "Yes, that Katie was quite a digger!"

Animals are not what they seem. Our world is not what it seems. There is comfort, order, and grace in the universe. Animals are more magical than any of us could ever dream; so is your world . . . and so are you! No one knows where Mozart's Sonata in C Major was before he composed it, or where David was hiding before Michelangelo freed him from a slab of marble. Where was Middle Earth before Tolkien released it from his imagination? Do artists work alone? Or are they surrounded by invisible cherubs who might be sporting more than wings? Perhaps their muses have whiskers or hooves or fluffy tails or sharp claws with tufts of fur between their toes. Do any of us work alone?

Maybe, just maybe, you've got an angel on your shoulder, too, giving you the impetus to write, to paint, to sing, to dance, to design one more website, to see one more patient, to heal an aching relationship, or even just to "dig" through the paperwork on your desk. Close your eyes and say "hello" to someone who still loves you, a spirit sweetheart who may have left her body on earth, but not her soul.

BUTTON UP YOUR OVERCOAT

WE'RE GOING FOR A RIDE. Those who only see the outer edges of living beings are not concerned with the interior life or the afterlife. If you've gotten this far into this book, you've proven you are not one of those people. Let's move now into Nature's most glorious dance, our ability to walk between the worlds.

Take out the photo of an animal who's gone to heaven and hold the picture in your lap quietly. Our quest is to locate what psychological programs you're running, turn them off, then download the program of the animal you'd like to contact.

Our goal is to completely silence your mind, shut down the program that reflects your experience of life on earth (Explicate Order), and let yourself melt into a spaceless, timeless void of bliss (Implicate Order). Once you've removed yourself from your own identity, from Explicate Order, and have expanded your consciousness out into the Implicate Order, we will learn how to navigate through the Dreamspace, then synch up and become even more connected.

In the words of our hero astronaut, "In quantum lingo, the wave-particle duality implies that quanta have both wave and particle characteristics, meaning that a 'packet' of energy has a finite amount of energy, and is associated with a particular frequency. We know that a quantum hologram consists of groups of such packets, of different frequencies and different phase relationships." That gives each quantum hologram a distinct character. So I'm asking you to send out a frequency that will access the quantum holograms of your animal, no matter where she is in space and time. You will cease to be a particle and will become a wave, instead. In this way, you will join with the animal in the photo and form Resogenesis on this arc of energy.

You will develop your own style of communicating with animals and clients; it depends on what techniques you like, what you do well, and what you explore on your own. Your personal style will depend on what you love. Be precise about what you're trying to accomplish, and your results will be more detailed and noteworthy. Make a list of questions so that you'll have direction for your inquiry. Don't just go free-floating into the void.

The meditation that follows was offered to us as a gift from my South African protégé Wynter Worsthorne. Here we can practice tuning into the animals who've "gone on to higher ground" and even ask them if and when they want to come back.

JOURNEY INTO THE LIGHT

I felt a need to write this meditation while helping people deal with the death of their beloved animal companions. The one thing so common in these cases is the sense of guilt that people carry with them — even though, more often than not, they did nothing wrong. In this meditation you can meet up again in a safe, beautiful place, and you can see for yourself where your beloved's spirit spends his time. You can talk to him and get messages back from him in a space where no guilt exists — a space where there is only love and freedom.

Sit comfortably and close your eyes. Quiet your mind. Slowly take yourself back to the place where you met your spirit guide. Step into the light ... feel the peace and protection you have here. Call your personal spirit guide to be with you on this journey.

See your spirit guide coming toward you and thank him for being with you. Ask him to guide you to this special place. Let him go in front of you . . . let him lead you. You are following him through a dense forest; it is a quiet and peaceful place, a place full of magical potential. The ground is soft beneath your feet; the air is warm and full of forest smells. Other animals may come and be with you, to give you their love and warmth.

In the distance you see the most beautiful light streaming through the trees. As you move toward the light, the trees start thinning out and you emerge from the forest into a gentle meadow. The light is shining onto you, flowing over you. Step into it. You are transported into a world of light, a world so full of love and peace it takes your breath away. Stay there for a while, drinking in the light and love that surrounds you. Then start moving forward into this world; as you move you start seeing things that are familiar to you. You know this place; you've been here before.

Look up and see who is before you. There he is — the beloved animal whom you thought had gone from you forever. As you move toward him, he moves toward you. You meet and reunite with a warmth you had almost forgotten. Feel the love flowing between you, feel the warmth and joy of being together again.

He is young again. He is healthy; there is no pain, no sorrow — only lively joy. He is here as whole and as happy as he ever was.

Spend time with him now and tell him everything you want him to know. He understands you and will listen. This is no place for sorrow, no place for guilt. Only joy and happiness exist here. Once you have finished saying what you need, be still and listen. He has a message for you. Listen with your heart, listen with your soul.

Spend time being with him, stroke him in all the places he loves — scratch behind his ears, tickle under his chin, tickle his tummy, feel the softness of his body beneath your hand. Play together, run together, play the games you used to play.

Others may join you, possibly family and friends who have crossed over into the light. Listen to them. They have all come to tell you that they are with you always; this world of light is part of your world. It is as easily accessible as stepping through a door. You can come and be with them at any time.

Know, too, that the one who met you is *with* you — he comes to visit you from this place as often as he wants, and he is pleased that now you have found your way to him. Know that whenever you need to, you can be here in an instant. All it takes is a thought.

Spend some more time there with your loved ones. Feel their warmth and love, take heed of their messages, and know that they are with you forever and always.

The animal friend who met you stays with you as you walk back toward the light through which you came. Your spirit guide is waiting to lead you back through the forest. Your friend goes with you for some of the way, to show you that he is next to you and can come to you when you need him. He leaves you with that knowledge, the knowledge that your spirits are together for eternity.

Walk back through the forest with your guide; he is next to you, giving you strength and warmth and love. Smell the forest smells; hear the music of the birds. Soon you come to the place where you were met by your guide. Many animals are with you, acknowledging you and thanking you for letting yourself back into nature.

Step through the light that brings you back to your physical body. Slowly become aware of the sounds in the room. Become aware of your breath, your heartbeat. Wiggle your toes. Move your fingers, and when you are ready, open your eyes.

AMBASSADOR OF MIRACLES

YOU CAN USE THIS MEDITATION to attract the gifts of heaven. But prayer and intentionality only work when all doubts and fears are put aside. When you have a problem, say, "I have an opportunity for self-expression, and God *does* know what to do about it." You are always in the mind of God, so your problems are in the mind of God. Divine Intelligence has every answer. You are not struggling alone. You are in partnership with the only power that is. Instead of telling yourself, "I don't know what to do about it," say, "God knows what to do." Put your problems on the altar of faith.

In the next chapter, I focus on practical day-to-day life and what you can do to employ some of these new ideas. I'll introduce to you my heroes and best friends, the champions of the animal rights movement, who have devoted all their attention to saving innocent creatures everywhere. I look at our spiritual concepts on an earthly level and explain how activism may enhance our lives and save the lives of the animals we love.

CHAPTER ELEVEN

The Big Picture

> Cowardice asks the question, Is it safe? Expediency asks
> the question, Is it politic? Vanity asks the question, Is it popular?
> But conscience asks the question, Is it right? And there comes
> a time when one must take a position that is neither safe,
> nor politic, nor popular; but he must take it because
> his conscience tells him that it is right.
>
> — MARTIN LUTHER KING, JR.

"THEY AREN'T JUST FINGS"

CHRISTY STABBED A PUPPY to death with a pair of scissors. Social workers counseled her until Christy felt remorse for her actions, but when the
idea finally sank in that the puppy had suffered, Christy tried to kill herself with the scissors. Christy was six years old at the time. She was put
in a hospital until the courts mandated that she live in St. Joseph's Children's Treatment Center in Dayton, Ohio, until such time she would not
harm herself or anyone else. My friend, Vickie, worked with Christy to
impart the knowledge that animals do have feelings, emotions, and love
for everyone — even those that hurt them.

As you know by now, my life sounds an awful lot like a fairy tale, from
staying in castles in England and lecturing in Vienna to visiting elephant
and tiger sanctuaries all over the world. But even in this avalanche of
opportunities, there's something special I've always wanted. Something
private. Something precious. Something that wasn't going to make the
NBC Nightly News. I've always wanted to talk to children like Christy. But

I feared that it was the one wish life would never grant me, because my work is too controversial. I never believed a professional psychic could be invited to speak to abused children, to hold tiny, sticky fingers and listen to tearful, stumbling stories.

Well, turns out God was online. Last year, my dream came true when I was invited to St. Joseph's, a high-security treatment center for severely abused children, some of whom had been abused by their own parents.

Vickie Schroeder, my super workshop coordinator in Dayton, Ohio, has been running a pet-assisted therapy program at St. Joseph's for the last four years. Through her self-created pet therapy program, she's brought an array of animals into the intensive treatment unit — a facility that is so high security that every single room is secured with locks. Vickie's mission, with the assistance of her three glorious golden retrievers and one yellow Labrador retriever, has been to convey the importance of compassion and to allow these kids to commune with animals even if they can't make meaningful connections with other humans.

The day I visited, the four dogs showed me the ropes. Abbie, Jake, Jesse, and Ellie May flopped down on the carpet, grinning, while dozens of little hands caressed their shaggy butterscotch bodies. The children, totally entranced, knelt around the dogs to pet them. The dogs' golden fur, sparkling eyes, warm licks, and sloppy kisses created a safe oasis for these kids who had been so unforgivably betrayed by the world.

I didn't get to meet Christy. After Vickie's tutelage, Christy had moved on, but not before she had made it her job to explain to all the new children that animals can think and feel, so they must be treated with the utmost gentleness and respect. Bravo, Vickie and Christy, for a miracle well done!

The children I met that day were no less spellbinding, and their stories were no less tragic than Christy's. The morning before I visited St. Joe's, I sat silently praying in my hotel room, bracing myself for whatever horror stories the afternoon could bring. When I asked God to show me my assignment for the day, I heard a voice in my head. "Matthew," it said. The name was crystalline and the voice was loud. "Matthew," I whispered. "Got it."

An hour later I was kneeling down, shaking hands with ten kids huddled around the dogs, and I asked them to introduce themselves. One twelve-year-old, blue-eyed blonde boy was particularly excited to see me. If you met this good-looking, cheerful, articulate kid on the sidewalk, you'd never guess he lived in an intensive treatment unit. Our eyes locked as he took my hand. "Hi. I'm Matthew," he said. My heart melted.

I asked the children if they had ever hurt animals. One precious little boy with a lisp said he put the cat in the microwave . . . but only for a second, and the cat was "o-tay!" A few more told remorseful stories of how they had killed hamsters and turtles. Then it was Matthew's turn: "Back when I was smoking [crack], I smashed a cat in the head with the butt of a shovel and crushed its skull. There was blood everywhere, and my mother took it to the emergency vet, but it died anyway."

I was careful to not let my face betray me. I asked him how he felt after he did it, and if he understood now that animals have feelings.

"Yeah, now I do!" he said excitedly. "I would never hurt another animal!"

"Me neither! Me neither!" they all chimed in.

I asked one talkative five-year-old girl what she thought animals think about all day. Her list was extensive and carefully detailed, but it ended with ". . . their families, mostly. They think about their families and how much they love them." The entire group agreed.

Some of these children are not allowed to see their parents at all, for fear that the parents will further abuse them. I marveled at the children's comprehension of animal sentience and wondered how many "normal," "healthy" kids would give this much credence to animals' emotions and intelligence. I asked them if they'd forgiven themselves for hurting animals in the past. The room went silent. I glanced around the circle of sad faces and downcast eyes.

I asked them if they'd ever rescued animals before. Pandemonium! A bird with a broken wing had been freed from a barbed wire fence! A squirrel had been rushed to the emergency vet! And so, so many insects had been rescued from swimming pools! I asked how it feels to help animals. "Great!" "Wonderful!"

The long-winded five-year-old summed it up: "It feelths ethspethally good to help wittle animals who can't help themthelves." And then the little lisping one topped it off, "They aren't just fings. They have feewings, too! It makths me happy to makth them happy!"

I explained that even when we can't help each other, or in those moments when we can't even help ourselves, we can always help animals . . . and it always feels good. I asked them what they wanted to be when they grew up.

"I'm going to be a vet!" I heard someone say. He said it calmly, but with great authority. I spun around to identify the owner of the voice. "I used to hurt animals, so now I'm going to spend the rest of my life healing them," he said.

"Yes," I said, taking his hand. "You're going to be a vet, Matthew. You're going to be the best vet in the entire world."

On the way to the car, Vickie explained to me that some of these precious children had been "placed" in twenty-five homes by the time they were twelve, and that my mild-mannered Matthew would fly into suicidal rages during which he would smash his head against a table and not be able to stop. The abuse he had suffered at others' hands was so atrocious, I won't mention it here.

Golden fur, sparkling eyes, warm licks, and sloppy kisses may be the only safe oasis these children have in the entire world. Here they can love and not be hurt — until, God willing, the day may come where that loving connection expands to include humans once again.

Leaving Matthew in there utterly broke my heart. But at least I knew he would be in the safekeeping of the loving staff at St. Joseph's and enjoy coveted visits from Vickie and her four golden angels. I promised to see them again when I returned to teach in Dayton the following year.

Then one of the staff members gave me some news that was even more heartbreaking. The funding for St. Joseph's has been cut and the hospital was about to shut its doors. Sure enough, St. Joseph's recently closed and the children were relocated. Many were sent home. Those children needed our help, and we didn't get there in time.

"What can I do?" This is the one question I hear more than any other, every single place I teach. Vickie Schroeder wasn't sitting on her couch, waiting for someone to tell her what to do. She took her four dogs and her own life to a higher level, and she did it all by herself. This time we have on earth is not about what you can *take*. It is only about what you can *give*. People come to me from all over the world asking me to dictate their life's work. I can't. I don't have assignments for any of you. I don't know what you should do with your life. But *you* do. Your desires are God's desires trying to manifest through you. Act on them.

A NEW SCIENCE, A NEW RELIGION

AS WE BEGIN THIS NEW MILLENNIUM, we need an entirely new way of looking at our world, a paradigm where science and religion can stand hand in hand, without cruelty, without the misconceptions of the past, recognizing truth while honoring consciousness as fundamental in all living things. We could call it a new philosophy, the Language of Miracles, one in which we treat our fellow earthlings with love and reverence, and honor the "supernatural" abilities inside ourselves. We're four hundred years late in updating our scientific beliefs about animals and their consciousness and sorely dragging our feet in our own spiritual evolution.

Descartes may have deemed that other animals are nonthinking, nonfeeling automatons — less significant than we well-oiled human machines — but for a bunch of abused kids in Dayton, Ohio, four golden dogs were the center of their universe one wonderful afternoon; and by bringing those children and dogs together, Vickie Schroeder was able to help those children feel that they, too, have a place in a universe that is more than a machine. And these children wouldn't agree with Descartes; they know that animals are a big part of the compassion found on this planet. By restoring the dignity of the animals, we might be able to reinstate their rightful place in this world. But can we evolve quickly enough to shepherd and protect earth's animals and to save endangered species from extinction?

The chorus to a favorite song we sing in church is "What would love do here? Would it turn away in fear?" I'd like to introduce you to some of my heroes, the maverick, whoop-ass activists who have created a blueprint for my life and taught me by example to never turn away in fear. Each one of these heroes has a lesson for me, and I hope that together these people and the affirmations they inspire will motivate you to help change the world. Our affirmation for Vickie is "My job is to inspire positive change."

THE CHEETAH GODDESS

ONE OF THE MOST INSPIRING of my heroes is a drop-dead gorgeous powerhouse named Annie Beckhelling. She invited me down to Cheetah Outreach, the sanctuary she founded in Cape Town, South Africa, to work with her spotted angels. There I fell in love, live and in person, with God's feline masterpiece — the fastest cat on earth. When I met her cats, who were playing in spacious pens, I marveled at how seamlessly the sanctuary functions. I've never seen big cats so happy in captivity.

When I asked Annie how she started this glorious sanctuary, she told me that in 1991 she found one single orphaned cheetah in Namibia, Africa. Shadow was just a baby then, sick and alone in a cage. His parents and siblings had been killed by poachers, and he was for sale. This orphaned cub motivated Annie to learn more about the plight of the cheetah and to ultimately found Cheetah Outreach. When I quizzed her about what on earth possessed her to believe she could start a cheetah sanctuary all by herself, with no prior experience, she said, "I didn't know the first thing about cheetahs, and I didn't know anything about how to run a charity. I only knew one thing. I knew I could. And I knew it would work."

It did work. Annie conceptualized promoting the case of the cheetah by introducing tame cheetahs as "ambassadors" to the cheetah-phobic community to increase awareness and education. In January 1997 Annie launched the project with a hectare of land provided by Spier Wine Estates, located in Stellenbosch, South Africa. A six-year-old male cheetah named Inca joined her team, so educational efforts began with two cheetahs: Shadow, who traveled to community events, and Inca, whose role was to greet Spier visitors. Cheetah Outreach then set out to introduce cheetahs to the South African community. Shadow was the first ambassador to be taken into schools, children's hospitals, and community events. She educated children as well as adults, including farmers who shot cheetahs that wandered onto their property in search of prey.

In the first year alone, Cheetah Outreach and Shadow visited more than fifty thousand men, women, and children by traveling to educational facilities, community clubs, hotels, malls, and various public events. At Spier, with an average annual visitorship of 350,000 people, Inca was able to greet more than 10 percent of the guests touring the lovely estate.

Annie's goals with the Cheetah Outreach program were to promote the survival of the free-ranging South African cheetah and to plant the seed of the conservation ethic in the process. Along the way she hoped to increase the respect and pride that disadvantaged South African youth have in their indigenous animals by using the cheetah as an ambassador species. Annie Beckhelling has quickly become an icon in the world of animal conservation. My visit to Cheetah Outreach became the first step in my own quest to help sustain the survival of the cats that I consider to be Mother Nature's masterpiece, and Annie does need our help — yours as well as mine. Even with her successful breeding program in place, some experts predict that the cheetah will be extinct by 2015. That is simply unacceptable in my world.

I had the thrill and honor of having one of Annie's ambassador cheetahs attend my Cape Town workshop as our guest teacher, and during that visit I also went from pen to pen at Annie's sanctuary, where I worked with each of her cats. A cheetah named Zaza told me that her best friend was a black and white dog and she was crazy about a man named Bob. Even I doubted myself when I heard about these far-fetched friendships. But one of the volunteers at the sanctuary confirmed that a black and white dog had grown up with Zaza and was her favorite playmate. I was stunned. I didn't know cheetahs played with dogs. More astounding still was when the volunteer told me Zaza had a new keeper named Bob. But then, in the midst of our conversation, Zaza disappeared.

One minute she was sitting in front of me, letting me scratch her glorious wiry fur and wildly licking my fingers. The next minute, she had dematerialized. The volunteer pointed across the field and laughed. A man was riding a bicycle down the sidewalk just outside Zaza's pen a quarter mile away, and Zaza had decided to chase him off — at about thirty-five miles an hour. I've never seen such poetry in motion.

If it weren't for Annie, Zaza wouldn't even be alive. So let's consider this: If love itself found an orphaned cheetah, dying in a cage, waiting for a cruel and untimely death, what would love do here? Ask Annie Beckhelling. Love would rescue the cat. Lots of people say animals are important to them. But if you show me your calendar and your checkbook, I'll show you what's important to you.

Sincere intention will release us from the bondage of outdated and destructive habits of the past. If we are going to live creatively, then we have to create new patterns. Don't settle for what you're given. Your conscious thought is vital and important and allows you to make choices deliberately and to direct your own good fully and completely. We are taught that the quality of grace comes from God. Grace gives us the ability to be confident, calm, poised, and in charge, and do the right thing at all costs. Grace provides us with the confidence of knowing that when you step forward with courage to protect less fortunate beings, God will protect you; but understand that grace is at its greatest when it is tested under fire. Our affirmation in honor of Annie is "I choose to live my life at the level of grace in the face of all apparent obstacles."

THE QUEEN OF PURRING COMPASSION

ONE OF THE BIGGEST COMPLIMENTS I've ever been given was at a book-signing: someone slipped me a note that said "The founder of PAWS LA (Pets Are Wonderful Support — Los Angeles) is in your front row." I hadn't even invited her. This accomplished woman showed up all by herself. Nadia Sutton quickly became one of my favorite women on the planet. PAWS LA is a charity dedicated to helping people living with AIDS and other life-threatening or disabling illnesses keep their beloved pets by providing services such as veterinary care, pet food, and grooming. A group of caring volunteers deliver the food when necessary and help with such tasks as walking the dog, changing the kitty litter, or transporting the pet to veterinary appointments if the person is homebound or incapacitated. Some volunteers called "buddies" are assigned to one person so that they can establish a more personal relationship.

Without PAWS those suffering people would have to give up their beloved little animals who give them so much unconditional love and healing energy.

When I asked Nadia how on earth she founded this amazing program, she said that back in 1989 she had a friend who was in the hospital and was dying of AIDS. He suddenly took a turn for the better and was told he could be discharged and go home. He said to the doctors, "No, I'd rather stay here and die." When they asked him why, he said, "My cats have already been taken away." PAWS all began when Nadia got his cats back for him. Under the direction of Nadia's friend, the wonderful Pamela Magette, PAWS LA is thriving and caring for 1,800 clients and their 2,400 animal companions. The organization has expanded to help low-income seniors keep their animals when they need them the most. With the help and mentoring of PAWS LA and PAWS San Francisco, many similar organizations have been started nationwide.

Nadia never sat around thinking "I'm going to start one of the most successful charities in America." Something needed to be done, so she did it. She had the gumption to get up off her fanny and take the first step. What made her do this? What was Nadia listening to? The voice of love inside her own heart — the quiet, persistent voice of love. An act of kindness so simple and small turned into a divine destiny to bless the entire country.

When you have the desire to help someone, human or animal, don't question your competence or credentials. Just do it. If you give 30 percent, the Universe will come soaring in to give 70 percent and champion your cause. I promise. Another way to look at it is this: there are thousands of people out there who care about the same things you do, but they need you to be their leader. People will come up the gangplank to help you, but you can't find your crew unless you're willing to be the captain of the ship.

Our affirmation in honor of Nadia is "I am here to be in command of my own life." And equally regal is Nadia's inspiration and passion, a resplendent Maine coon cat, Lady MacDuff, whose only affirmation is "I am here to be in control of Nadia." Such a team!

THE SUPERHERO

ONE OF THE MASTER KEYS that unlocks the doors to the power of the universe is passion. So, here is my tribute to Mr. Passion himself, the most controversial animal rights activist in America, the man whose life is a living tribute to the glory and triumph that only courage, patience, persistence, stubborn fury, fearless power, and endless compassion can bring.

We all have heroes. Mine spent twenty-three days in solitary confinement for a nonviolent civil rights protest against a university that was torturing animals in lab experiments so heinous they defy all description. He got arrested for locking arms with other animal lovers and refusing to leave the campus until they got a meeting with the dean. While in prison he met the convicted murderers Richard Ramirez and the Menendez brothers. When they asked, "What are you in for? Murder?" he answered in his tough, deep Brooklyn accent, "No, I rescue bunny rabbits — got a problem with that?"

This hero is Chris DeRose, the president of a charity called Last Chance for Animals. A former police officer, Chris uncovers atrocities against animals and tries to bring them to the attention of the public. He is best known for busting theft rings of criminals who steal dogs and cats out of people's own yards and sell them to laboratories. Yes, it really happens. Some laboratories appreciate the acquisition of "tame" animals because they are more docile while they're being hurt or killed under the guise of experimentation. A one-man police force for animals in distress, Chris is the Bodhisattva savior of all animals everywhere, and the only man I know who should go through life wearing a cape. But he spends a lot of time in jail, instead.

I'd like to share his latest success with you. I ran into him recently in the Dallas–Fort Worth International Airport. I was on tour and only in this airport for a quick plane change. Something told me to walk down the concourse and sit in a particular chair. So I did. Not even reading a book, I sat at a gate that wasn't mine, wondering why Spirit had told me to sit there. Two minutes later, I found out. I heard a voice say, "Amelia? What are you doing here?" Chris and I both live in Los Angeles, so this chance meeting in a huge airport in a distant city among tens of thousands of travelers was pretty stunning.

"That's not the question. What are *you* doing here?" I asked. He literally jumped up and down, grinning with a smile that would light up all of Dallas as he told me. Now, this is a big Italian man with a black belt in karate, an ex–New Jersey cop, not the kind of guy who cries in movies, but his eyes filled with tears of joy as he told me the news. "You know that bastard I've been chasing for the last eight years? The one who steals people's pets and sells them for experiments all around the country to universities and hospitals. The one who kills or lets die of neglect about five hundred dogs and cats a year and sells about six thousand of these stolen pets a year to research — he's the one we nailed. He *was* the most feared animal trafficker in northern Arkansas and southern Missouri. No more — he is finished once and for all. The largest Class B licensed dealer is permanently out of business and has lost all his money and holdings — over two million dollars worth and a lot more too. I got him! I got him! I got him! I finally got the bastard!" His voice trembled and I burst into tears as I leaped out of my chair to give him a trumphant hug. He explained he was flying around the United States on a press tour to tell the media about his success.

So far in this book, I've made a point of not telling you any gruesome stories that would break your heart, but we need to get real now. Please look at it this way: the more conscious the system, the more freedom of action. Either we create our own reality, or our reality gets created for us. The rule of thumb here is "Act, or get acted upon." As long as we have choice, our world is not a mechanistic, predetermined system. We've got to be conscious and look the evil in the eye, or we can never take back our world from the animal abusers.

When I saw Chris, he was jumping for joy over the conviction of a man he'd been chasing for eight years, a man who kept puppies in hideous conditions to sell to laboratories, including those of prestigious universities, and who even stole puppies and kittens from the front yards of their own homes. In Chris's book *In Your Face*, he gives his account of what he experienced out at the Baird ranch, a puppy farm from which several hundred thousand animals had been sold to labs. Here Chris found live puppies piled high on the carcasses of dead puppies, and all up to their eyeballs in their own feces. He said the stench from all the animal carcasses could be smelled from a block away. "Perhaps these suits and university 'Nazi doctors' have no eyes or hearts or consciences, but they do have noses," he wrote.

Now let's get clear on what's going on here in case any of this is new to you. Most of you are probably aware that animals like rats and monkeys are used in laboratory testing at universities, hospitals, and pharmaceutical companies. But you might not realize that these same labs experiment on dogs just like yours in the name of science. These are called "puppy labs" or "dogs labs."

Even if the dogs at the Baird ranch had been healthy and cared for as puppies, they still would have been sold to labs where they would face a terrible life. Technically, lab animals are not always killed. Allowing them to die would mean that the corporation would lose its investment; if subject number 666 dies in the cage, "it" has to be replaced. (They number instead of name the animals to help the lab assistants and students not get "attached" to them and try to rescue them. Instead, they try to keep the animals alive so that their anguish is seemingly endless while atrocities beyond your wildest nightmares are performed on them in the name of "medicine" or "science" or "improved products." So no matter what heinous conditions the puppies survived at the Baird ranch, it was no match for the anguish they were about to endure for the rest of their lives in these labs.

For example, one university in Southern California was breaking the legs of animals and subjecting them to third-degree burns with no anesthesia so that the students could face "realistic situations" during their final exam. So many students told their parents, who tipped off animal rights activists, that the exam dates had to be changed again and again to avoid public exposure. I think the students' time would be better spent under the tutelage of real vets performing necessary surgeries. Other puppy-lab "research" has been funded by tobacco companies, whose researchers pump smoke into the dogs' lungs so that they can breath nothing but smoke while the scientists monitor how quickly the dogs heal.

Chris DeRose's career as an animal rights activist began when a malamute dog, tortured beyond all definition, died in his arms in a soundproof lab where no one could hear the desperate cries of the animals. Chris had invited himself in to take photographs and shoot some videotape. His forbidden footage was aired on CNN, allowing some viewers to actually identify their own animals on the news. They stormed the lab to reclaim their stolen dogs. The public is not supposed to know about the "Nazi-doctor" behavior that takes place behind closed doors in these corporate research organizations, universities, and hospitals, but Chris changed that, at least for one special moment in time. He was able to reunite some of the humans with their dogs. Other heartbroken people were only able to get the collars and tags of their missing dogs.

Mahatma Gandhi said, "The greatness of a nation and its moral progress can be judged by the way its animals are treated. Vivisection is the blackest of all black crimes that man is at present committing against God and his fair creation." And Chris DeRose said, "I want my country to return to greatness." My affirmation for Chris is "My thoughts and actions matter. I am the embodiment of God's love, and I champion the innocent at all costs."

THE MAVERICK

I MET DR. MARC BEKOFF at the very same SPCA convention in San Francisco where I met Bernie Siegel. Now, mind you, after my upbringing in rural Texas and Louisiana, I had my own ideas about the evils of "sciii-yunce" and how animals are treated in the name of medicine. I read in the program that Marc was a former Guggenheim Fellow and author of sixteen books, including *The Encyclopedia of Animal Rights and Welfare*, but he was a professor of... oh, my God... "sciii-yunce."

None of his animal rights credentials had any credence in my mind;

as far as I was concerned it was all lip service. As I settled down to hear him speak, all I could think was "He's a biologist. He cuts up cats for a living, right?"

I decided to sit through his talk, just so I could yell at him later. But as he launched into his lecture, the cloud of gloom started lifting off of me. By the time he started his slide presentation, the piss and vinegar had begun to drain out of me and was getting replaced by something sweet and effervescent — like cerebral champagne. I found him talking about animals as I talk about them, caring about animals as I care about them, seeing animals and perceiving their rich emotional lives as I perceive them, loving them as I love them — no excuses, no objectifying, no equivocating, no exceptions. The bottom line: Dr. Bekoff's life's work revolves around stopping torturous animal experiments.

"But wait," I wanted to yell out, "I thought scientists were supposed to believe..."

He quoted from an article he'd written:

I believe holistic and heart-driven science is needed, deep science that is impregnated with spirit and compassion. Holistic, heartfelt science reinforces a sense of togetherness in which the seer and seen are one. It fosters the development of deep and reciprocal relationships among humans, other animals, and other nature, softening our tendencies to control and manage almost everything in sight.

A pluralistic and open view will help get us past speciesism. A new paradigm in which science and spirituality are viewed as equals will allow for the development of a deep sense of unity and kinship, as well as the formation and maintenance of deep and meaningful interconnections among all animals and all life. I envision a seamless tapestry of oneness, a unity of communities in which we are all one, the seer and the seen.

Marc went on to talk about students who were protesting heinous experiments, bowing out of programs that demanded they participate in "dog labs." And he pointed out that these students were *not* getting kicked out of premed programs. I whistled through my teeth and mumbled, "So, maybe I was born too soon."

He went on to describe sadistic experiments in which baby chimps are put in isolation tanks away from their mothers so that their panic, grief, confusion, terror, rage, and inevitable depression can be rationally "monitored." But Marc didn't talk only about how gruesome and ultimately fruitless these experiments are. He spoke about how to *stop* them. He cited numerous successes and many more impending successes because he and others like him are championing the welfare of animals against the work of his fellow unenlightened scientists. He closed his lecture with the words, "Compassionate people who push the envelope can easily engender the wrath of small minds." Our affirmation for Marc is "I choose to act as if the God in all life matters."

THE PIONEER

NOW, PERHAPS YOU ARE WONDERING if animal experimentation might really be necessary. Thanks to brilliant computer programs, like Rat Stack, med school students are finally able to simulate animal dissection without the use of live animals. But is that really enough? If you're asking yourself if science requires painful animal research, let's ask the man whom I consider to be the best vet in America.

Can you get your master's degree in animal behavior after you've told your professors that you refuse to perform any experiments that harm animals? And then graduate from Cornell University College of Veterinary Medicine maintaining an open compassionate heart for all animals? Dr. Allen Schoen did. He went on to pioneer acupuncture, acupressure, and complementary medicine in animals over the course of the last two decades, but not without getting attacked at every turn.

Allen was the star vet scheduled to speak at the SPCA seminar where I first heard Marc Bekoff speak. After Marc's captivating lecture, I thumbed greedily through Allen's book *Love, Medicine and Animal Healing* and found it to be a stunningly beautiful account of the opposition he's faced from the traditional medical community.

A key passage leaped off the page at me. Allen had refused to perform any painful or unethical experiments on animals in order to earn his degree. Therefore, for his research experiment, he had been assigned the prestigious job of petting baby pigs to monitor how their growth was influenced by human contact. That he was able to do this surprised me. "Pig Petting 101" had not been an elective in the premed program when I was growing up. This was the only reason I hadn't become a vet, which had been my lifelong goal. I refused to kill the frog in my high school biology class, and that put an end to my career in medicine. My eyes welled with tears as I read Allen's account. I would have coveted the opportunity to caress one hundred baby Wilburs to see if a "same pig" would become a "some pig," (as stated in *Charlotte's Web*) or better yet, a "somebody" instead of a slab of "something" lying beside a piece of French toast. Yes, there *should be* a way to become a vet or a doctor without having to hurt or kill lab animals and keep a freezer stocked with dissected cats. Our affirmation for Allen is "I am a powerful agent of change in this world and my words have power. As I speak the truth and defend innocent creatures, justice will prevail and free them from suffering."

Enlightenment comes about slowly, but all I want is for all vivisection to stop *now*. We're not there yet, but we must get there. The United States is lagging far behind the rest of the world in reducing this cruelty. Animal rights activists are influencing the movement in media-grabbing protests and laboratory raids, but another group of caring people is working from inside the establishment. These are the thousands of scientists and educators who are striving to eliminate the need for live animal experimentation. You never hear about them, but I know they are there; I know some personally, like my own mother, Dr. Melinda McClanahan, who radically reduced the number of frogs killed in the comparative anatomy labs at the university where she once taught. These good people refuse to accept the old research methodology and look at every chance to use new techniques sans animals. Day by day, little by little, these scientists and teachers are trying to change entrenched attitudes about the "necessity" of animals in research and science education.

Into the Jungle

My final story is about a heroic animal champion who runs a self-created Newfoundland dog rescue program in Memphis, Tennessee. She's not a scientist; she's a therapist, but she still risked her career to champion my beliefs. She is also a sterling writer, and the world is soon to hear much more from Ms. Beth Boyett, MFA, MSSW, LCSW.

People often ask me if I ever work on murder cases where animals were present at the scene of the crime. If an animal witnessed a murder, couldn't the animal identify the murderer? Well, I'll let Beth tell you herself.

"You will never work as a forensic witness again." My friend and former mentor, a headhunted neuropsychologist who now stumps for one of the world's largest pharmaceutical companies, chuckled. He handed back the flyer I was distributing to friends and co-workers about Amelia Kinkade's upcoming animal communication workshop that I was hosting in my own town, Barbecue Capital of the World, Memphis, Tennessee.

"Of course," he added, "I've always thought you were too expressive for court testimony. You're not poker-faced. But that's what makes disturbed people talk to you. And you're one of the best emergency psychiatric assessors I've ever trained. So, enjoy your vacation, and help some animals. But you know, if you start hearing animals talk, you'll have to commit *yourself*, and that'll be another first around here."

I was not insulted. This man was a brilliant psychologist who had trained some of the best psychiatry residents in emergency care for the mentally ill. He was honestly describing the mental health world as we both knew it: people who hear voices are psychotic; people who hear *animal* voices are described by a term we were never supposed to use in diagnosis, but which we could attest to in court: *insane.*

I recalled just a few months previously when a patient in the psychiatric ER requested to see a surgeon to remove a cat who had taken up residence in her head. The cat was having kittens, she explained, and she did not want them to die in her brain. The woman was pouring milk down her ears to feed the mama cat, but she did not think enough milk was reaching the kittens because the mother cat was quite skinny. "I try to pour a half-gallon down each ear, but most of it comes out," she said. *Most of it comes out, indeed*...Five minutes later I had her admitted to the in-patient psychiatric unit, and, of course, I have never doubted that call. She thanked me profusely when my supervisor okayed she receive a CAT scan (absolutely no pun intended) before she was sent up to the unit. We wanted to rule out any brain abnormality, but she took the name of the procedure — "CAT" scan — literally and was grateful I had listened to her story.

I was willing to hear anybody out, it was true; it had been that way all my life. Besides, I liked the daily challenge my new profession (that of emergency psychiatric assessor) afforded me: to constantly define and redefine "What is reality?" Reality is not always as clear cut a definition as one would suppose, particularly when one is on call twelve hours per night and is often jolted out of sleep to face what looks to be a well-groomed, albeit hyperverbal citizen who has just declared, "After they took me down off the cross, they let me have one phone call. I called my dog to tell him I'd be late coming home."

In that case, the psychiatric residents howled when, at the patient's request, I called the man's neighbor to check his baseline functioning. I suspected what used to be called "manic depression" as opposed to the residents' immediate diagnosis of schizophrenia. The neighbor of this client actually confirmed that this man (who functioned quite well when he took his medicine for bipolar disorder) had indeed been involved in a church's outdoor Easter play that evening in which he was tied (willingly) to the cross but then had become extremely manic, and the police had to be called. He further reported that the man's dog will bark unceasingly if the man is late getting home, and the neighbor can only get the dog to calm down if the man calls home and talks over the answering machine so the dog can hear his guardian's voice. The neighbor also told me that it was the dog who alerted her when the man last made a suicide attempt by hanging. The psychiatric residents were chastised by the department chair: the social work intern had beaten them to the diagnosis only because I had listened and followed up on a story. The man needed only a few days of observation and reinstatement of his medication, not a ninety-day commitment or a trip to court. As the man was leaving for the short-term unit, he explained, "Jesus wasn't on lithium. I was trying to be like Jesus." Poor judgment, perhaps, but still Reality, take it or leave it... And the part about the dog: I believed all of it. I knew the healing and protective powers of animals from my own home.

After eight years of post-secondary school and two graduate degrees, I started a Newfoundland Big Dog Rescue with my friend Miss Sally Banks, a remarkable woman who had founded Memphis's first Humane Society in the 1950s. As stress relief, protection, and a diversion for my overtaxed brain, I had adopted (and even helped deliver) two Newfoundland puppies and had become involved with Newfoundland Rescue, a national organization that helps place abandoned or abused Newfoundlands. At the same time, as I dealt with so many of the abused dogs who landed at "Miss Sally's Bark & Breakfast," I encountered so much animal behavior that I could not understand; unfortunately, unlike my patients at the ER, the dogs could not tell me what was wrong, or so I thought!

Call it a miracle, call it magical thinking, but here are the facts: I was on vacation in rural Alabama when I chanced upon a bookstore's pet section and a maroon book with a smiling woman on its cover literally fell down in front of me when I tripped and jostled a bookshelf. The author's confident and playful smile led my eye to the subtitle: *How to Talk to Animals and Get Answers*. The eyes of the author were not those of a psychotic person. If nothing else, I figured, it would be interesting reading for my long layover in the Atlanta airport. And so it was.

When I found Amelia's book, I already knew that animals had great healing effect on many people, but neither education nor religion ever prepared me for the miracles that can occur daily, even within the so-called "sane" reality. The animals and Amelia have taught me that. When I began my big dog rescue, my hope was to

place these unwanted "wooly mammoths" to equally loving companions who needed them. But the animals are scared sometimes. I've
never had a Newfoundland or Saint Bernard come to my rescue center with any mean tendencies, but I have seen sadness and fear in
their eyes. So it can be hard to get them to trust people again. That's
what I hoped to learn from reading Amelia's book. Although I
thought that she was using a symbolic version of "talk" in the subtitle, the "get answers from animals" I had already experienced many
times over.

My first rescue was a part-Newfoundland shaggy boy who was
abandoned at a gas station in 103 degree heat. He answered immediately when I drove up, opened my car door, and said, "Hey, Big Boy,
you want a ride?" He bounded into the front seat, sat up, and licked
my cheek. No animal voices, but an answer just the same. Big Boy
answered again three weeks later when the parents of a fifteen-year-
old young man with Down Syndrome came to meet him. "You want
to go home and be our son Timmy's best friend?" Boy got up and
did a luxurious stretch, tapped at his leash with his front paw,
and looked back at the surprised dad. Taking no chances, Boy then
grabbed the leash in his teeth and walked over to the man. Boy looked
at the man's truck, licked my hand, and jumped in, just as he had with
me. He'd made a decision, and no educated part of my brain doubts
that. Boy was rechristened "Wolf" by Timmy, and I get a Christmas
card every year "from Wolf and his best boy Timmy."

So I never expected to *hear* an animal voice, and I never even
wanted to, given my profession and my attachment to sanity. But when
I entered Amelia's world, I would have to get used to the broader reality, the one in which the animals live. I first contacted Amelia through
her website when something happened that was so horrible that it
seemed to have been scripted for a movie drama: A couple in the
Northeast had contacted me about adopting two Newfoundland-mix
brothers at my rescue. I had checked the couple's references thoroughly, and a contact with the Northeast Atlantic Region Newfoundland Club was scheduled to interview them as well. We were already
discussing transportation for the pups when the couple stopped all
communication. I wondered, but waited to hear from them.

A month later the woman, whom I'll call Jane, phoned. Her daughter had been murdered in England. She and her husband were still in shock and did not know for sure who the murderer was. To make matters worse, their daughter's dogs had been present at the murder scene and had witnessed the event. Jane and her husband, whom I'll call Ted, had brought the dogs back to Boston with them, but the dogs were traumatized, crying constantly, pacing everywhere. Needless to say, she was calling to say that because they had adopted their daughter's dogs, they could not adopt my pups. But I wasn't concerned about that. Jane and Ted needed help and they needed answers.

I had barely finished Amelia's book, and though I didn't believe *I* could hear animals, with all Amelia's endorsements, I thought there must be something to this. I was not about to put two grieving parents through a reading, though, before I experienced one myself. I was having trouble placing my newest rescue, a beautiful, abandoned Saint Bernard (whom, coincidentally, I had named Amelia Tallulah when she had first come to my rescue, nine months before I ever heard of Amelia Kinkade). I wrote an email, and the next thing I knew, I mailed Amelia Kinkade a photo, and my Saint Bernard and I had an appointment. My dog, Amelia T, was snoring beside my bed when I first called, but she sat up just as we began talking. Amelia Kinkade was right about everything she told me about Amelia T, but one thing left me utterly speechless: "Amelia T said that the most important people in her life are Rachel, you, and Lynn."

I had never told Amelia Kinkade how I got Amelia T. My little neighbor Rachel had lost her dog, and her mother was ill. Her mother asked me to take Rachel to the pound to make sure their dog was not there. While there, Rachel saw Amelia T, who was scheduled to be put to sleep, and little Rachel took me to her. "Look, Miss Beth, that dog is smiling at you!" Amelia T was eaten up with heartworms, she'd just had a litter of pups, and she weighed sixty pounds when she should have weighed at least one hundred. But that dog pulled back her jowls, tossed her head, and hoisted her weary body up. She walked to the door of that cage and made a sound like "ROO!" She put her paw up as if to shake. Clearly we weren't leaving without her.

It took two hours and some pleading with the animal shelter director to convince her that I would pay for heartworm treatment and have the dog spayed by my own vet, Dr. Lynn. I had three dogs at home and two in my rescue kennel, and I knew I was out of my mind. But that dog wanted to live, and I knew she would be great with a special needs adopter. I thought I was doing something for someone else.

Instead, Amelia T gave me the greatest gift: she refused to leave my home, even though she was friendly to the children who came to meet her. She was placed in four different homes for one-week stays, and each time, the parents who brought her back said the same thing, "She would lie on the floor and not pay any attention to anybody, and she hasn't eaten for five whole days!" And now Amelia Kinkade had just given me the names of Amelia T's most significant humans, Rachel and Dr. Lynn, and there was no way she could have known that.

Amelia Kinkade continued. "She says she loved her birthday party, especially the big cake." I had taken Amelia T to a care home just the day before, and it was a resident's birthday. Amelia T had plopped herself down right beside the client who was celebrating a birthday, and that huge hunk of a dog had sat up and grinned when everybody sang "Happy Birthday." When the cake was cut, she began to howl until somebody brought her a piece. As if specific names and the birthday party were not enough, Amelia T upped the ante by suddenly jumping on the bed and licking Amelia Kinkade's book cover. She sat there with a rather smug look, cradling the book in her front paws. I took a picture shortly after she raised her head, and you can see it on Amelia Kinkade's website. That dog has never shown an interest in any other book before or since.

There were other hints, but the point of all this is that I contacted Jane and Ted and said, "I don't know how she's doing it, but Amelia Kinkade is doing it. Call her." They did. Amelia Kinkade was able to give them enough information to convince them that somehow she was tapping into their daughter's murder through the dogs' point of view. Amelia gave them specific names of their daughter's neighbors and friends, all people who had been with their daughter shortly before she was murdered. And, yes, Amelia identified the main suspect by name. After the reading, the daughter's dogs began to calm down. Jane has read Amelia's first book and says she gets telepathic pictures from the dogs, knows what they're scared of, and even what they want to eat. Like other sane people around the world who have taken Amelia's course, Jane says that sometimes she can hear the dogs in her mind, talking in English words. This woman is not insane, but, yes, it defies reality as most of us know it.

And now for a confession that my old mentor would say puts the nails in the coffin of my forensic career, but along with my vet who sometimes looks up to see her deceased dog standing at her desk, and with others who come forward in this book and are not hallucinating: yes, it happened once to me.

Now, mind you, I have never had auditory, visual, olfactory, or any other kind of hallucinations. I had no substances on board at the time this happened. I was writing the day's treatment notes when I heard a very loud and distinct, "Beth!" I live alone, there was nobody else in my home at the time, and the voice was so loud I thought it was some kind of intruder. I jumped up and grabbed my emergency Louisville slugger (a sturdy baseball bat). "Beth!" It was coming from the floor; was he under the bed? I reached for the phone and froze. A fierce little black dog was looking up at me, a new rescue somebody had named Janis Joplin. I'd been fostering Janis for a while, but nothing like this had ever happened to me in my life. She simply wanted my attention, and I "heard" her call my name as if it were out loud!

An even more stunning incident occurred even more recently, while Amelia Kinkade was fostering a cat who belonged to Ellen DeGeneres's mother. "Butch" had taken up residence under Amelia's bed until he could be safely relocated to his old home in Ojai, California. Amelia emailed to say she had renamed the cat. I emailed back to say I had concentrated on the cat and thought his name should be Dr. Winston Johnson. Amelia called excitedly to say she had already named him Dr. Winston Mitchell. When she asked him his name, he had replied "Winston," but she wanted to name him after one of her wise and gentle mentors, Dr. Mitchell. Her other favorite mentor, who is also a septuagenarian and looks and thinks suspiciously like Dr. Mitchell, is her reverend, Dr. Tom Johnson. Although I did not get the last name correct, Amelia assured me that I picked up on the frequency and personalities of the men and her desire to name the cat after one of her spry mentors. The first name and the doctor-status were unprecedented successes for me.

Suddenly I had a big career decision to make: I had to choose between working as a forensic witness or hearing Amelia's cats call themselves *by name* and hearing my own dog call me by name. What do you think I did? Well, let's just say you can call me "Ms. Beth."

Our affirmation for Beth is "My courage and compassion bless every living being on my pathway."

WHAT WOULD LOVE DO HERE?

I'VE OFFERED EXAMPLES of the people I most admire who have founded charities, started sanctuaries, and risked everything in order to save animals' lives. Your destiny may not be to travel to Africa or go to jail in order to defend animals. Your next step may be to volunteer once a week to walk the dogs at your local animal shelter. You might decide to tithe 10 percent of your income to one of the spectacular charities I've spotlighted in this chapter, or devote goods and services toward one of these organizations or to another of your choice. You might commit to purchasing only free-range eggs and meat, or even take the leap and become a complete vegetarian. You might opt to throw out that jacket with the real fur trim and spoil yourself with a new fake fur coat. You may vow to never buy another household product or tube of lipstick that was tested on animals. These choices may sound small, but I'm a big believer in the Butterfly Effect. Your choices matter. You matter.

Or your next step may speak to you through silence as well as action. Even as I write this, someone is sleeping in my lap, gazing up at me adoringly with sultry green eyes and reaching toward the ceiling with her little white paws to "make biscuits" in the air. Her motorboat purr punctuates my point. *This love matters.* Maybe your destiny is to turn off the TV, unplug the phone, then simply look over at the furry loved one sitting beside you . . . and listen. Perhaps the biggest risk you'll ever take is to reclaim the sanctity of these moments and learn to take this love seriously.

Now, a lot of people will tell you that you should be doing more "important" things, like making money and getting caught up in the chaos of the human world. It takes a pile of courage to defy authority and replace all that negative brainwashing with bliss. Should I be doing something more "constructive" than sitting in silence, sharing love with my cat, playing with the tufts of fluff between her toes, and quietly listening to her tell me about her day? Naah. And Flo would agree. I can spend hours gazing at her whiskers, her furry lips, her sublime design, and merely thanking God that I get to live on a planet alongside such beauty. It's in these moments the magic happens. Someone who is not human needs to speak to you. Do what love would do. Fulfill your destiny. Listen.

Recommended Reading

Anderson, Allen and Linda, *Angel Dogs: Divine Messengers of Love*. Novato, CA: New World Library, 2005.

Barker, Raymond Charles, *The Power of Decision*. Camarillo, CA: DeVorss Publications, 1968.

Bekoff, Marc. "Animal Emotions: Exploring Passionate Natures," *BioScience* 50: 2000.

———. *Encyclopedia of Animal Rights and Welfare*. Westport, CT: Greenwood Publishing Group, Inc., 1998.

———. *Strolling With Our Kin: Speaking For and Respecting Voiceless Animals*. Jenkintown, PA: AAVS/Lantern Books, 2000.

Bekoff, Marc, Colin Allen, and Gordon Burghardt, eds. *The Cognitive Animal*. Cambridge, MA: MIT Press, 2001.

Bekoff, Marc, and John Byers, eds. *Animal Play: Evolutionary, Comparative and Ecological Approaches*. New York, Cambridge University Press, 1998.

Bohm, David. *Wholeness and the Implicate Order*. New York: Ark Paperbacks, 1983.

Braden, Gregg. *Awakening to Zero Point: The Collective Initiation*. Bellevue, WA: Radio Bookstore Press, 1997.

Campbell, Joseph. *The Hero with a Thousand Faces*. Princeton, NJ: Princeton University Press, 1949.

Chopra, Deepak. *Quantum Healing*. New York: Bantam Books, 1990.

Davies, Paul. *About Time: Einstein's Unfinished Revolution*. New York: Simon & Schuster, 1995.

DeRose, Chris. *In Your Face: From Actor to Animal Activist*. Los Angeles: Duncan Publishing, 1997.

Dossey, Larry. *Meaning & Medicine*. New York: Bantam Books, 1991.

———. *Space, Time & Medicine*. Boston: Shambhala, 1985.

Fox, Emmet. *Alter Your Life*. San Francisco: HarperSanFrancisco, 1994.

———. *Power through Constructive Thinking*. San Francisco: HarperSan Francisco, 1989.

Goodall, Jane, and Marc Bekoff. *The Ten Trusts*. San Francisco: HarperSanFrancisco, 2002.

Greek, Ray C., and Jean Swingle Greek. *Species Science: How Genetics and Evolution Reveal Why Medical Research on Animals Harms Humans*. New York: Continuum, 2002.

Holmes, Ernest. *The Science of Mind: A Philosophy, a Faith, a Way of Life*. New York: Penguin Putnam, 1998.

Johnson, Tom. *You Are Always Your Own Experience*. Los Angeles: Arboles, 1982.

Kinkade, Amelia. *Straight from the Horse's Mouth: How to Talk to Animals and Get Answers*. Novato, CA: New World Library, 2005.

Kohanov, Linda. *Riding between the Worlds*. Novato, CA: New World Library, 2003.

McElroy, Susan Chernak. *Animals as Teachers & Healers*. New York: Ballantine Books, 1996.

Myerson, John, and Robert Greenebaum. *Riding the Spirit Wind: Stories of Shamanic Healing*. Framingham, MA: LifeArts Press, 2003.

Mitchell, Edgar. "Nature's Mind: The Quantum Hologram," *International Journal of Computing Anticipator Systems* 7: 2000, 295.

———. *The Way of the Explorer: An Apollo Astronaut's Journey through the Material and Mystical Worlds*. New York: Putnam, 1996.

Orloff, Judith. *Second Sight*. New York: Warner Books, 1996.

Peat, F. David. *Einstein's Moon: Bell's Theorem & The Curious Quest for Quantum Reality*. Chicago: Contemporary Books, 1990.

Penrose, Roger. *Shadows of the Mind*. Oxford: Oxford University Press, 1994.

Pearsall, Paul, MD. *The Heart's Code*. New York: Broadway Books, 1999.

Pribram, Karl H. "Quantum Holography: Is It Relevant to Brain Function?" *Information Sciences* 115: 1999, 97–102.

Quinn, Gary. *Living in the Spiritual Zone: 10 Steps to Change Your Life and Discover Your Truth*. Deerfield Beach, FL: Health Communications, 2005.

———. *May the Angels Be With You: Access Your Spirit Guides and Create the Life You Want*. San Diego, CA: Jodere Group, 2003.

Russell, Peter. *From Science to God: A Physicist's Journey into the Mystery of Consciousness.* Novato, CA: New World Library, 2003.

Scully, Matthew. *Dominion: The Power of Man, the Suffering of Animals, and the Call to Mercy.* New York: St. Martin's Press, 2002.

Sheldrake, Rupert. *Dogs That Know When Their Owners Are Coming Home.* New York: Three Rivers Press, 1999.

Siegel, Bernie S. *101 Exercises for the Soul.* Novato, CA: New World Library, 2005.

———. *Peace, Love, and Healing.* New York: Harper & Row, 1989.

———. *Prescriptions for Living.* New York: Harper Perennial, 1998.

Somé, Malidoma Patrice. *Of Water and Spirit: Ritual, Magic, and Initiation in the Life of an African Shaman.* New York: Penguin Compass, 1994.

Talbot, Michael. *The Holographic Universe.* New York: HarperCollins, 1991.

———. *Mysticism & The New Physics.* New York: Penguin Books, 1981.

Teish, Luisah. *Jambalaya.* San Francisco: HarperSanFrancisco, 1995.

Tucker, Linda. *Children of the Sun God.* Milpark, South Africa: Earthyear Books, 2001.

Schoen, Allen M. *Kindred Spirits.* New York: Broadway Books, 2001.

Schoen, Allen M., and Pam Proctor. *Love, Miracles, and Animal Healing.* New York: Fireside, 1996.

Wise, Steven M. *Rattling the Cage: Toward Legal Rights For Animals.* Cambridge, MA: Perseus Publishing, 2000.

Wolf, Fred Alan. *The Dreaming Universe.* New York: Simon & Schuster, 1994.

Wright, Machaelle Small. *Behaving As If the God In All Life Mattered.* Warrenton, VA: Perelandra, 1987.

Zukav, Gary. *The Dancing Wu Li Masters: An Overview of the New Physics.* New York: William Morrow, 1979.

Professional Interspecies Communicators

Reyon Laurie Anderson
P.U.R.R.F. (Puddha Speaks)
Oceanside, CA
(619) 271-9461, (760) 845-3288
puddysplace@yahoo.com

Julie Barone
Kingston, NY
(845) 338-4115
juliebarone@yahoo.com

Julia Bertram
England
mavericks@ameliakinkade.com

Matthew Collister
Malew, Isle of Man
talk2animals@manx.net

Leslie Anne Connell, RN, LMT, and Shen
Atlanta, GA
(678) 530-0360
leslie@drshen.us

Elaine Downs
Lancashire, England
(44) 017 0621 0257
animalmatters@aol.com

Patty Gibbons
Central Islip, NY
(631) 768-9172
info@pattygibbons.com
www.pattygibbons.com

Jamie Greenebaum
Medway, MA
(508) 395-6682, (508) 533-5075
jamie@g2partners.com
http://jamiesanimalcommunication.com

Ronda Holst
Healing Paws
Cottonwood, CA
(530) 347-5216
rholst@c-zone.net

Lorraine Kenyon
England
(44) 016 9829 4209
lorraine@lorrainekenyon.com
www.lorrainekenyon.com

Yvette Anne Knight
docdoolittle@manx.net

Kathryn Ronayne
London, England
(44) 020 8444 5498
info@kathrynronayne.com
www.kathrynronayne.com

Vickie Schroeder
Fairborn, Ohio
vschroeder2@woh.rr.com

Marcel Stoller
Steffisburg, Switzerland
(41) (0) 33 437 32 42
(41) (0) 79 333 30 79
marcel.stoller@hispeed.ch
http://homepage.hispeed.ch
/STOLLER-MARCEL

Lisbeth Tanz
St. Louis, MO
(636) 461-1690
lisbeth@allanimalz.com

Heidi Wright
Malin, OR
(530) 640-0686
Heidi@CritterConnections.net
www.CritterConnections.net

Wynter Eberheart Worsthorne
Cape Town, South Africa
(27) (0) 78 115 4894
wynter@animaltalk.org.uk
www.animaltalk.org.uk

Esther Yesudas
listen_to_animals@freenet.de

Acknowledgments

NOTHING COULD BE MORE CHALLENGING than trying to list all the people I love on a couple of pages, but there are some humans and one furry animal without whose help this book would not have been possible. I'd like to thank my editor, Jason Gardner, for his laser-sharp mind, loving heart, and gentle guidance, but most of all for his wicked sense of humor. No other editor on earth would have allowed my bozons to keep their unicycles. Jason, your generosity is astounding, and you are a blessing to all animals everywhere. Thank you for having the courage to champion innocent animals and publish such a controversial book.

I'm also grateful for my copyeditor, Patricia Heinicke, whom I thank for her hawk eyes, smart questions, and creative style sheet. (Whether or not to capitalize newly invented words like "bearbeezbooze" are questions that require careful consideration.)

Thank you to the entire adventurous team at New World Library, who support my work, love animals, and dare to think outside the box.

Aside from New World Library, I had two other editors who carefully pored over every page of this book. I'd like to thank one of my best friends, author and editor Linda Sivertsen, who lay on her couch with her red pen in hand and her four wonderful dogs at her feet. Linda laughed and cried in all the right places and patiently plowed through passages that needed her wise nips and tucks. She also lost her most precious dog in the midst of this editing. Linda, Brodie's spirit lives on through this book.

Next in line was a champion who took me by surprise. At the ninth hour, I received the meticulous help of a scientist who spent her life teaching comparative anatomy, radiation biology, and genetics to countless pre-med students. She is also the only professor I know who can explain the difference between a pentaquark and a tetraquark while rolling out a homemade crust for her famous lemon meringue pie. She also happens to be my mother. Dr. Melinda McClanahan, I'm sure Einstein smiled down from heaven as we made wild assumptions about his intentions. If he were still alive, he probably wouldn't even notice me, but boy, would he have a crush on you!

I'd like to thank every single student who contributed their heartfelt stories to this book. It's my hope that their courageous stories will help their careers soar all over the world. I also extend my deepest appreciation to my workshop coordinators around the globe, who have made my teaching possible, and to the vivacious Connie Zimet, who produced my meditation CD as well as many peals of laughter when I needed them most.

On the personal front, I'd like to thank a Harvard graduate, author, and shaman whose guidance and protection have utterly transformed my life. Dr. John Myerson, you are a blessing to every life you touch. Thank you for your loyalty and healing magic.

To Karl Gnass, my art teacher at the American Animation Academy, I'd like to thank you for every stunning and beautiful lecture I ever plagiarized.

To my treasured friend, author Gary Quinn, I am grateful for every smile, every chuckle, and for every tear you've dried from my eyes. Thank you, Gary, for fueling my spirit with joy and keeping me airborne just off your wingtips.

It is with great sorrow that I make these final acknowledgments. No sooner had I typed the last words of this manuscript than the love of my life, Florabelle, joined the angels. Her paw print is on every page of this book. Thank you, Flo, for loving me in ways no one else could. *The Language of Miracles* is yours, little one, and although I typed the words, the message of harmony and hope between humans and animals was your idea all along.

I'd like to extend our appreciation to our veterinarian, Dr. Karen Martin, who battled valiantly to save Flo's life, but whose gentle wisdom ultimately allowed Florabelle the sanctity of a peaceful passage at home in my arms.

And I'm eternally grateful for the generosity of my dear friend, actress Amy Smart, who provided a tranquil rose garden in her backyard as Flo's final resting place. Amy, you light the world with your radiant beauty, but it is what shines from within you that warms my heart.

And finally, I need to thank Amy's two handsome boy cats, Yogi and Nala, who bravely watch over little Flora's grave . . . until we meet again.

About the Author

AMELIA KINKADE is an internationally renowned animal communicator, speaker, teacher, and author. She is celebrated by veterinarians, animal rescue organizations, and animal lovers for her ability to bridge the communication gap between species. In 2002 she was privileged to accept an invitation to Buckingham Palace to work with Queen Elizabeth's cavalry and to the British Midlands to translate for the hunting horses of Prince Charles. She was also featured in the book *The 100 Top Psychics in America*.

Amelia's unique abilities have been featured in hundreds of magazines and newspapers, including the *New York Times*, *Chicago Tribune*, *London Sunday News*, *Good Housekeeping*, *ABC Online*, and the *Boston Northshore Sunday*. She has appeared on television programs such as *The View with Barbara Walters*, *The Other Half* with Dick Clark, *VH1*, *BBC News*, and numerous other broadcasts in the United States, the United Kingdom, Europe, Africa, and Australia. She is the author of *Straight from the Horse's Mouth: How to Talk to Animals and Get Answers*. She lives in North Hollywood.

NEW WORLD LIBRARY is dedicated to publishing books and other media that inspire and challenge us to improve the quality of our lives and the world.

We are a socially and environmentally aware company, and we make every attempt to embody the ideals presented in our publications. We recognize that we have an ethical responsibility to our customers, our employees, and our planet.

We serve our customers by creating the finest publications possible on personal growth, creativity, spirituality, wellness, and other areas of emerging importance. We serve our employees with generous benefits, significant profit sharing, and constant encouragement to pursue our most expansive dreams. As members of the Green Press Initiative, we print an increasing number of books with soy-based ink on 100 percent postconsumer waste recycled paper. Also, we power our offices with solar energy and contribute to nonprofit organizations working to make the world a better place for us all.

Our products are available
in bookstores everywhere.
For our catalog, please contact:

New World Library
14 Pamaron Way
Novato, California 94949

Phone: 415-884-2100 or 800-972-6657
Catalog requests: Ext. 50
Orders: Ext. 52
Fax: 415-884-2199

Email: escort@newworldlibrary.com
Website: www.newworldlibrary.com